ADVENTURES IN

Jewish
COOKING

ADVENTURES IN

Jewish
COOKING

Jeffrey Nathan

CLARKSON POTTER/PUBLISHERS
NEW YORK

Published by Clarkson Potter/Publishers, New York, New York.
Member of the Crown Publishing Group, a division of Random House, Inc.
www.randomhouse.com

CLARKSON N. POTTER is a trademark and POTTER and colophon are registered trademarks of Random House, Inc.

Printed in the United States of America

Design by Jane Treuhaft

LIBRARY OF CONGRESS CATALOGING-IN-PUBLICATION DATA
Nathan, Jeffrey.
    Adventures in Jewish cooking / Jeffrey Nathan.—1st ed.
        p.   cm.
    Includes bibliographical references.
    1. Cookery, Jewish.   I. Title.
TX724.N366   2002
641.5'676—dc21   2002025134

ISBN 0-609-61068-6

10 9 8 7 6 5 4 3 2 1

First Edition

THIS BOOK IS DEDICATED TO MY MOM,
Harriet Nathan.

She was never-ending in her love
and absolute in her confidence. She offered the
guidance and steady support
that put me on this adventurous path.

I love you, Mom!

—J.N.

acknowledgments

No matter what words I may write within these pages to thank my wife, Alison, and our kids, Chad and Jaclyn, it would never truly convey how much I've valued their support and encouragement. They've urged me to always reach for one more goal, and they've eaten every experiment I've ever presented to them. All my dreams are coming true because of them. My family life, restaurant, television series, and certainly this cookbook would not have been possible without Ali's devotion and passion. She is truly the driving force behind the scenes.

Words alone cannot adequately thank my friends at Jewish Television Network. The opportunity afforded me by Jay Sanderson and Harvey Lehrer is truly what a chef dreams of. Their confidence in me as chef/host of *New Jewish Cuisine* propelled me toward yet another dream come true—my first cookbook. Our friendships go beyond the excitement of filming groundbreaking cooking shows; they have given Ali and me wonderful West Coast friendships that transcend the distance and time zones without losing a beat.

Though the restaurant business varies with the seasons, my fortune in having two wonderful partners has been constant. Harvey Riezenman and I have been partners through two decades and half a dozen restaurants. He and his wife, Charlotte, are friends beyond measure. Bob Ross, the new addition to our trio, guided us into the kosher world, and what an enjoyable journey it's been! Both Harvey and Bob offered invaluable encouragement to bring kosher cooking into the twenty-first century, and held down the fort while I worked on this book.

The loyalty and trustworthiness of my staff, especially my general manager, Jigi Mathew, has turned him into a treasured friend. From the day Abigael's began, Jigi has been full steam ahead. He runs the day-to-day operations with such finesse and detail, I feel we can accomplish anything! Thank you, Jigi, for caring just as much as I do.

A great chef can accomplish nothing without his chef de cuisine, and this is certainly true in my case. For more than twenty years and several restaurants, Ramón Mercedes has been my chef de cuisine, enabling me to further my career with his constant willingness to transform the recipes in my head into delicacies in his sauté pan.

David Frank, my pastry chef, has been a constant help with his enthusiasm and passion. My cooking demonstrations, which often feature recipes from within this book, would not run as smoothly without David's assistance and perfection in packing.

The many others who must also be thanked for their direct and not-so-direct involvement in writing this cookbook are: sous-chef José (Tony) Guzman; line cooks Junior Figlio and Eric Pablo; Abigael's number-one Mashgiach (kosher supervisor), Mendy Segal; and

Mary Goodman, who handled my countless phone calls and appointments. And to the many waiters, waitresses, busboys, and dishwashers who kept Abigael's running at a top-notch level whether I was present or not; to all of you, I give my utmost thanks for your tireless work and devotion.

Special thanks are due to Rick Rodgers and his assistant, Diane Kniss. A cookbook author and culinary teacher, Rick translated my babble into words that portray my passion for cooking and tested every recipe in the book to make it perfect. We learned an immeasurable amount from each other and became friends in the process.

Every great adventure needs someone to get the ball rolling. For *Adventures in Jewish Cooking*, that person was Bob Tabian, my literary agent. Bob brought me into the world of publishers, writers, and editors, and steered me toward the well-conceived *shidduchs* with my publisher and collaborator.

My editor, Pam Krauss, and her assistant, Adina Steiman, took over where Bob Tabian left off. Each woman was a pleasure to work with in her own right. The team of devoted staff members at Clarkson Potter also deserves a heartfelt thank-you for the attention to detail shown in every aspect of this cookbook.

Alan Richardson's photographs tantalize the eye with hints of the tastes to come, by bringing the dishes I've created to life. His photographic talents are evident in every picture in this book. We spent many a photographic moment together envisioning, creating, and developing the images you see, each appreciating what the other brought to the table.

I would also like to thank my food stylist, Jee Levine, and prop stylist, Betty Alfenito, who added the nuances that helped the photos really shine.

Two special people have always encouraged me and had faith in my ideas and ventures. For that unwavering support I must thank my in-laws, Monney and Selina Siegel. Just knowing that they were behind us with a smile of approval and a pat on the back made our sometimes overwhelming work that much easier. They also convinced us to save every recipe we ever thought of because, "Who knows, maybe one day you'll want to write a cookbook." Above all else, their ready willingness to baby-sit helped make this cookbook a reality.

Much thanks must also be bestowed upon my friends Rabbis Harvey, Danny, and Ari Senter at the Kof-K Supervisory Board. Rabbi Senter and his sons have gladly shared their knowledge of kashrut and the beauty of our faith. My incessant questions and their devotion to detail have helped Abigael's to become one of New York's finest dining establishments and made *Adventures in Jewish Cooking* the informative and creative cookbook it is.

The special thanks I hold in my heart and in my soul are for the higher powers that have brought me to this place in my life, blessed with family, partners, co-workers, and friends. Through my faith, I am reminded to appreciate each and every one of the blessings bestowed upon me.

contents

Introduction

The title of this book could conjure up the image of a chef (that would be me) risking life and limb in the pursuit of a great recipe. Maybe you can see me swinging through the jungle on a vine, climbing up a steep mountain, or fending off a wild animal. While I did plenty of traveling to collect these recipes, I guarantee that the delicious adventures I had were completely safe.

Perhaps the title should be *Adventuresome Jewish Cooking*. The goal of this book is to awaken American cooks to the great, big, wide, and wonderful world of Jewish cooking. Jewish-American cooking traditions aren't the only ones observed by Jewish cooks. Over the years, my experiences as a chef brought me not only to the varied foods of the world, but to the cooking of my heritage. This led to my creating Abigael's, a Manhattan restaurant that celebrates the best of kosher cooking, and hosting my show, *New Jewish Cuisine*.

Believe me, I was the perfect example of a guy who thought that Jewish cooking meant a pastrami sandwich on rye or bagel with a

schmear. I grew up in New York, and in our household Jewish cooking was personified by my family's recipes for matzo ball soup, stuffed cabbage, and blintzes. Our culture sprang from the Ashkenazic branch of Judaism, with roots in Central and Eastern Europe (did you know that *Ashkenaz* is an old Hebrew word for Germany?). To generalize, for there are many subcultures under the Ashkenazic umbrella, this hearty cooking uses ingredients that thrive in cool climates: rye, potatoes, beets, cabbage, and freshwater fish. I didn't really know that there were many other kinds of Jewish cooking.

Or did I? My childhood neighborhood, Howard Beach in Queens, New York, was predominantly Italian. I remember that one of my favorite treats as a kid was to visit my friend Gary's house for Sunday dinner. The table was filled end to end with platters of chicken, meatballs, and so many other dishes, including my favorite, broccoli rabe (the more garlic and olive oil, the better), which we spread in a thick layer on a slab of crusty bread.

As an adult chef, I discovered Sephardic Jewish culture and its cuisine, and it was like a homecoming for my taste buds. You might say it is the Jewish version of the so-called Mediterranean cuisine. The word "Sephardic" comes from *Sepharad*, Hebrew for Spain, the country from which the Jews were evicted in 1492. These Jews migrated to other countries around the Mediterranean, including Italy, a country with a cuisine that still influences what I like to cook and eat. Seasoning is very important in Sephardic cooking, and you'll find cinnamon, saffron, ginger, basil, garlic, and other herbs and spices used with joyous abandon, along with vegetables like tomatoes and sweet peppers (and broccoli rabe!).

My professional career began as a dishwasher (I'm proud of this because it shows how I worked my way up the ladder) at Villa Russo, an Italian restaurant in Queens, which thrives to this day. There, despite the piles of dirty pots and pans, I discovered a passion for cooking.

I joined the Navy as a cook, and Uncle Sam paid for my first round of traveling and recipe collecting. I became the personal chef to the captain and officers, a position that allowed me to shop in the local markets of the different ports of call and to try my hand at more upscale recipes. After four years at sea, I signed up at the Culinary Institute of America, in Hyde Park, New York, also compliments of Uncle Sam.

Upon graduation, I worked in all kinds of restaurants and bakeries (some of them for knowledge, not salaries), gathering new skills and tastes along the way. As the chef at The New Deal in Soho, I made my mark with a menu specializing in wild game, allowing me to expand my culinary horizons again.

Years later my friend and partner Harvey Riezenman came to me with a surprising proposition to buy a kosher restaurant that was for sale. At first, I wasn't interested, but soon my interest was piqued, almost in spite of myself. Here was a whole new culinary frontier to pioneer. I didn't want to serve the same old dishes that everyone expected, but an updated, fresh version of kosher cooking. This was going to be "new Jewish *cuisine*," elegant and delicious renditions of food from the entire Jewish diaspora, from Yemen to Ethiopia, from Italy to Morocco, from Israel to Brooklyn.

Abigael's thrived, first at a location in midtown and now on Broadway, right at the edge of Times Square. My vision of a new Jewish cuisine began to blossom. I found that it was exciting to devise kosher versions of nonkosher dishes, such as my chicken and veal pâté, and refining old-fashioned food by giving it an updated twist kept my creative juices flowing. It's not all about innovation though; I derive just as much satisfaction from taking a recipe from my heritage and making it the best it can be, and you'll find a number of these tried-and-true favorites scattered throughout this book. At Abigael's I began to put some Sephardic dishes on the menu, exposing many of my customers to this spicy, exciting cuisine for the first time. I searched out the best purveyors of kosher products, and with the help of my rabbinical supervisor, learned to navigate the intricacies of kosher cooking with confidence.

I want our customers to think of Abigael's not as a kosher restaurant, but as a great restaurant that just happens to be kosher. In this book, you will find a number of recipes for Abigael's most famous dishes, presented just as they are served at the restaurant. I promise that there are many, many recipes that you will be able to prepare for a weeknight meal, but for special occasions, you may enjoy the challenge of creating a kosher meal with restaurant flair. You will also learn little tricks that you can apply to less complicated meals, like using dried mushrooms as a crust for simply sautéed fish fillets. Or perhaps you'll cook my spicy cilantro-braised brisket, but skip some of the garnishes.

When I came upon Abigael's, I had been in the restaurant business for almost twenty years, but my exploration of modern Jewish cooking was the beginning of a new chapter in my development as a chef...and as a person. Over the years, I admit that I had been jumping around a bit, getting recognition as a wild game chef, and even as an Italian cook. But Abigael's was my *beshert*—it's where I was destined to find myself. As I honed the recipes for Abigael's menu, I realized that I had come home, both spiritually and professionally. The fact

that my unique way of cooking was tied to my religion made that discovery much more satisfying.

Today, *New Jewish Cuisine,* my television show, gives me a platform to share my approach to kosher cooking with millions every week. The response has been incredibly gratifying, as more and more home cooks take part in this delicious celebration of a people and their food.

Appetizers

It's no accident that many Jewish delis are known simply as "appetizing stores." The array of smoked fish; spreads and dips for schmearing onto breads, bagels, and matzo; knishes filled with deliciously savory stuffings; and tangy pickles is tantalizing.

For today's cook, those old favorites are great building blocks for first courses. I like to take an old favorite and turn it inside out. A smoked salmon cheesecake with slices of homemade bialy loaf is a terrific way to start a meal—and it's not bad at a Yom Kippur break fast, either. If you think that you can't look at another piece of gefilte fish served straight from the jar, try my gefilte fish terrine with carrot and beet salads in a horseradish vinaigrette.

Appetizers cover a lot of ground. They can be the first course to a sit-down dinner or noshes and nibbles at a big bash. It is their job to set the mood for the meal. An elegant appetizer, such as the salmon cakes with spicy tomato sambal or the Latin American ceviche, lets the guests know that they are in for an extra-special meal. Anytime you serve fork-free fare, like baked stuffed mushrooms or fried asparagus, a subliminal signal is sent to relax.

Good hosts often offer their guests something to drink. I've included a heady rum punch that is guaranteed to put life into any party. But today's responsible host is aware that not all of the guests may be drinking alcohol, and it's important to offer nonalcoholic beverages, too. Any one of the Persian coolers (shall it be strawberry or sour cherry?) may have the tipplers asking for a sip, too.

Baked Mushrooms
with Spicy Pastrami Filling

Recently a friend served these at a dinner party of food writers where he was asked to contribute an appetizer. He reported that everyone declared these the best stuffed mushrooms they ever had. The pastrami really puts them over the top. Plus, you can make them well ahead of serving and just pop them into the oven when you're ready to roll.

16 medium cremini or "gourmet stuffing" button mushrooms (about 1 pound), trimmed

2 tablespoons extra-virgin olive oil, plus more for drizzling

1/2 cup finely diced onion

1/2 cup finely diced red bell pepper

2 ounces sliced pastrami, finely diced

2 garlic cloves, minced

1/4 teaspoon hot red pepper flakes

1/2 cup dry white wine

2/3 cup seasoned bread crumbs, divided

1 tablespoon chopped fresh parsley

1 tablespoon chopped fresh oregano

1 tablespoon chopped fresh basil

Kosher salt and freshly ground black pepper to taste

1. Remove the stems from the mushrooms; reserve the caps and finely chop the stems (or pulse them in a food processor). Heat the oil in a large skillet over medium-high heat. Add the onion and red bell pepper and cook, stirring occasionally, until softened, about 3 minutes. Add the chopped mushroom stems, pastrami, garlic, and red pepper flakes. Cook, stirring occasionally, until the mushrooms give off their juices, about 5 minutes. Pour in the wine and cook over high heat until almost completely evaporated, about 3 minutes.

2. Remove from the heat and stir in 1/3 cup of the bread crumbs, the parsley, oregano, and basil. Season with salt and pepper. Let stand to cool.

3. Lightly oil a baking sheet. Stuff the mushroom caps with the pastrami mixture, pressing the filling firmly so it adheres to the cap. Pour the remaining 1/3 cup bread crumbs into a small bowl. Dip the top of each filled mushroom in the bread crumbs and place on the baking sheet. (The mushrooms can be prepared up to 8 hours ahead, covered and refrigerated.)

4. Position a rack in the center of the oven and preheat the oven to 350°F.

5. Drizzle the mushroom caps with oil. Bake until the tops are golden brown, about 20 minutes. Cool slightly and serve warm.

Chicken and Veal Pâté

MAKES
8
SERVINGS

Pâté certainly belongs in the Appetizer Hall of Fame, but many are made with pork. This pork-free pâté has every bit of the flavor and richness of the French bistro classic. Serve it in the classic style with grainy mustard and toast or with a salad of baby greens, tomatoes, and a mustard vinaigrette. It is also is a fine representative of the meatloaf family, and can be served hot or chilled in a sandwich.

1. Heat 2 tablespoons of the oil in a medium skillet over medium heat. Add the onion, red bell pepper, and garlic and cook, stirring occasionally, until the onion is translucent, about 6 minutes. Stir in the thyme and oregano. Transfer to a large bowl.

2. Heat the remaining 1 tablespoon oil in the skillet over medium heat. In batches, stir in the spinach, with the water still clinging to the leaves, cooking each batch until wilted. Cook until the spinach is tender, about 5 minutes. Drain in a sieve, rinse under cold water to cool, and squeeze gently to remove excess liquid. Chop coarsely and add to the bowl of vegetables.

3. Position a rack in the center of the oven and preheat the oven to 350°F. Oil a 9 × 5-inch loaf pan.

4. Add the chicken, veal, livers, bread crumbs, egg, nutmeg, salt, and pepper to the vegetables and mix well. Transfer to the loaf pan and smooth the top. Cover with aluminum foil.

5. Bake until an instant-read thermometer inserted in the center of the loaf reads 165°F., about $1^{1}/4$ hours. Cool completely in the pan on a wire rack.

6. Unmold the pâté and wrap tightly in aluminum foil. Refrigerate overnight and up to 3 days.

7. Cut the pâté into thin slices, then into halves or quarters. Serve with an assortment of crackers, chutney, and mustard.

3 tablespoons olive oil

1 large yellow onion, cut into $^{1}/4$-inch dice

1 large red bell pepper, cored, seeded, and cut into $^{1}/4$-inch dice

4 garlic cloves, minced

1 tablespoon chopped fresh thyme

1 tablespoon chopped fresh oregano

1 pound spinach, stems removed, well washed but not dried

1 pound ground chicken

8 ounces ground veal

4 ounces chicken livers, trimmed and ground until smooth in a food processor

$^{1}/2$ cup seasoned dried bread crumbs

1 large egg, beaten

$^{1}/4$ teaspoon freshly grated nutmeg

$1^{1}/2$ teaspoons kosher salt

$^{1}/2$ teaspoon freshly ground black pepper

Crackers, flatbreads, or toast points, chutney and prepared mustard, for serving

heritage recipe

Classic Chopped Liver

**MAKES
12
SERVINGS**

In Jewish New Yorkese, we have an expression: "What am I, chopped liver?" I never could understand why it was bad to compare yourself to such a delicious appetizer. Not that there aren't secrets to a good chopped liver. First, be sure to use lots of onions, and brown them well to bring out their sweetness. Also, serve your chopped liver with lots of garnishes so your guests can personalize each serving.

1½ pounds chicken livers, well trimmed
⅓ cup vegetable oil
4 medium onions, finely diced
¼ cup brandy
6 large eggs, hard-boiled and halved
1 teaspoon sugar
Kosher salt and freshly ground black pepper to taste
Assorted crackers (matzo, lavash, and other flatbreads) and breads, for serving
Additional garnishes: hard-boiled eggs (whites and yolks separated and chopped), chopped onion, schmaltz and gribenes (see page 165), grated black radish, chopped fresh parsley

1. Position the rack 6 inches from the source of heat and preheat the broiler. Place the chicken livers on a lightly oiled broiler rack. Broil, turning once, until well done, about 5 minutes per side. Set aside.

2. Heat the oil in a large skillet over medium-high heat. Add the onions and cook, stirring occasionally, until deep golden brown, 8 to 10 minutes. Stir in the chicken livers. Pour in the brandy, and averting your face, ignite the brandy with a match. Let burn until the flame extinguishes, about 1 minute. Remove from the heat and cool slightly.

3. In batches, transfer the chicken liver mixture and eggs to a food processor, and pulse just until coarsely chopped. Do not overmix. Transfer to a large bowl. Stir in the sugar, and season with the salt and pepper. Cover tightly and refrigerate for at least 2 hours and up to 2 days to chill and blend the flavors.

4. Remove from the refrigerator about 1 hour before serving. Serve with the crackers and whatever condiments your family likes.

Latin American Ceviche

MAKES
6
SERVINGS

While brainstorming ideas for a new Passover appetizer, I developed this gefilte fish alternative. The added crunch from the matzo incorporates tradition into this New World creation. For fancy affairs, I serve the ceviche in a coconut shell—it saves on washing dishes!

1. To make the ceviche, cut the salmon and red snapper or halibut into wide slices, cutting them very thinly on a bias across the slant grain. Combine the salmon, snapper, lime juice, and lemon juice in a large, nonreactive (glass, ceramic, or stainless-steel) bowl and toss well. Cover tightly with plastic wrap. Refrigerate, stirring occasionally, until the fish looks opaque, 20 to 25 minutes. Drain the fish, discarding the juices.

2. To make the salad, combine the fish, 1 crumbled matzo, the mango, oranges, tomatoes, onion, jalapeños, red and green bell peppers, oil, orange juice, lime juice, and cilantro. Mix gently, and season with salt and pepper. Cover and refrigerate for at least 1 and up to 6 hours.

3. Carefully fold in the remaining crumbled matzo. Divide the baby lettuces among 6 martini glasses or salad plates, top with equal amounts of the ceviche, and garnish with the matzo shards.

CEVICHE
8 ounces skinless salmon fillet
8 ounces skinless red snapper
  or striped bass fillet
1/4 cup fresh lime juice
2 tablespoons fresh lemon juice

MATZO SALAD
3 matzos, 2 broken into large
  chunks and 1 broken into
  long shards
1 mango, pitted, peeled, and
  cut into long, thin strips
2 oranges, cut into supremes
  (see page 141)
1 cup diced plum tomatoes
1/2 red onion, thinly sliced
2 jalapeño peppers, seeded and
  minced
1/2 cup red bell pepper, cut into
  long, thin strips
1/2 cup green bell pepper, cut
  into long, thin strips
3 tablespoons extra-virgin olive
  oil
3 tablespoons fresh orange juice
2 tablespoons fresh lime juice
2 tablespoons chopped fresh
  cilantro
Kosher salt and freshly ground
  black pepper to taste
6 ounces mixed baby greens

Nori-Wrapped Salmon
with Pea Shoot Salad

Of all the dishes I've created over the years, I think I'm proudest of this one, which combines many elements I learned when I worked in a Japanese restaurant. It looks like a million bucks, with sliced medallions of bright pink salmon wrapped with dark seaweed surrounding a pea shoot salad. But appearance is only half the story, because it tastes terrific, too. The salmon will be cut and stuffed, so buy a thick center cut that you can divide by yourself into 6 servings—you may need two pieces instead of one large one. Pea shoots (sometimes called pea leaves) are available in the spring and summer in Chinese markets. If you wish, substitute finely shredded boy choy or napa cabbage. You'll find kosher nori and wasabi at Kosher Depot (see Sources, page 250).

WASABI REMOULADE

1 tablespoon wasabi powder
1 tablespoon water, as needed
$^{1}/_{2}$ cup mayonnaise
$1^{1}/_{2}$ tablespoons soy sauce
$^{1}/_{2}$ teaspoon dark Asian sesame
   oil

PONZU SAUCE

$^{1}/_{3}$ cup soy sauce
$^{1}/_{3}$ cup water
$^{1}/_{3}$ cup fresh lemon juice
3 tablespoons fresh orange juice
1 tablespoon honey
1 teaspoon peeled and minced
   fresh ginger

1. To make the remoulade, mix the wasabi powder and water in a small bowl to make a paste. Stir in the mayonnaise, soy sauce, and sesame oil. Cover and refrigerate to blend the flavors. (The remoulade can be prepared up to 1 day ahead.)

2. To make the ponzu, mix the soy sauce, water, lemon juice, orange juice, honey, and ginger in a small bowl. Cover and refrigerate until well chilled. (The ponzu can be made up to 5 days ahead.)

3. To prepare the vegetables for the salmon, heat 2 tablespoons of the oil in a large skillet over medium-high heat. Add the ginger and stir until fragrant, about 30 seconds. Add the mushrooms, carrot, and snow peas, and stir-fry until crisp-tender, about 2 minutes. Add the sesame oil and gently toss to combine. Cool completely. (The vegetables can be prepared up to 2 hours ahead if stored at room temperature.)

4. Cut the salmon fillets lengthwise into 6 pieces, each about 5 inches long by 1 inch wide. With a paring knife make a "pocket" slit lengthwise along the middle of each salmon piece, leaving $^1/_2$ inch remaining uncut on each side. Do not cut through the salmon. Stuff each fillet with the vegetables.

5. Place a nori sheet on a work surface, shiny side down. Brush the nori with soy sauce. Place a stuffed fillet horizontally on the bottom third of the nori. Fold over the sides and roll from the bottom up to form a cylinder, ending with the seam side down. Repeat with the remaining nori and salmon. (The salmon can be prepared up to 3 hours ahead, covered tightly with plastic wrap, and refrigerated.)

6. Heat the remaining 2 tablespoons oil in a 12- to 14-inch nonstick skillet over medium-high heat. Add the salmon rolls and cook, turning occasionally, until seared on all sides (the nori will turn a darker shade), about 3 minutes. If you like rare salmon, it is ready to serve. For medium salmon, reduce the heat to medium-low and cook, turning occasionally, for another 3 to 4 minutes.

7. While the salmon is cooking, make the salad. In a medium bowl, toss the pea shoots, red bell pepper, mushrooms, sesame seeds, $^1/_4$ cup of the ponzu sauce, and sesame oil.

8. To serve, cut each roll into 1-inch-thick slices. Mound a portion of salad on each of 6 plates. Arrange the salmon slices around the salads, and top with a drizzle of the wasabi mayonnaise. Serve with small bowls of the remaining ponzu sauce for dipping.

SALMON

4 tablespoons peanut or vegetable oil

1 tablespoon peeled and minced fresh ginger

4 shiitake mushroom caps, cut into long, thin strips ($^1/_2$ cup)

1 medium carrot, cut into long, thin strips ($^1/_2$ cup)

12 snow peas, cut into long, thin strips ($^1/_2$ cup)

1 teaspoon dark Asian sesame oil

$1^1/_4$ pounds skinless, center-cut salmon fillets

6 sheets of nori (seaweed sheets for sushi)

$^1/_4$ cup soy sauce, as needed

PEA SHOOT SALAD

$4^1/_2$ cups (about 9 ounces) loosely packed pea shoots, available at Chinese produce stores

1 medium red bell pepper, cored, seeded, and julienned

4 stemmed shiitake mushrooms, julienned

1 tablespoon sesame seeds, toasted (see page 66)

1 teaspoon dark Asian sesame oil

Gefilte Fish Terrine
with Carrot and Beet Salads

Talk about "not your Grandma's gefilte fish"! This is absolutely one of the classiest ways you could ever serve the holiday classic. When I made it on my television show, I got hundreds of requests for the recipe. This is only worth making with the freshest fish possible. Do think ahead—the terrine is easiest to slice if it is well chilled.

2 tablespoons vegetable oil
1 large onion, chopped
1¹/2 pounds skinless whitefish fillet
1¹/2 pounds skinless pike fillet
1 cup cold water
5 large eggs, lightly beaten
7 tablespoons matzo meal
2 tablespoons sugar
1¹/2 tablespoons kosher salt
1¹/2 teaspoons freshly ground white pepper
1 medium carrot, shredded
1 pound carrots, peeled
1 pound beets, peeled

1. The day before serving, position a rack in the center of the oven and preheat the oven to 325°F. Lightly oil two 8 ¹/2 × 4¹/2-inch loaf pans.

2. Heat the oil in a small skillet over medium heat. Add the onion and cook, stirring occasionally, until translucent, about 2 to 3 minutes. Set aside to cool.

3. In batches, process the fish in a food processor fitted with the metal blade until ground into a paste. Combine the ground fish, onion, water, eggs, matzo meal, sugar, salt, and pepper in the bowl of a heavy-duty electric mixer fitted with the paddle blade. Mix on low speed until well combined, scraping down the sides of the bowl as needed. Using a rubber spatula, fold in the shredded carrot. Spread in the loaf pans and cover each with aluminum foil. Arrange the loaf pans inside a larger roasting pan.

4. Slide the rack halfway out of the oven. Place the roasting pan on the rack. Pour enough water into the pan to reach ¹/2 inch up the sides of the loaf pans. Carefully slide the rack back into the oven. Bake until an instant-read thermometer inserted in the center of the loaf reads 140°F., about 50 minutes.

5. Remove the loaf pans from the water and cool on a wire rack. When the pans are cool, wrap each one tightly in plastic wrap and refrigerate until chilled, at least 4 hours or overnight. (The terrines can be prepared up to 1 day ahead.)

6. To make the salads, shred the carrots with a mandoline fitted with the julienne blade. Transfer to a medium bowl. Shred the beets and transfer to another bowl.

7. To make the vinaigrette, whisk the vinegar, mustard, horseradish, and shallots in a small bowl. Gradually whisk in the oil. Season with salt and pepper. Toss each shredded vegetable with half of the vinaigrette and season again with salt and pepper. (The salads can be prepared up to 2 hours ahead, covered, and refrigerated.)

8. To serve, divide each terrine into eight to ten slices. On each plate, place a slice of terrine with mounds of the beet and carrot salads. Sprinkle the salads with the chives. Garnish each plate with small spoonfuls of the horseradishes. Serve chilled.

HORSERADISH MUSTARD VINAIGRETTE

3 tablespoons balsamic vinegar
2 teaspoons prepared mustard
2 teaspoons prepared white horseradish
2 tablespoons finely chopped shallots
$2/3$ cup extra-virgin olive oil
Kosher salt and freshly ground black pepper to taste
2 tablespoons finely chopped chives, for garnish
Prepared white and beet horseradishes, for garnish

WASHING VEGETABLES

According to the laws of kashrut, insects are at the top of the list of forbidden foods . . . not that any cook looks forward to a big plate of roasted whatevers. Nonetheless, it is very important to wash all fruits and vegetables well before using to remove any trace of insects. I recommend a commercial all-natural produce cleanser like FIT, which does not have any chemical or soapy aftertaste.

Take special care with vegetables with tight buds that could harbor the little guys, such as cauliflower, broccoli, and asparagus. Mushrooms should be washed very quickly so they won't soak up water. Perhaps the best way to clean fresh fungi is to fill a large bowl with cold water and a splash of FIT. Add the mushrooms and agitate them briskly. Lift the mushrooms out of the water and into a colander, leaving the grit to fall to the bottom of the bowl.

Salmon Cakes with Mango Coulis

MAKES
8
SERVINGS

I am a sucker for exotic spices and the interplay of hot and sweet. This appetizer has layer after layer of flavor, and is one of my favorites. It makes a tantalizing dinner-party first course, or serve several cakes with a rice pilaf as a main course.

MANGO COULIS

1 ripe mango, pitted, peeled, and coarsely chopped

2 tablespoons fresh lime juice

2 tablespoons water

SALMON CAKES

1½ pounds salmon fillet, skinned, tiny bones removed

1 quart Vegetable Stock (page 43) or water

⅓ cup mayonnaise

2 tablespoons fresh lemon juice

1 tablespoon Dijon mustard

1 teaspoon Worcestershire sauce

1 scallion (green and white parts), finely chopped

2 tablespoons chopped parsley (or better still, a combination of fresh parsley, oregano, basil, and thyme)

½ teaspoon pure ground chipotle chile powder or 1 teaspoon chili powder

½ teaspoon freshly ground black pepper

¼ cup crushed corn flakes

2 ounces sliced smoked salmon, diced

½ teaspoon kosher salt

½ cup vegetable oil

1. To make the coulis, purée the mango chunks, lime juice, and water in a blender. (The coulis can be prepared up to 2 days ahead, covered, and refrigerated.)

2. To make the salmon cakes, place the salmon fillet in a large skillet and add the vegetable stock. If needed, add water to the stock to barely cover the salmon. Bring to a simmer over medium-high heat, then reduce the heat to medium-low. Cover and cook just until the salmon is slightly pink in the center when prodded with the tip of a knife, 6 to 8 minutes. Using a slotted spatula, transfer the salmon to a plate to cool. (The cooking liquid can be used in another recipe as a fish stock.) Using a fork, break the salmon into flakes.

3. In a medium bowl, whisk the mayonnaise, lemon juice, mustard, and Worcestershire sauce. Stir in the scallion, fresh herbs, chipotle powder, and pepper, then the corn flakes. Fold in the flaked salmon, then the smoked salmon, being careful not to overmix. Season with the salt. Cover and refrigerate for at least 1 and up to 8 hours.

4. Shape into eight 3-inch cakes. Heat the oil in a 12-inch skillet over medium heat. Have ready a shallow dish of the flour, a shallow dish of the beaten eggs, and a shallow dish of the panko. Dredge each cake in the flour, coat with the eggs, then the panko. Add the cakes to the hot oil and cook, turning once, until golden on both sides, about 5 minutes.

5. Place a salmon cake on each of 8 serving plates. Garnish with a dollop of the sambal and a small mound of greens. Drizzle the coulis around the salmon cake and serve immediately.

^{1}/2 cup all-purpose flour
3 large eggs, beaten
1 cup panko (Japanese bread crumbs); see Note page 173
1^1/2 cups Curried Tomato Sambal (recipe follows)
8 ounces mixed baby greens (mesclun), for garnish

Curried Tomato Sambal

PAREVE
MAKES ABOUT 4 CUPS

Sambal is a beautifully spiced Indian condiment that I use like ketchup on meats, grilled fish, poultry, and anything else I can think of. Keep it in your refrigerator for up to 1 month.

^{1}/3 cup plus 2 tablespoons extra-virgin olive oil
^{1}/2 cup finely chopped red onion
1 tablespoon minced fresh ginger
1 tablespoon curry powder
1 teaspoon ground cumin
One 28-ounce can crushed tomatoes
^{1}/4 cup soy sauce
2 tablespoons rice wine vinegar
1^1/2 tablespoons sugar
^{1}/2 teaspoon hot red pepper flakes
^{1}/2 cup chopped fresh cilantro

Heat 2 tablespoons of the olive oil in a large stockpot over medium heat. Add the onion and ginger. Cook, stirring often, until the onion is translucent, about 3 minutes. Stir in the curry powder and cumin, then the tomatoes, soy sauce, rice wine vinegar, sugar, and red pepper flakes. Bring to a boil.

Reduce the heat to medium-low and cook at a brisk simmer, stirring often, until reduced to 4 cups, 30 to 45 minutes. Cool completely.

Transfer the sambal to a blender and add the cilantro. With the machine running, gradually pour in the remaining ^{1}/3 cup olive oil and blend until smooth. (The sambal can be prepared up to 1 month ahead, stored in an airtight container, and refrigerated.)

Smoked Salmon Cheesecake

MAKES
12
SERVINGS

When I first started serving this easy, do-ahead cheesecake, I had a hard time winning over people who were used to sweet cheesecakes. After the first bite, they became believers. Served in thin slices (it's rich!), perhaps with a spoonful of roasted pepper vinaigrette, it works as a dinner appetizer or a brunch main course. (For a real treat, serve it with toasted slices of the Bialy Loaf on page 199.) Offer it on a platter with lavash or other flatbreads, and it's a great spread—just the thing to come home to for a Yom Kippur break fast.

2 tablespoons unsalted butter, melted

3 tablespoons freshly grated Parmesan cheese

3 tablespoons seasoned dried bread crumbs

2 tablespoons vegetable oil

1/3 cup finely chopped onion

1/3 cup finely chopped red bell pepper

1/3 cup finely chopped green bell pepper

1 teaspoon kosher salt

1/2 teaspoon freshly ground black pepper

1 1/2 pounds cream cheese, at room temperature

4 large eggs, at room temperature

8 ounces sliced smoked salmon or smoked salmon scraps (available at some delicatessens), chopped

2 tablespoons chopped fresh dill

1/2 cup (4 ounces) shredded Havarti cheese

1/3 cup heavy cream

1. Position a rack in the center of the oven and preheat the oven to 350°F. Generously brush an 8-inch springform pan with the melted butter. Wrap the bottom of the pan in a double thickness of aluminum foil.

2. In a small bowl, mix the Parmesan cheese and bread crumbs. Pour into the pan, and tilt to coat the pan halfway up the sides. Pat the crumbs in the bottom of the pan into an even, thin layer.

3. Heat the oil in a medium skillet over medium heat. Add the onion and the red and green bell peppers. Cook, stirring occasionally, until softened, about 6 minutes. Stir in the salt and pepper. Cool completely.

4. Beat the cream cheese in a heavy-duty electric mixer fitted with the paddle attachment on medium-low speed until smooth, about 1 minute. Scrape down the sides of the bowl with a rubber spatula. Add the vegetables. With the mixer running, add the eggs, one at a time, just until blended, scraping the bowl as needed. Add the smoked salmon, dill, Havarti, and heavy cream, and mix just until blended. Spread evenly in the springform pan. Place the pan in a large roasting pan. Slide the rack halfway out of the oven.

Pour enough water in the roasting pan to come halfway up the side of the springform pan. Slide the rack back into the oven carefully.

5. Bake until the edges are puffed and golden but the center still seems slightly unset, about 1¹/2 hours. Run a knife around the edge of the cheesecake to release it from the sides of the pan. Cool completely on a wire rack.

6. Remove the sides of the pan. Wrap the cheesecake tightly with plastic wrap. Refrigerate until chilled, at least 4 hours or overnight. (The cheesecake can be made up to 2 days ahead.)

7. Cut into thin slices and serve on plates, garnishing each serving with frisée, cherry tomatoes, and red onions, along with crackers for spreading. Pass the vinaigrette on the side, if desired.

Frisée (pale curly endive), cherry tomatoes, and finely sliced red onion, for garnish

Crackers, lavash, flatbreads, matzo, or sliced toast, for serving

Red Pepper and Tomato Vinaigrette (page 136), optional

ROASTING PEPPERS

Why bother to roast bell peppers? Several reasons . . . and each will make your recipes even more delicious. Roasting loosens the tough skin, giving peppers a silky smooth texture, and it brings out the flavor, too. Red and yellow bell peppers are the best candidates for roasting, as the procedure doesn't do anything special for green peppers.

To roast peppers, position a broiler rack 6 inches from the source of heat and preheat the broiler. Place the peppers on the rack. Broil, turning the peppers occasionally, until the skin is charred on all sides—take care not to burn through the pepper flesh. Don't worry about a few naked spots, as roasting will still loosen the skin in those areas even if they aren't blackened. Transfer the peppers to a paper bag and fold the end to seal. Let cool until easy to handle, about 20 minutes. Using a small knife as an aid, peel off the blackened skin. *Don't* rinse the peppers under water to help remove the skin—you'll only rinse away flavor, and a few specks of blackened skin isn't a big problem. Remove and discard the ribs and seeds. The peppers are now ready for use . . . and your kitchen will smell wonderful.

Smoked Whitefish Pinwheels

MAKES
ABOUT 36
PINWHEELS

As the chef in the family, it's my job to trim the smoked fish. The larger the number of diners, the more fish that needs to be skinned and filleted. So one day, in the middle of cleaning a mountain of fish (and wondering just how many smoked fish there must be in the sea), I threw together an impromptu wrap with the smoked fish and a few other ingredients. It was so tasty, it ended up on my menu as an hors d'oeuvre.

¹/₃ cup plus 1 tablespoon
   mayonnaise
1¹/₂ tablespoons prepared white
   horseradish
Six 10-inch flour tortillas
2 cups flaked smoked whitefish
   (from 1 large smoked
   whitefish, skinned and
   boned)
2 ounces alfalfa sprouts
1 ripe avocado, pitted and
   thinly sliced
¹/₂ cup finely chopped red
   onion
1 cup Tomato Salsa (page 155)

1. In a small bowl, mix the mayonnaise and horseradish in a small bowl. Spread a tortilla with 1 tablespoon of the mayonnaise. About 2 inches from the bottom of the tortilla, sprinkle ¹/₃ cup of the whitefish in a thick strip. Layer with a tangle of sprouts, a few avocado slices, and a sprinkle of onion. Top with about 2 tablespoons of the salsa. Starting at the bottom, roll up tightly and place on a baking sheet, seam side down. Repeat with the remaining tortillas and filling ingredients. Cover tightly with plastic wrap and refrigerate until chilled, at least 30 minutes and up to 4 hours.

2. Using a sharp knife, trim the ends (save for noshing), and cut each roll crosswise into 6 pieces. Arrange on a platter and serve chilled.

Matzo-Crusted Asparagus

This recipe began life as an "oops," and turned into a "wow!" One of my assistant chefs at Abigael's accidentally mixed up the directions for a couple of recipes, and ended up with these lightly battered spears. The batter fries into a lacy, thin pattern, which allows the asparagus flavor and color to come through. This method also works well with fresh, trimmed okra pods. You can serve these with just the lemon wedges or make a roasted red bell pepper dip (roast a red pepper as directed on page 27, peel, seed, and purée it in a blender, then stir into ¹/₂ cup mayonnaise).

1. Position a rack in the center of the oven and preheat the oven to 200°F. Line a baking sheet with paper towels. Pour enough oil to come halfway up the sides of a Dutch oven and heat the oil to 350°F.

2. Mix the matzo meal, onion and garlic powders, salt, pepper, and nutmeg in a large bowl. Whisk in the pineapple juice and egg, then enough of the water to make a thick batter about the consistency of baby cereal.

3. In batches, dip a few asparagus spears in the batter (it should be just thick enough to coat each spear; adjust the thickness with more juice as needed). Without crowding, carefully lower the spears into the oil and fry until golden, about 2 minutes. Transfer the cooked asparagus to the baking sheet and keep warm in the oven while frying the remaining spears. Serve hot with the lemon wedges.

Vegetable oil, for deep-frying
1 cup matzo meal
1 teaspoon onion powder
1 teaspoon garlic powder
¹/₂ teaspoon kosher salt
¹/₄ teaspoon freshly ground
    black pepper
¹/₈ teaspoon freshly grated
    nutmeg
¹/₂ cup canned unsweetened
    pineapple juice, or more as
    needed
1 large egg, lightly beaten
³/₄ cup water, as needed
1¹/₂ pounds fresh asparagus,
    trimmed of woody stalks
Lemon wedges, for serving

Potato and Cabbage Knishes

MAKES 24
APPETIZER-
SIZED
KNISHES

It's hard to find a good knish these days, even from street vendors in New York, where they used to be one of the great snacks. This recipe, based on one from the justly famous and still excellent Yonah Schimmel Knishery on Manhattan's Lower East Side, brings the knish back to its days of glory. The spicy dip is optional, but a really nice touch when serving these as a passed hors d'oeuvre at a cocktail party.

FILLING

1¼ pounds baking (Burbank or russet) potatoes, peeled and cut into 2-inch chunks

4 tablespoons (½ stick) pareve margarine

1 medium onion, chopped

2 cups shredded red cabbage

½ teaspoon fennel seed

½ cup water

1 teaspoon sugar

1 teaspoon balsamic vinegar

1 teaspoon red currant jelly

Kosher salt and freshly ground black pepper to taste

One 17-ounce box frozen puff pastry, thawed according to package instructions

1 large egg, beaten

1. To make the filling, place the potatoes in a medium saucepan and add enough lightly salted cold water to cover. Bring to a boil over high heat. Cook, partially covered, until tender, about 20 minutes. Drain well and mash.

2. Meanwhile, heat the margarine in a medium skillet over medium heat. Add the onion and cook, stirring often, until translucent, about 5 minutes. Stir in the cabbage and fennel seed, then the water, sugar, vinegar, and jelly. Reduce the heat to medium-low. Cover and cook, stirring occasionally, until the cabbage is tender, about 30 minutes. Uncover during the last 5 minutes to evaporate any excess liquid; drain, if necessary. Stir into the mashed potatoes and season with salt and pepper. Cool completely. Transfer to a pastry bag (do not fit with a tip) or a resealable plastic bag (snip off about a 1-inch-wide opening from one corner).

3. Position a rack in the center of the oven and preheat the oven to 350°F. Line a large baking sheet with parchment paper.

4. On a lightly floured surface, roll out one pastry sheet into a 12×9-inch rectangle. Cut the rectangle lengthwise in half to make two 12×4½-inch rectangles. Working with one rectangle at a time, pipe the filling about 1 inch above the bottom edge. Brush the pastry above the filling with beaten egg. Starting at the bottom, roll up the pastry to make a log, turning the log seam side down. Cut into six 2-inch lengths. (The knishes can be frozen at this point for up to 1 month. Thaw, then bake as directed.)

5. Mix the mayonnaise, mustard, parsley, and horseradish in a small bowl. Cover and let stand at least 1 hour to blend the flavors. (The dip can be made up to 1 day ahead, covered and refrigerated. Serve at room temperature.)

6. Place the knishes on the baking sheet 1 inch apart, seam side down. Brush the tops of the knishes with beaten egg to glaze them. Bake until the knishes are golden brown and the pastry looks cooked through, about 25 minutes. Cool slightly and serve warm.

DIP
1 cup mayonnaise
2 tablespoons prepared mustard
2 tablespoons chopped fresh parsley
1 tablespoon prepared horseradish

Roasted Red Pepper Hummus

MAKES
ABOUT
2½ CUPS

Roasted red peppers transform plain hummus into something special. Serve it with pita bread wedges and crudités for a snack, or use it as an ingredient in my Mediterranean Pizza on page 210.

1 cup dried garbanzo beans
   (chickpeas)
1 red bell pepper, roasted (page
   27), skinned, seeded, and
   coarsely chopped
⅓ cup tahini (sesame paste)
⅓ cup fresh lemon juice
3 garlic cloves, minced
½ teaspoon ground cumin
Pinch of ground hot red
   (cayenne) pepper
2 tablespoons extra-virgin olive
   oil
2 tablespoons chopped fresh
   parsley
Kosher salt and freshly ground
   black pepper to taste

1. In a medium bowl, place the beans and add enough cold water to cover by 2 inches. Let stand at room temperature for at least 8 and up to 12 hours. Drain well.

2. Place the drained beans in a medium saucepan. Add enough fresh water to cover by 1 inch and bring to a boil over high heat. Reduce the heat to medium and simmer until the beans are tender, about 1 hour. Drain, reserving ½ cup of the cooking liquid. Rinse the beans under cold running water to cool.

3. Purée the cooked beans, roasted pepper, tahini, lemon juice, garlic, cumin, and cayenne in a food processor, then add the oil. With the machine running, add enough of the reserved cooking liquid to make a thick, fluffy spread. Add the parsley and pulse to combine. Season with salt and pepper. Cover and refrigerate to blend the flavors, at least 1 hour. (The hummus can be prepared up to 1 week ahead.) Serve at room temperature.

Vegetarian Chopped Liver

**MAKES
ABOUT
4 CUPS**

The year my sister Shelly went to Florida and came back with a Southern accent, she became a vegetarian for a while, too. Mom was forced to come up with some vegetarian dishes that the entire family would like. This recipe is actually one that has been around for decades—it is said to have been one of Isaac Bashevis Singer's favorites. It still gets high marks from Shelly, even though she is no longer a vegetarian, or a Southern belle. In the spirit of sibling rivalry, I have to say that I can't believe that Shelly and I actually like the same thing!

1. Position a rack in the center of the oven and preheat the oven to 400°F. Line a shallow baking dish with aluminum foil and lightly oil the foil.

2. Place the apples in the baking dish and bake until tender (they will split open), about 30 minutes. Cool. Discard the skin.

3. Cook the green beans in a large pot of rapidly boiling, salted water over high heat until tender, about 6 minutes. Drain and rinse under cold running water until cooled.

4. Heat the vegetable oil in a medium skillet over medium heat. Add the onion and cook, stirring occasionally, until golden brown, 6 to 8 minutes.

5. In batches, pulse the apples, green beans, onion, and eggs in a food processor together just until coarsely chopped, scraping down the side of the work bowl as needed. Transfer to a bowl. Return all of the chopped ingredients to the processor with the corn flakes and pulse again a few times to combine. Season with the salt and pepper. Cover and refrigerate until chilled, at least 2 hours. (The spread can be made up to 2 days ahead.)

6. Serve chilled or at room temperature, with the crackers and fresh vegetables for spreading.

2 Granny Smith apples, cored
1¼ pounds green beans, trimmed
1 tablespoon vegetable oil
1 large onion, chopped
2 large eggs, hard-boiled and peeled
2 cups (2 ounces) crushed corn flakes
Kosher salt and freshly ground white pepper to taste
Crackers, matzo, cucumber slices, and celery ribs, for serving

Persian Pickled Vegetables

**MAKES
4
QUARTS**

Ruben Bazargan-Fard, the Mashgiach (kosher supervisor) at Abigael's, is from Iran. This is his favorite snack food. This recipe makes a big batch, but the idea is to have a container of pickles in the refrigerator always at the ready to serve to guests. Be sure to wash all of the vegetables well before using.

1 small head of cauliflower, cut into small florets

1/2 pound turnips, cut into 1-inch cubes

1 head of celery, cut into 1 1/2-inch lengths

2 pounds carrots, cut into 1-inch lengths

1 green bell pepper, cored, seeded, and cut into 1-inch pieces

1 red bell pepper, cored, seeded, and cut into 1-inch pieces

4 ounces green beans, trimmed and cut in half

1 cup pearl onions, peeled

10 cups white vinegar

2 cups water

One 2-inch length of fresh ginger, peeled and sliced

3 tamarind pods (see Note) or 3 limes, cut in quarters

3 garlic cloves, peeled

1 cup fresh mint leaves

2 tablespoons kosher salt

2 teaspoons golpar (see Note)

2 teaspoons siyah-daneh (see Note)

1 teaspoon coriander seeds

1/2 teaspoon hot red pepper flakes

1. Bring a large pot of lightly salted water to a boil over high heat. Add the cauliflower and turnips and cook for 3 minutes (they should remain crisp). Drain well. Place the cauliflower, turnips, celery, carrots, green and red bell peppers, green beans, and pearl onions in a large crock or plastic container.

2. In a large, nonreactive saucepan, combine the vinegar, water, ginger, tamarind, garlic, mint, salt, golpar, siyah-daneh, coriander, and red pepper flakes. Bring to a boil; then reduce the heat to low and simmer for 5 minutes. Pour over the vegetables. The vegetables must be completely submerged. Cool completely, then cover tightly and refrigerate for at least 2 weeks before serving. (The pickles can be refrigerated for up to 2 months.)

NOTE: Tamarind pods, the fruit of the tamarind tree, have a sticky, fibrous pulp with a unique, acidic flavor. They are worth searching out. You can find them at ethnic grocers and produce stands. Golpar and siyah-daneh can be found in grocers that specialize in Mediterranean foods. If it is unavailale, substitute dried marjoram for the former, and fennel seed for the latter.

Fresh Berry Iced Tea

Here is the iced tea we serve at Abigael's, always refreshing, fresh, and natural. Make it the way we do, and change the fruits with the seasons. For example, in the winter, substitute chopped cranberries and orange segments for the summer berries.

1. Combine the water, tea bags, and mint in a covered container. Refrigerate overnight.

2. Remove the tea bags and mint. Stir in the apple juice, raspberries, and strawberries. Refrigerate for 2 hours. Stir well, and pour over ice cubes to serve.

1½ quarts cold water
12 orange pekoe tea bags
12 large mint sprigs
2 cups apple juice
½ pint raspberries
1 cup sliced strawberries

Hot Apple Cider

Mulled cider is the ultimate warmer-upper, and is very welcome at winter holiday parties. My version is infused not only with spices, but with dried citrus zest. Drying the zests isn't extraneous; it really brings out the citrus flavor, and takes very little effort. If you like, add a splash of dark rum or even red wine.

1. The day before making the cider, preheat the oven to 300°F. Using a vegetable peeler, remove the zests from the orange and lemon. Spread the zests on a baking sheet and bake until curled and leathery, about 10 minutes. Turn off the oven and let the zests stand, uncovered, overnight in the oven until dried and brittle.

2. In batches, grind the cloves, allspice, cinnamon sticks, and zests together to a powder in an electric coffee grinder or mini food processor.

3. Bring the cider, brown sugar, and spices to a simmer in a large pot over medium heat. Serve warm, garnishing each serving with a cinnamon stick.

1 large seedless orange
1 large lemon
12 whole cloves
6 allspice berries
Four 3-inch cinnamon sticks, coarsely broken into pieces, plus whole cinnamon sticks for garnish
½ gallon apple cider
6 tablespoons light brown sugar

Strawberry Cooler (Sharbat)

Many Middle Eastern cultures make fruit syrups to mix with iced water or club soda to create a refreshing drink. This fruity thirst-quencher is called sharbat, from which we get the English word "sherbet." Here is a basic strawberry syrup with a sour cherry variation. Each batch makes a generous quart, which will yield about 15 coolers, depending on how much syrup you use. This is not just a kid's drink.

**MAKES
ABOUT 15
SERVINGS**

2 quarts strawberries, hulled
    and coarsely chopped
4 cups sugar
2 cups water
1 vanilla bean, split lengthwise

Chilled water or club soda, as
    needed

1. Bring the strawberries, sugar, water, and vanilla bean to a boil in a large saucepan over medium heat, stirring often to dissolve the sugar. Cook, stirring occasionally, until the liquid has thickened to a very light syrup, about 15 minutes.

2. Strain through a sieve into a large bowl. Press hard on the solids, but do not rub the solids through the sieve. Scrape the tiny seeds from the vanilla pod into the syrup. Skim off and discard the foam on the surface. Cool completely. Transfer to a bottle or covered container. Refrigerate until ready to use. (The syrup can be prepared up to 2 months ahead.)

3. To serve, pour about ⅓ cup of the syrup into a tall glass and mix with water or seltzer, adjusting the amount of syrup to taste. Add ice and serve.

SOUR CHERRY SYRUP

Sour cherries, which are tarter and smaller than Bing cherries and have a translucent cast, give this syrup its authentic flavor. They can be found during their short midsummer season at farmer's markets and farmstands in cherry-producing regions. For the syrup, use 4 cups sugar; 3 cups water; 1 vanilla bean, split lengthwise; and 1 star anise pod. Substitute 2 pounds unpitted sour cherries, crushed in a bowl with a potato masher or large spoon, for the strawberries. Makes about 5 cups syrup.

Prize-Winning Rum Punch

This heady rum punch was the result of a recipe contest I ran a few years back. It's wonderfully delicious and dangerously potent—the day after the competition, everyone was late to work. Instead of a little glass of schnapps, serve this punch at festive holiday gatherings, such as Purim. You'll never go back to schnapps again!

1. Combine the wine, orange juice, lime juice, triple sec, rum, brandy, schnapps, and sugar in a large container. Cover and refrigerate until well chilled, at least 4 hours.

2. Pour into a punch bowl. Stir in the soda, strawberries, and orange. Serve chilled.

One 750-ml bottle fruity red wine, such as Merlot or Shiraz

$1\frac{1}{2}$ cups fresh orange juice

$\frac{1}{2}$ cup Rose's lime juice

$\frac{1}{3}$ cup triple sec or other orange-flavored liqueur

$\frac{1}{3}$ cup dark rum

$\frac{1}{4}$ cup brandy

$\frac{1}{4}$ cup peach schnapps

$\frac{1}{4}$ cup superfine (bartender's) sugar

2 cups lemon-lime soda (such as 7-Up), chilled

1 pint strawberries, thinly sliced

1 orange, quartered and thinly sliced

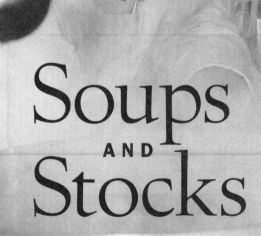

Soups

AND

Stocks

My nana was famous for her chicken soup.

Everyone, not just Jewish grandmothers, knows that chicken soup will cure just about anything. So whenever Nana visited, my sister and I would pretend that we were sick, just to ensure that she wouldn't leave without making a batch of her specialty. Of course, the soup never failed to magically appear. It took us years to figure out that my parents, who also loved Nana's soup, stocked the fridge with all the necessary ingredients. It wasn't magic after all!

Soup can be many things—an elegant first course, a hearty supper, a light lunch, a midnight snack, a cure-all. No matter when it is served, it is always welcome and satisfying. I see no reason for making a small pot of soup. Go ahead and make enough for an army, and freeze any leftovers. There will be many a time when you are glad your freezer holds a meal that can be ready in no time.

The backbone of any soup is a good stock. In fact, many dishes succeed or fail based on the quality of the stock used in the recipe. Canned broth (broth is made from meaty bones and seasoned, but stock is made from bones alone and unseasoned) is okay in a pinch, but stock is easy to make. Stock is unsalted because it will be an ingredient in a finished dish that will eventually get seasoned anyway. Homemade stocks don't have the preservatives, artificial flavors, or high sodium content found in commercial broth and bouillon cubes. Get in the habit of simmering up a batch on a relaxed weekend, and freeze it in one- to two-pint covered containers so you can defrost what you need without any waste.

Chicken Stock

There's no sense in making a small batch of this basic pantry item, so cook up a big pot and freeze it in quart containers. Your homemade stock will be much tastier than any canned broth or bouillon cube you can buy. Get in the habit of freezing chicken bones and trimmings for a cost-efficient way to make stock, or simply buy chicken parts when you see them at a good price.

3 pounds chicken necks, backs, or wings
1 large onion, chopped
1 large carrot, chopped
2 large celery ribs, chopped
1 large leek (white part only), trimmed, chopped, and well rinsed
1 garlic clove, smashed
Seasoning Sachet: 12 fresh parsley sprigs, 1 teaspoon dried thyme, 1/2 teaspoon whole black peppercorns, and 2 bay leaves, wrapped in cheesecloth and tied into a bundle
1 gallon water, as needed

1. Place the chicken, onion, carrot, celery, leek, garlic, and seasoning sachet in a large pot, and add enough cold water to cover by 1 inch. Bring the stock to a boil over high heat, skimming off the foam that rises to the surface.

2. Reduce the heat to low and simmer until full-flavored, at least 2 and up to 4 hours, occasionally skimming off the foam on the surface.

3. Strain the stock into a large bowl and discard the solids. Let stand until warm. Cover and refrigerate until chilled, at least 8 hours. Remove the chilled, hardened fat from the surface and save it as schmaltz, if desired. Refrigerate the stock for up to 3 days, or freeze for up to 2 months.

TURKEY STOCK

Substitute 3 pounds turkey wings for the chicken parts.

Beef Stock

MAKES
ABOUT
3 QUARTS

In my opinion, there is no substitute for homemade beef stock. I should know, because in my years as a chef, many a restaurant supplies salesperson has tried to sell me an "instant" replacement for the real thing. These products taste like many things, but beef isn't one of them. You won't have that problem with this essential of the well-stocked kitchen. Three pointers: Use thoroughly browned bones, keep the stock at a bare simmer, and allow plenty of time to extract every drop of flavor.

5 pounds beef bones
2 tablespoons vegetable oil
1 large onion, coarsely chopped
1 large carrot, coarsely chopped
1 large celery rib, coarsely chopped
1 gallon water, as needed
Seasoning Sachet: 12 fresh parsley sprigs, 1 teaspoon dried thyme, $1/2$ teaspoon whole black peppercorns, and 2 bay leaves, wrapped in cheesecloth and tied into a bundle
2 garlic cloves, smashed
1 tablespoon tomato paste
Kosher salt and freshly ground black pepper to taste

1. Position a rack in the top third of the oven and preheat the oven to 425°F. Spread the bones in a large roasting pan and toss with the oil. Roast until the bones are beginning to brown, about 30 minutes. Pour off the fat in the pan.

2. Stir in the onion, carrot, and celery. Roast until the bones are nicely browned and the vegetables are tender (don't worry if they are a bit scorched), about 30 minutes. Transfer the bones and vegetables to a large pot.

3. Pour the fat from the pan. Place the pan over high heat on the stove. Add 2 cups water and scrape up the browned bits in the pan with a wooden spoon. Pour the liquid into the pot. Add the seasoning sachet, garlic, and the tomato paste. Add enough cold water to cover the ingredients by 1 inch.

4. Bring to a boil over high heat, skimming off the foam that rises to the surface. Reduce the heat to low and simmer, uncovered, until full-flavored, at least 3 and up to 5 hours. Season lightly with salt and pepper.

5. Strain the stock into a large bowl, discarding the solids. Let stand for 5 minutes and skim the fat from the surface. To store the stock, cool until warm. Cover and refrigerate for up to 3 days, or freeze for up to 2 months.

VEAL STOCK
Substitute veal bones for the beef bones.

Fish Stock

MAKES
1½
QUARTS

Fish stock is made from thin bones, so it takes much less time to simmer than other stocks that use thick bones. Any good fish store will be happy to sell you the frames and heads for the stock, but avoid oily fish like salmon and mackerel, and use only the bones from mild-flavored fish like bass or whitefish. If the heads include the gills, ask the salesperson to snip them out, or do it yourself at home with a pair of sturdy kitchen scissors.

2 tablespoons vegetable oil

1 medium leek (white part only), or 1 medium onion, chopped

1 medium celery rib with leaves, chopped

1½ pounds fish frames and/or heads, gills removed, well rinsed

1½ quarts water, as needed

Seasoning Sachet: 6 fresh parsley sprigs, ½ teaspoon dried thyme, ¼ teaspoon whole black peppercorns, and 1 bay leaf, wrapped in cheesecloth and tied into a bundle

1. Heat the oil in a large saucepan over medium heat. Add the leek and celery, and cover. Cook, stirring, until softened but not browned, about 5 minutes.

2. Add the fish frames and cover. Cook, stirring occasionally, until the bones begin to give off some juices, about 5 minutes.

3. Add enough cold water to barely cover the bones, and add the seasoning sachet. Bring to a boil over high heat, skimming off any foam that rises to the surface. Reduce the heat to low. Simmer, uncovered, for 30 minutes.

4. Strain the stock into a large bowl, and discard the solids. Let stand for 5 minutes and skim the fat from the surface. To store the stock, cool until warm. Cover and refrigerate for up to 3 days, or freeze for up to 2 months.

Vegetable Stock

MAKES ABOUT 4 QUARTS

To avoid using meat in pareve dishes, some cooks resort to water instead of stock, which almost guarantees bland food. A simply prepared vegetable stock will add just the right nuance to any savory recipe.

1. Heat the vegetable oil in a large saucepan over medium-high heat. Add the onions, shallot, and garlic, and cook just until the onions begin to wilt, about 3 minutes. Stir in the mushrooms, tomatoes, carrots, celery, leek, and seasoning sachet. Pour in the water and bring to a boil over high heat.

2. Reduce the heat to low and simmer for 45 to 60 minutes, skimming off any foam that rises to the surface. Season lightly with salt and pepper.

3. Strain into a large bowl and discard the solids. To store the stock, cool until warm. Cover and refrigerate for up to 3 days, or freeze for up to 2 months.

2 tablespoons vegetable oil
2 large onions, thinly sliced
1 shallot, thinly sliced
5 garlic cloves, minced
1 pound white button mushrooms, quartered
$^1/_2$ pound ripe plum tomatoes, quartered
4 medium carrots, cut into 1-inch pieces
4 medium celery ribs, cut into 1-inch pieces
1 large leek (white part only), split lengthwise into quarters and rinsed
Seasoning Sachet: 12 fresh parsley sprigs, $^1/_2$ teaspoon dried thyme, $^1/_2$ teaspoon whole black peppercorns, and 2 bay leaves, wrapped in cheesecloth and tied into a bundle
1 gallon water
Kosher salt and coarsely ground black pepper to taste

Monney's Beef Borscht

MAKES 12 SERVINGS

This is my favorite soup in the world. Not only is it everything a soup should be, it is the soup that made me propose to my wife. We had been dating awhile, and I was finally invited to her family's house for dinner. For the first course, we were served this borscht, which was her father, Monney's, specialty. It was full of vegetables and chunks of short ribs, which I politely ate around, leaving the bones in the bowl. When I saw everyone at the table pick up the bones and start slurping, I knew this was the family for me!

2 tablespoons vegetable oil

2 medium onions, thinly sliced

4 pounds cross-cut beef short ribs (flanken)

1 pound beef bones

4 garlic cloves, thinly sliced

1/2 medium head of thinly sliced green cabbage (5 cups)

1 small fennel bulb, thinly sliced (1 1/2 cups)

One 28-ounce can canned crushed tomatoes

Seasoning Sachet: 8 parsley sprigs, 1 tablespoon dried thyme, 1/4 teaspoon black peppercorns, and 2 bay leaves, wrapped in cheesecloth and tied into a bundle

1 tablespoon sweet paprika

2 teaspoons pure ground mild chile

1 teaspoon kosher salt, plus more to taste

1/4 teaspoon ground hot red (cayenne) pepper

3/4 teaspoon sour salt (see Note), plus more to taste

Freshly ground black pepper to taste

1. Heat the oil in a large soup pot over medium-high heat. Add the onions and cook uncovered, stirring occasionally, until golden brown, about 6 minutes. Add the flanken, beef bones, and garlic. Cook without stirring for 3 minutes. Stir well, then cook until the beef begins to lose its raw look, about 3 more minutes.

2. Stir in 3 quarts water, the cabbage, fennel, crushed tomatoes, the seasoning sachet, paprika, ground chile, 1 teaspoon kosher salt, and cayenne. Bring to a boil over high heat. Reduce the heat to low.

3. Simmer, occasionally skimming off the foam and fat that rises to the surface, until the flanken is very tender, about 3 hours. Discard the sachet. Remove from the heat and let stand for 10 minutes. Skim off the fat from the surface of the soup. Stir in the sour salt. Season with the pepper, and additional sour salt and kosher salt. (The soup is best if cooled to room temperature, covered, and refrigerated overnight. Reheat before serving.)

4. Ladle into bowls and serve hot. If you feel like slurping the bones, go ahead.

NOTE: Not really a salt, sour salt (also called citric salt) is processed from citrus fruit. If it is unavailable, substitute 3 to 4 tablespoons fresh lemon juice.

Hungarian Goulash Soup

MAKES 8
GENEROUS
SERVINGS

My wife, Alison, loves to cook the dishes of her heritage, which includes Hungary. One time we chanced upon a Hungarian market on New York's Upper East Side, bought a collection of different paprikas, and ended up cooking for the rest of the weekend. Here is one of our favorite recipes from that experience. It is not only delicious, but authentic, for true Hungarian goulash is always thin and souplike, and never prepared as a thick stew.

1. Heat the oil in a large saucepan over medium-high heat. Add the onions and fennel. Cook uncovered, stirring occasionally, until golden, about 6 minutes.

2. Add the beef and cook, stirring occasionally, until the meat loses its raw look, about 5 minutes. Add the paprika and caraway seeds, and stir for 1 minute. Stir in half of the potatoes, the tomatoes, 2 green bell peppers, 2 carrots, the garlic, and the bay leaves. Add the stock and bring to a simmer over high heat, skimming off the foam that rises to the surface.

3. Reduce the heat to medium-low. Simmer until the beef is barely tender, about $1^{1}/2$ hours.

4. Add the chicken wings and the remaining potato and carrot. Increase the heat to high and return the soup to a boil. Return the heat to medium-low and simmer until the chicken wings are cooked through, about 45 minutes.

5. Stir in the remaining green pepper. Season with the salt and pepper. Remove from the heat and let stand for 5 minutes. Skim off the fat on the surface of the soup. (The soup can be prepared up to 2 days ahead, cooled, covered, and refrigerated. Reheat before serving.)

6. Ladle into bowls, being sure each serving gets a chicken wing, and serve hot.

$^{1}/4$ cup vegetable oil

2 large onions, chopped

1 cup chopped fennel bulb

2 pounds beef chuck or flanken, cut into 1-inch chunks

$^{1}/3$ cup sweet Hungarian paprika

1 teaspoon caraway seeds

3 large red-skinned potatoes, peeled and cut into 1-inch cubes

4 plum tomatoes, seeded and cut into 1-inch dice

3 green bell peppers, cored, seeded, and cut into $^{1}/2$-inch dice, divided

3 carrots, cut into $^{1}/2$-inch dice, divided

5 garlic cloves, minced

2 bay leaves

8 cups Chicken Stock (page 40)

8 chicken wings

Kosher salt and freshly ground black pepper to taste

heritage recipe

Classic Chicken Soup
with Matzo Balls

MAKES
8 TO 12
SERVINGS

Many a chicken soup has been made with only one chicken and its feiselach (Yiddish for feet) simmered in a pot of water—that's the way Great-Grandma Baba used to make it. But for deep-flavored, golden, prize-winning soup, make yours with chicken stock. And for the lightest matzo balls around, fold beaten egg whites into the batter, another of Baba's secrets.

MATZO BALLS

6 large eggs, separated
$1/2$ cup vegetable oil, plus
 additional for oiling hands
$1/4$ cup chopped fresh parsley
$1/4$ cup water
2 tablespoons kosher salt
$3/4$ teaspoon freshly ground
 black pepper
2 cups matzo meal
1 teaspoon baking powder

1. To make the matzo balls, bring a large pot of salted water to a boil over high heat. In a medium bowl, whisk the yolks, oil, parsley, water, salt, and pepper. In another medium bowl, whisk the whites just until soft peaks barely begin to form. Pour the whites into the yolk mixture. Stir the matzo meal and baking powder together, then fold into the eggs. Let stand until firm enough to handle, about 20 minutes (or about as long as it takes for the water to come to a boil).

2. Moisten your hands lightly with vegetable oil and form the matzo mixture into 24 walnut-sized balls. Carefully drop the matzo balls into the water. Reduce the heat to medium and cover. Simmer gently until the balls are cooked through, about 45 minutes. Using a skimmer or slotted spoon, transfer the matzo balls to a large bowl of cold water.

3. Meanwhile, make the soup. Bring the stock, chicken, onions, carrots, celery, parsnip, and turnip to a boil in a large pot over medium-high heat, skimming off the foam that rises to the surface. Reduce the heat to medium-low. Simmer, partially covered, until the chicken is cooked through and the vegetables are tender, about 45 minutes. With tongs, transfer the chicken to a plate.

4. When the chicken meat is cool enough to handle, cut into bite-sized pieces, discarding the skin and bones, and return the meat to the soup. Stir in the dill and season with salt and pepper.

5. When ready to serve, drain the matzo balls. Place the balls in the simmering soup and cook until heated through, about 10 minutes. (The soup can be prepared up to 2 days ahead, cooled, covered, and refrigerated. Reheat before serving.)

6. Ladle the soup and matzo balls into bowls and serve hot.

PASSOVER VARIATION

Of course, at Passover, one cannot eat leavened foods, so delete the baking powder from the matzo balls.

CHICKEN SOUP

3 quarts Chicken Stock (page 40)

One 4-pound chicken, cut into 8 serving pieces

2 medium onions, cut into $1/2$-inch dice

3 medium carrots, cut into $1/2$-inch dice

3 celery ribs, cut into $1/2$-inch dice

1 medium parsnip, peeled and cut into $1/2$-inch dice

1 medium turnip, peeled and cut into $1/2$-inch dice

2 tablespoons chopped fresh dill

Kosher salt and freshly ground black pepper to taste

Sephardic Chicken Soup
with Sofrito and Saffron Matzo Balls

MAKES
8
SERVINGS

When preparing a Hanukkah dinner at the James Beard House, I was inspired by my chef de cuisine, Ramón Mercedes, to jazz up the traditional chicken soup and matzo balls with Latin flavors. It was such a hit, hardly anyone touched the latkes! (Only kidding…)

SAFFRON MATZO BALLS
6 large eggs, separated
1/2 cup vegetable oil, plus additional for moistening hands
1/4 cup water
1/4 cup chopped fresh cilantro
2 tablespoons kosher salt
1/2 teaspoon crumbled saffron threads
3/4 teaspoon freshly ground black pepper
2 cups matzo meal
1 teaspoon baking powder

3 quarts Chicken Stock (page 40)
One 4-pound chicken, cut into 8 serving pieces

1. To make the matzo balls, bring a large pot of salted water to a boil over high heat. In a medium bowl, whisk the egg yolks, oil, water, cilantro, salt, saffron, and pepper. In another medium bowl, whisk the whites just until soft peaks barely begin to form. Pour the whites into the yolk mixture. In a separate bowl, stir the matzo meal and baking powder together, then fold into the eggs. Let stand until firm enough to handle, about 20 minutes (or about as long as it takes for the water to come to a boil).

2. Moisten your hands lightly with vegetable oil and form the batter into 24 walnut-sized balls. Carefully drop the matzo balls into the water. Reduce the heat to medium and cover. Simmer gently until the balls are cooked through, about 40 minutes. Using a skimmer or slotted spoon, transfer the matzo balls to a large bowl of cold water.

3. Meanwhile, make the soup. Bring the stock and chicken pieces to a boil in a large pot over medium-high heat, skimming off the foam that rises to the surface. Reduce the heat to medium-low. Simmer, partially covered, until the chicken is cooked through, about 45 minutes. Remove the chicken from the soup. When cool enough to handle, remove and discard the skin and bones. Cut the chicken into bite-sized pieces, and return it to the pot.

4. To make the sofrito, while the soup is simmering, heat the oil in a medium skillet over medium heat. Add the onion, tomatoes, red and green bell peppers, cilantro, and garlic. Cook, stirring occasionally, until the vegetables in the sofrito are tender but not browned, about 8 minutes. Add the red pepper sauce, if using. Set the sofrito aside.

5. When ready to serve, stir the sofrito into the soup. Drain the matzo balls and place on a work surface. Using a knife, coarsely chop the balls, then stir into the soup. Simmer until the balls are heated through, about 5 minutes. (The soup can be prepared up to 2 days ahead, cooled, covered, and refrigerated. Reheat before serving.)

6. Ladle the soup into bowls and serve hot.

SOFRITO

2 tablespoons extra-virgin olive oil
1 small yellow onion, cut into 1/4-inch dice
1/2 cup diced (1/4-inch) plum tomatoes
1/2 cup diced (1/4-inch) red bell pepper
1/2 cup diced (1/4-inch) green bell pepper
2 tablespoons chopped fresh cilantro
4 garlic cloves, minced
1 teaspoon hot red pepper sauce (optional)

Japanese Miso Chicken Soup

MAKES
8
SERVINGS

Asian flavors are not usually found in Jewish cooking. To my mind, this combination, especially in this Japanese-accented chicken soup, is the perfect blend of old and new. There are many different kinds of miso available, but I prefer the mellowness of a light brown or red variety for this soup.

ASIAN CHICKEN STOCK

One 4-pound chicken, rinsed
   and patted dry
3 scallions (green and white
   parts), chopped
1 small celery rib, coarsely
   chopped
1 small carrot, coarsely
   chopped
4 ($1/4$-inch) rounds of fresh
   ginger
$1/4$ teaspoon whole black
   peppercorns
$2^1/2$ quarts water

1. To make the Asian stock, using a sharp, heavy knife or cleaver, separate the chicken wings from the breasts. Chop into pieces between the joints. Cut off the leg quarters, then separate the drumsticks and thighs. Set aside.

2. Using a sharp, thin knife, cut the breast meat from one side of the rib cage in one piece. Pull off the skin. Repeat with the other side of the chicken. Wrap the chicken breast meat in plastic wrap and refrigerate. Using the heavy knife, chop the remaining bony pieces of the chicken (the rib cage and back) into large pieces.

3. In a large pot, place the wings, thighs, drumsticks, chopped rib cage and back, scallions, celery, carrot, ginger, and peppercorns. Add the water and bring to a boil over high heat, skimming off any foam that rises to the surface. Reduce the heat to low and simmer, uncovered, until full-flavored, about 3 hours. (If desired, remove the thighs and drumsticks after 45 minutes; remove the meat for another purpose, and return the skin and bones to the stock.) Strain the stock into a bowl. Skim off any fat on the surface. You should have about 3 quarts. If necessary, boil the stock over high heat to reduce. (The soup can be made up to this point 1 day ahead, cooled, covered, and refrigerated. Reheat to simmering.)

4. Bring the stock to a simmer over medium-high heat. Rinse the reserved breast meat under cold water. Cut into thin strips about $1/2$ inch wide and 3 inches long. Stir the breast strips, mushrooms, tofu, and soy sauce into the simmering soup, and cook until the chicken is cooked through, about 4 minutes. Remove from the heat.

5. Whisk 1 cup of the soup together with the miso in a small bowl to dissolve the miso. Stir into the soup and add the scallions and sesame oil. Reheat gently, if needed, but do not allow the soup to boil after adding the miso. Serve hot.

4 large shiitake mushroom caps, cut into $1/4$-inch strips

4 ounces firm tofu, cut into $1/2$-inch dice

2 teaspoons soy sauce

$1/2$ cup brown or red miso (available at Asian and specialty markets and health food stores; see Mail-Order Sources, page 250, for kosher brands)

6 scallions (white parts only), sliced diagonally into $1/4$-inch pieces

2 teaspoons dark Asian sesame oil

DEMYSTIFYING MISO

Miso is an essential ingredient in Japanese cooking, and more and more American cooks are discovering its complex flavor. Miso is made from soybeans that have been salted and fermented with rice or barley, then ground into a paste. The exact combination of ingredients dictates its color, flavor, and aroma. Miso is a powerhouse of rich, salty flavor, and is always used in small quantities. The three main varieties of miso are white (made from rice and soybeans, and actually pale to deep yellow in color), red (soybeans with rice or barley, and ranging in color from reddish, mahogany brown to dark brown), and mamemiso (made from soybeans alone, with a deep red color and chunky texture). Store opened miso in a tightly covered container in the refrigerator, where it will keep for a few months.

Salmon Corn Chowder

MAKES
8
SERVINGS

I consider this a summer soup, for it is at its best with sweet Jersey corn and aromatic basil from the farmer's market. Add some whole grain or sourdough bread and a green salad, and you have quite a meal.

3 tablespoons unsalted butter

1 medium yellow onion, cut into ¹/₂-inch dice

3 celery ribs, cut into ¹/₂-inch dice

1 red bell pepper, cored, seeded, and cut into ¹/₂-inch dice

1 tablespoon all-purpose flour

4 cups Fish Stock (page 42)

1 cup heavy cream

1 tablespoon chopped fresh basil leaves

¹/₂ teaspoon sugar

Kosher salt and freshly ground black pepper to taste

¹/₂ pound new potatoes, scrubbed but unpeeled, cut into ¹/₂-inch dice

1 pound salmon fillet, skinned and cut into 1-inch pieces

2 cups fresh corn kernels (about 4 ears)

1. Melt the butter in a large saucepan over medium heat. Add the onion, celery, and red bell pepper. Cook, stirring occasionally, until softened but not browned, about 3 minutes. Sprinkle in the flour and cook, stirring constantly, for 1 minute.

2. Stir in the stock and heavy cream, basil, and sugar. Season with the salt and pepper. Add the potatoes. Bring to a simmer over high heat.

3. Reduce the heat to medium-low. Simmer, partially covered, until the potatoes are tender, about 20 minutes. Stir in the salmon pieces and corn, and simmer until the salmon is cooked through, about 10 minutes. Season again with salt and pepper. Serve hot.

Sweet-and-Sour Cabbage Soup

**MAKES
10 TO 12
SERVINGS**

If you've ever messed up a recipe, this story should make you feel better. I made my mother's sweet-and-sour cabbage rolls perfectly for years, but I finally overcooked a batch. Never one to waste food, I transformed it into a soup. Lo and behold, it has become one of my most requested dishes.

1. Place the flanken and crushed tomatoes in a large soup kettle. Add enough water to cover by 1 inch. Bring to a boil over medium heat, stirring often and skimming off the foam that rises to the surface. Reduce the heat to medium-low and cover. Cook until the meat is tender, about 1 hour.

2. Place the ground beef in a large saucepan and add enough cold water to cover. Bring to a boil over medium-high heat, stirring often to break up the clumps of meat. Reduce the heat to medium-low and simmer until the meat is thoroughly cooked, about 12 minutes. Drain in a colander.

3. Stir the cabbage, onion, cranberries, currants, ketchup, sherry, maple syrup, garlic, and onion and garlic powders into the tomatoes. Increase the heat to high and bring to a boil. Return the heat to medium-low and cover. Simmer, stirring often, until the cabbage is tender, about 30 minutes.

4. While the cabbage is cooking, bring 1½ cups water to a boil in a small saucepan over high heat. Stir in the rice. Cover tightly and reduce the heat to low. Cook until the rice is tender and absorbs the water, about 15 minutes.

5. Stir the rice and ground beef into the soup and return to the simmer. Season with salt and pepper. Serve hot.

2 pounds cross-cut beef short ribs (flanken), cut between the ribs into large chunks

One 28-ounce can crushed tomatoes

1 pound ground beef chuck

6 cups shredded green cabbage

1 medium onion, halved lengthwise and sliced into thin half-moons

1 cup fresh or frozen cranberries

½ cup dried currants, soaked in hot water to cover for 20 minutes, then drained

½ cup ketchup

3 tablespoons dry sherry

3 tablespoons maple pancake syrup

2 garlic cloves, minced

1½ teaspoons onion powder

1½ teaspoons garlic powder

½ cup long-grain rice

Kosher salt and freshly ground black pepper to taste

Loaded Baked Potato Soup

A plain baked potato is not very interesting—it needs to be "loaded" with sour cream, cheese, salsa, and other goodies. I feel the same way about potato soup. Move over, vichyssoise, and make room for a potato soup with chutzpah. This soup can be adapted for pareve or meat menus, too—just follow the simple changes at the end of the recipe.

6 large (9 ounces each)
   Burbank or russet baking
   potatoes, scrubbed
6 tablespoons unsalted butter
2 tablespoons extra-virgin olive
   oil
1 large red onion, chopped
6 shallots, thinly sliced
2 medium leeks (white part
   only), split, rinsed, and
   chopped
1/2 cup all-purpose flour
8 cups Vegetable Stock
   (page 43)
Kosher salt and freshly ground
   black pepper to taste
Sour cream, chopped fresh
   chives, shredded Cheddar
   cheese, and tomato salsa, for
   garnish

1. Position a rack in the center of the oven and preheat the oven to 450°F.

2. Bake the potatoes directly on the oven rack until tender when pierced with the tip of a sharp knife, about 1 hour. Cool completely. Peel the potatoes, leaving some of the skin attached (it gives the soup a rustic look), and chop into 1-inch pieces.

3. Heat the butter and oil in a large saucepan over medium heat. Add the onion, shallots, and leeks. Cook, stirring occasionally, until the onion is translucent, about 6 minutes. Reduce the heat to low, sprinkle in the flour, and cook for 2 minutes, stirring constantly, being careful not to brown the flour.

4. Gradually whisk in the vegetable stock, being sure to scrape the bottom of the pot and fully blend all of the flour mixture into the stock. Increase the heat to medium-high and bring to a simmer, stirring often to prevent scorching. Add the potato flesh and simmer for 15 minutes, whisking often, allowing the potatoes to dissolve into the soup. (Don't worry if you have some small pieces of potato that didn't dissolve. Under no circumstances should you purée the soup in a blender, which will ruin the texture.) Season with the salt and pepper. (The soup can be prepared up to 2 days ahead, cooled, covered, and refrigerated. Reheat gently over low heat, stirring often. If too thick, thin with additional vegetable stock.)

5. Ladle into bowls and serve hot, passing bowls of sour cream, chives, cheese, and salsa for topping.

PAREVE VARIATION
Substitute margarine for the butter and omit the dairy garnishes.

MEAT VARIATION
I love this soup topped with pastrami cracklings. To make the cracklings, heat 2 teaspoons vegetable oil in a large nonstick skillet over medium-high heat. Add 4 ounces thinly sliced pastrami, coarsely chopped. Cook, stirring occasionally, until the pastrami is crisp, about 4 minutes. Add the cracklings to the pareve version of the soup.

Wild Mushroom and Barley Soup

MAKES
8
SERVINGS

What I love about this soup is that it can (and should) taste a little different every time you make it. It all depends on the exact combination of mushrooms, which should be chosen according to what looks good in the market when you go shopping. For a pareve version, use the vegetable oil and vegetable stock.

6 tablespoons schmaltz (see page 165) or vegetable oil

3/4 cup pearl barley

1 ounce dried porcini mushrooms (about 1 cup)

1 pound assorted mushrooms (such as button, cremini, and stemmed shiitake), thinly sliced

1 medium onion, cut into 1/2-inch dice

2 medium celery ribs, cut into 1/4-inch dice

1 medium carrot, cut into 1/4-inch dice

1 medium leek (white part only), cut into 1/4-inch dice

2 quarts Chicken Stock (page 40) or Vegetable Stock (page 43)

Seasoning Sachet: 8 fresh parsley sprigs, 1/2 teaspoon dried thyme, 1/2 teaspoon whole black peppercorns, and 2 bay leaves, wrapped in cheesecloth and tied into a bundle

1/4 cup chopped fresh parsley

Kosher salt and freshly ground black pepper to taste

1. Heat 1 tablespoon of the schmaltz or oil in a medium saucepan over medium-high heat. Add the barley and cook, stirring occasionally, until lightly toasted, about 4 minutes. Add 2 quarts water, salt lightly, and bring to a boil. Reduce the heat to medium-low and cover. Cook until almost tender, about 40 minutes. Drain in a sieve and rinse under cold water.

2. Meanwhile, place the dried porcini in a small bowl and cover with hot water. Let stand until softened, about 20 minutes. Drain in a sieve lined with a moistened paper towel, reserving the soaking liquid.

3. Melt the remaining 5 tablespoons of the schmaltz or oil in a large pot over medium heat. Add the sliced mushrooms, onion, celery, carrot, and leek, and cover. Cook, stirring occasionally, until tender, about 10 minutes. Stir in the stock, cooked barley, porcini mushrooms, porcini liquid, and the seasoning sachet. Bring to a boil over high heat, then reduce the heat to medium-low. Simmer, uncovered, until the vegetables are tender, about 30 minutes. Stir in the parsley. Remove the sachet. Season with the salt and pepper.

4. Ladle into bowls and serve hot.

Moroccan Yellow Split Pea Soup

MAKES
12
SERVINGS

The Moroccan Jews, who were often spice traders, strongly influenced the way the Sephardim ate. To this day, Moroccan cooks love to use a blend of many spices in their cooking. Even something as familiar as split pea soup can get a lift from this way of seasoning. For a meat-free dish, this soup is quite filling.

1. To make the topping, mix the yogurt, curry powder, and honey in a small bowl with a rubber spatula. Cover and let stand at room temperature while making the soup.

2. Heat the oil in a large soup pot over medium heat. Add the onion, celery, carrot, potato, and ginger. Cook, stirring occasionally, until the onion is translucent, about 6 minutes. Add the yellow peas, curry powder, turmeric, red pepper flakes, cinnamon, and bay leaf and stir until fragrant, about 30 seconds.

3. Stir in the stock and bring to a boil over high heat. Reduce the heat to low. Simmer uncovered, stirring occasionally, until the split peas are very tender, about 1 hour.

4. Purée the soup directly in the pot with a hand-held blender, or purée batches of the soup in a standing electric blender (use caution when blending hot liquids) and return to the pot. Season with salt and pepper. (The soup can be prepared up to 2 days ahead, cooled, covered, and refrigerated. Reheat before serving, stirring often.)

5. Ladle into bowls and serve hot, topping each serving with a dollop of the curried yogurt topping and a sprinkling of cilantro leaves.

PAREVE VARIATION

Omit the yogurt topping. Garnish with cilantro leaves.

CURRIED YOGURT TOPPING
1 cup plain yogurt
1 teaspoon curry powder
1 teaspoon honey

3 tablespoons extra-virgin olive oil
1 large onion, chopped
2 celery ribs, chopped
1 large carrot, chopped
1 large baking potato (russet or Burbank), peeled and cut into 1-inch chunks
2 tablespoons peeled and finely chopped fresh ginger
1 pound yellow split peas, rinsed and sorted
1½ tablespoons curry powder
1 teaspoon ground turmeric
¼ teaspoon hot red pepper flakes
One 3-inch cinnamon stick
1 bay leaf
3 quarts Vegetable Stock (page 43)
Kosher salt and freshly ground black pepper to taste
Chopped fresh cilantro, for garnish

Tomato-Wild Rice Soup

MAKES
6 TO 8
SERVINGS

Basically a tomato bouillon, this light and delicate soup gets additional flavor and texture from robust wild rice. Be sure to cook the rice separately—if cooked in the soup, it will soak up too much of the liquid. For more on wild rice, see page 74.

²/₃ cup wild rice, rinsed and drained

2 tablespoons extra-virgin olive oil

4 celery ribs, cut into ¹/₂-inch dice

1 small onion, cut into ¹/₂-inch dice

1 garlic clove, smashed

4 ripe plum tomatoes, seeded and cut into ¹/₂-inch dice

1 tablespoon sugar

2¹/₂ cups tomato juice

3 cups Vegetable Stock (page 43)

1 tablespoon fresh lemon juice

Kosher salt and freshly ground black pepper to taste

1. Bring 3 cups lightly salted water to a boil in a medium saucepan over high heat. Add the wild rice and reduce the heat to low. Cover tightly and cook until the grains are split and tender, and most of the water is absorbed, about 1 hour (the exact cooking time and rate of absorption depend on your particular brand of wild rice). Drain, if necessary.

2. Meanwhile, heat the oil in a large soup pot over medium-high heat. Reduce the heat to low and add the celery, onion, and garlic. Cook, stirring often, until the onion is translucent, about 5 minutes. Stir in the tomatoes and sugar. Cook until the tomatoes begin to soften, about 2 minutes. Stir in the tomato juice, stock, and lemon juice. Bring to a gentle boil over medium-high heat, then reduce the heat to low. Simmer, uncovered, until the vegetables are tender, about 30 minutes.

3. Stir in the wild rice and cook until heated through, about 2 minutes. Season with salt and pepper. (The soup can be prepared up to 2 days ahead, cooled, covered, and refrigerated. Reheat before serving.)

4. Ladle into bowls and serve hot.

Chilled Strawberry Soup
with Strawberry Salsa

MAKES
8
SERVINGS

Every summer, my family makes a ritual visit to a local strawberry farm, where we always buy more berries than we can feasibly eat. After we bake strawberry pies and make many jars of jam, we turn the leftovers into this cool and creamy soup.

1. To make the soup, purée the strawberries, 1/4 cup sugar, and ginger in a food processor fitted with the metal blade. Transfer to a large bowl.

2. Add the ginger ale, sour cream, and heavy cream, and whisk until well blended. Taste and sweeten with more sugar, if needed. Cover tightly with plastic wrap and refrigerate until well chilled, at least 3 hours or overnight.

3. Up to 2 hours before serving the soup, make the salsa. In a small bowl, mix the strawberries, blueberries (if using), onion, cilantro, lime juice, and balsamic vinegar. Cover and refrigerate for at least 20 minutes to blend the flavors.

4. To serve, mix the chilled soup well and ladle into bowls. Top each serving with a spoonful of the salsa, a dollop of sour cream, and a scattering of mint leaves.

SOUP

2 1/2 quarts strawberries, hulled
1/4 cup sugar, plus more to taste
2 teaspoons peeled and finely chopped fresh ginger
3 cups ginger ale
1/2 cup sour cream, plus more for garnish
1/2 cup heavy cream
Fresh mint leaves, for garnish

STRAWBERRY SALSA

1 cup hulled and coarsely chopped strawberries
1/4 cup coarsely chopped blueberries (optional)
1/4 cup finely chopped red onion
3 tablespoons finely chopped fresh cilantro
2 tablespoons fresh lime juice
1 teaspoon balsamic vinegar

Salads

How many times have you ordered a restaurant's house salad and been served nothing more than the ubiquitous "baby greens"? That kind of salad makes me fall asleep just looking at it. A salad should be more than just a handful of greens tossed with dressing. Add some red and yellow tomatoes for a splash of color, some almonds for crunch, currants for a sweet contrast, not to mention roasted garlic because everyone loves it—now we're talking salad! My salads are edible symphonies of flavor, texture, and color, and when it comes to selecting ingredients, it's my theory that more is better.

Most of the salads in this chapter, however, aren't typical green salads, but substantial dishes made from grains, pasta, and potatoes—"composed salads" in chef lingo. They can be served as first courses, side dishes, or on a buffet table. Of course, if you want to make one of the vinaigrettes used in these salads to toss on greens, go ahead—you'll love it.

One tip about composed salads: As these salads chill, they soak up the seasonings and their flavor changes. A salad that was perfectly seasoned when you mixed it can be lackluster a few hours later. How to fix this? Always reseason the salad just before serving with an additional splash of vinegar (or lemon juice or whatever acid the recipe calls for) and a generous dose of salt and pepper.

Abigael's House Salad

More than just lettuce with a chunk of tomato, the house salad at my restaurant has wonderful surprises in every bite—crunchy almonds and cucumbers, sweet currants, mellow roasted garlic, and tangy tomatoes nestled in the refreshing mixed greens. I admit it takes a little forethought to get all the components ready, so you may want to save the "all-out" version for company. But I bet that my easy balsamic vinaigrette will become your house dressing for every-night meals.

BALSAMIC VINAIGRETTE
1/4 cup balsamic vinegar
2 teaspoons water
1 1/2 teaspoons sugar
1/2 teaspoon Dijon mustard
1 garlic clove, minced
1/4 teaspoon salt
Generous pinch of freshly
   ground black pepper
1/2 cup extra-virgin olive oil

8 ounces mixed baby greens
   (mesclun)
1 ripe red beefsteak tomato, cut
   into 3/4-inch cubes
1 ripe yellow tomato (or an
   additional red tomato), cut
   into 3/4-inch cubes
1 cup (1/2-inch dice) seedless
   English cucumber
1 cup canned garbanzo beans
   (chickpeas)
1/2 cup sliced natural almonds,
   toasted (see page 175)
8 garlic cloves, roasted and
   peeled (see sidebar)
1/4 cup dried currants, soaked
   in water for 20 minutes,
   drained, and patted dry

1. To make the vinaigrette, combine the vinegar, water, sugar, mustard, garlic, salt, and pepper in a blender. With the machine running, gradually pour in the oil and blend until thickened.

2. In a large bowl, toss the greens, red and yellow tomatoes, cucumber, beans, almonds, roasted garlic, and currants. Add the dressing and toss again. Serve immediately.

ROASTING GARLIC

Garlic has a reputation for being a bully in the kitchen. Add a little too much to a dish, and everyone knows it. Roasting the garlic cloves mellows their flavor so much that they can even be spread onto bread.

To roast garlic, peel large, plump garlic cloves. Place in a small, shallow baking dish, and add enough olive oil to cover completely. Cover tightly with aluminum foil. Bake in a preheated 200°F. oven until the cloves are golden and tender, about 1 hour. Cool completely in the oil, then remove the garlic from the oil.

Be sure to save the garlicky oil for salad dressings and cooking. Refrigerate the oil in a covered container for up to 1 month. The oil will become cloudy and semifirm when chilled, but it will liquefy again at room temperature.

Tuna and Penne Salad
with Creamy Lemon Dressing

On a warm summer day, this is a tangy and refreshing lunch that can be tossed together with hardly any effort. Keep it in mind for a light supper or make a double batch to take to a picnic. Feel free to improvise. Sometimes I'll mix in some shredded iceberg lettuce just before serving, or jazz it up with capers, pitted olives, or fresh basil (not that it needs it). For this salad, do use canned tuna packed in olive oil—it has lots more flavor than the water- or vegetable-oil-packed variety, and it adds authentic Italian gusto.

1. Bring a large pot of lightly salted water to a boil over high heat. Add the pasta and cook, stirring occasionally, until tender, about 8 minutes. Drain and rinse under cold running water. Shake well in the colander to remove excess water.

2. Flake the tuna and its oil in a medium bowl. Add the drained pasta and toss. Add the tomatoes and onion and mix gently.

3. Whisk the mayonnaise, oil, and lemon juice in a small bowl until smooth and creamy. Pour over the pasta, sprinkle with the parsley, and mix gently. Season with salt and pepper.

4. Cover with plastic wrap and refrigerate until chilled, at least 2 hours. (The salad can be made up to 1 day ahead. Reseason with salt and pepper before serving.) Serve chilled.

8 ounces (about 2$\frac{1}{2}$ cups) tube-shaped pasta, such as penne

Two 6-ounce cans tuna in olive oil, undrained

1 cup cherry tomatoes, halved

$\frac{1}{2}$ medium red onion, cut into thin half-moons

$\frac{1}{4}$ cup mayonnaise

$\frac{1}{4}$ cup extra-virgin olive oil

2 tablespoons fresh lemon juice

3 tablespoons chopped fresh flat-leaf parsley

Kosher salt and freshly ground black pepper to taste.

Beet, Pear, and Fennel Salad
with Orange Vinaigrette

This elegant and colorful salad highlights autumn's bounty, with sweet pears and earthy beets brought together by a sweet-sour orange vinaigrette. If your beets come with the greens attached, don't throw them away. Rinse the greens well, and sauté them quickly with olive oil and chopped garlic until wilted. Eat them as is, or load the coarsely chopped greens on toasted sourdough bread and top with goat cheese.

**MAKES
6
SERVINGS**

ORANGE VINAIGRETTE
Grated zest of 1 orange
$1/4$ cup fresh orange juice
$2^1/2$ tablespoons fresh lime juice
1 tablespoon honey
$1^1/2$ teaspoons cider vinegar
$1/2$ cup extra-virgin olive oil
2 teaspoons chopped fresh
   mint
2 teaspoons chopped fresh basil
$1/4$ teaspoon fennel seeds,
   toasted (see page 66) and
   ground
Kosher salt and freshly ground
   black pepper to taste

SALAD
6 medium beets (about
   6 ounces each), scrubbed
   but unpeeled
1 medium fennel bulb, trimmed
8 ounces arugula, trimmed,
   well washed, dried, and
   torn into bite-sized pieces
3 ripe medium Anjou or
   Bartlett pears, unpeeled,
   cored, and thinly sliced
3 ounces feta cheese, crumbled

1. To make the vinaigrette, combine the orange zest and juice, lime juice, honey, and vinegar in a blender. With the machine running, gradually add the oil and blend until thickened. Transfer to a bowl and stir in the mint, basil, and fennel seeds. Season with salt and pepper. Cover and refrigerate until ready to use.

2. Position a rack in the center of the oven and preheat the oven to 400°F. Pierce each beet a few times with a fork, and place them on a foil-lined baking sheet. Bake until the beets are tender, about $1^1/4$ hours. When the beets are cool, peel them. Cover and refrigerate until chilled.

3. When ready to serve, cut the fennel in half lengthwise, then cut out the hard core. Using a mandoline or a sharp knife, cut the fennel crosswise into paper-thin slices. In a large bowl, toss the fennel and arugula with a few tablespoons of the vinaigrette and season with salt and pepper. In a medium bowl, toss the pears with a couple of tablespoons of the vinaigrette and season lightly.

4. Slice the beets $1/4$ inch thick. Arrange a beet on each of 6 plates, in a wide circle. Heap portions of arugula mixture in the center and top with the pears, then the feta cheese. Drizzle with the remaining vinaigrette and serve immediately.

Smoked Salmon Cheesecake
(recipe on page 26).

OPPOSITE TOP: Moroccan Yellow Split Pea Soup *(recipe on page 57)*. **OPPOSITE BOTTOM:** Sephardic Chicken Soup with Sofrito and Saffron Matzo Balls *(recipe on page 48)*.

ABOVE: Beet, Pear, and Fennel Salad with Orange Vinaigrette *(recipe on page 64)*. **LEFT:** Challah Panzanella Salad *(recipe on page 69)*.

LEFT: Dinner in a Pot *(recipe on page 82)*. BELOW: Grilled Lamb Rib Chops with Ratatouille *(recipe on page 100)*.

Latin Beef Brisket with Chimichurri (*recipe on page 78*).

A PASSOVER MENU

OPPOSITE: Rack of Veal with Wild Mushroom–Farfel Dressing *(recipe on page 98).* **ABOVE LEFT:** Mango-Date Haroset *(recipe on page 185).* **ABOVE RIGHT:** Matzo for Passover **RIGHT:** Gefilte Fish Terrine with Carrot and Beet Salads *(recipe on page 22).*

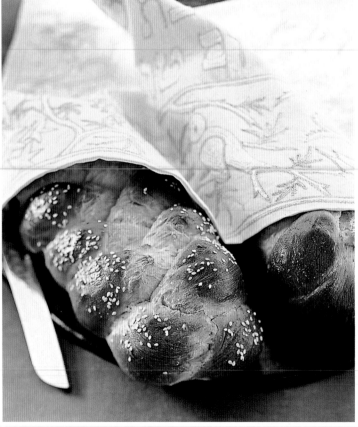

A SHABBAT MENU

ABOVE: Persian Pickled Vegetables *(recipe on page 34).* **LEFT:** Honey Challah *(recipe on page 202).*
OPPOSITE: Perfect Roast Chicken with Lemon and Rosemary *(recipe on page 108)* shown with Egg Barley with Roasted Portobello Mushrooms and Balsamic Drizzle *(recipe on page 164).*

OPPOSITE: Asian Duck Stir-Fry *(recipe on page 121).* **ABOVE:** Tuna au Poivre on Tomato-Onion Salad *(recipe on page 143).*

LEFT: Salmon Confit with Gazpacho Relish and Dill Oil *(recipe on page 130).* **BELOW:** Porcini-Crusted Striped Bass with Smoked Trout and Scallion Mashed Potatoes and Port Wine Syrup *(recipe on page 134).* **OPPOSITE:** Spaghetti Squash with Pine Nuts and Arugula *(recipe on page 157).*

OPPOSITE: Pumpkin and Pine Nut Risotto *(recipe on page 174)*. **ABOVE LEFT:** Moroccan Eggplant, Fennel, and Sweet Peppers Sauté *(recipe on page 184)*. **ABOVE RIGHT:** Acorn Squash with Ginger-Orange Glaze *(recipe on page 180)*. **LEFT:** New Mexican Rice Pilaf *(recipe on page 176)*.

ABOVE: Honey-Ginger Zabaglione Cream with Fresh Berries *(recipe on page 244)*. **RIGHT:** Passover Banana Cake with Strawberry-Marsala Compote *(recipe on page 222)*.

Hungarian Slaw
with Apples and Mint

Wilting the shredded cabbage gives this slaw a nice, tender texture, while apples, mint, and caraway seed add unexpected but truly harmonious flavors. If you haven't learned already, the easiest way to shred cabbage for a slaw is in a food processor. But use the thin slicing blade instead of the holes of the shredder, or you'll end up with cabbage purée.

1. Bring the water and 3 teaspoons of the salt to a boil in a large soup pot over high heat. Stir in the cabbage and remove from the heat. Place a plate or bowl directly on the cabbage to keep it submerged and let stand for 30 minutes. Drain well. A handful at a time, wrap the cabbage in a kitchen towel and squeeze to remove the liquid. Transfer the cabbage to a bowl.

2. In a large bowl, whisk the vinegar, lemon juice, sugar, and remaining 1 teaspoon salt. Gradually whisk in the oil. Add the cabbage, apple, onion, mint, and caraway seeds, and mix well. Taste and add more salt, if needed. Cover and refrigerate until well chilled, at least 2 hours. (The slaw can be prepared up to 1 day ahead.)

2 quarts water
4 teaspoons kosher salt, plus
   more to taste
One 2-pound head of green
   cabbage, cored and
   shredded
2 tablespoons cider vinegar
2 tablespoons fresh lemon
   juice
1 teaspoon sugar
$1/4$ cup canola or safflower oil
1 Golden Delicious apple,
   peeled, cored, and shredded
1 small red onion, halved
   lengthwise and sliced into
   thin half-moons
2 tablespoons chopped fresh
   mint
1 teaspoon caraway seeds,
   toasted (see page 66)

Asian Two-Cabbage Slaw

**MAKES
8
SERVINGS**

Not your corner deli cole slaw. Starting with the cabbage itself (tender napa and crunchy red), and with an Asian-inspired dressing, this slaw is loaded with unexpected, palate-exciting flavors.

1 cup mayonnaise

¹/4 cup rice wine vinegar

¹/4 cup soy sauce

2 tablespoons fresh lemon juice

2 tablespoons dark Asian sesame oil

1 tablespoon hot red pepper sauce

1 tablespoon peeled and shredded fresh ginger (use the large holes on a box grater)

4 cups shredded napa cabbage (¹/2 small head)

4 cups shredded red cabbage (¹/2 small head)

2 large carrots, trimmed and shredded

2 ounces snow peas, trimmed and cut on a sharp diagonal into ¹/8-inch strips

1 cup peeled, matchstick-cut jicama (optional)

4 scallions (white and green parts), finely chopped

3 tablespoons chopped fresh cilantro

Kosher salt and freshly ground black pepper to taste

3 cups fresh bean sprouts

Toasted sesame seeds (see sidebar), for garnish

1. In a large bowl, whisk the mayonnaise, vinegar, soy sauce, lemon juice, sesame oil, red pepper sauce, and ginger until combined.

2. Add the napa and red cabbage, carrots, snow peas, jicama (if using), scallions, and cilantro, and mix well. Season with salt and pepper. Cover and refrigerate until well chilled, at least 2 hours or overnight. (The slaw can be prepared up to 1 day ahead.)

3. Just before serving, add the bean sprouts. Sprinkle with the sesame seeds and serve chilled.

TOASTING SPICES

Spices are the seeds, bark, fruit, buds, roots, or stems of aromatic edible plants. Herbs, on the other hand, are the leaves of such plants. Most spices benefit from toasting. Seeds are oily, so toasting spices that are seeds (fennel, caraway, cumin, and the like) provides extra flavor because the heat brings their essential oils to the surface.

To toast spices and seeds (such as sesame), heat a small skillet over medium heat until hot. Add the spices or seeds and cook, stirring almost constantly, until they are very fragrant (you may see a wisp of smoke, but be careful not to burn them), about 2 minutes. Immediately transfer the seeds to a plate and cool completely. Grind the seeds with a mortar and pestle. Or use an inexpensive, blade-type electric coffee grinder as your kitchen spice grinder.

Israeli Couscous Salad with Summer Vegetables and Lime Vinaigrette

This bright salad was developed to accompany my Moroccan Sea Bass (page 136), but it is so good that it deserves to be considered on its own merit. For more on Israeli couscous, see page 137.

1. Bring a large pot of lightly salted water to a boil over high heat. Add the zucchini and yellow squash and cook just until crisp-tender, about 2 minutes. Scoop them out of the water with a sieve, reserving the boiling water, then rinse the vegetables under cold water and set aside.

2. Add the couscous to the boiling water and cook until tender, about 10 minutes. Drain, rinse well under cold running water, and drain well.

3. In a medium bowl, whisk the lime juice, curry powder, cumin, turmeric, mild chile powder, and hot chile powder. Gradually whisk in the oil. Mix in the couscous, zucchini, yellow squash, red, yellow, and green bell peppers, cilantro, and parsley. Season with salt and pepper. Cover and refrigerate until chilled, at least 1 hour. (The salad can be prepared up to 1 day ahead. Reseason with lime juice, salt, and pepper before serving.)

$^1/_2$ cup ($^1/_4$-inch dice) zucchini
$^1/_2$ cup ($^1/_4$-inch dice) yellow squash
2 cups (8 ounces) Israeli couscous
2 tablespoons fresh lime juice
2 teaspoons curry powder
1 teaspoon ground cumin
$^1/_2$ teaspoon ground turmeric
1 teaspoon pure ground mild chile powder, such as ancho (see page 131), or Texas-style chili powder
1 teaspoon pure ground hot chile powder, such as pasilla (see page 131), or
   $^1/_8$ teaspoon ground hot red (cayenne) pepper
$^1/_4$ cup extra-virgin olive oil
$^1/_2$ cup ($^1/_4$-inch dice) red bell pepper
$^1/_2$ cup ($^1/_4$-inch dice) green bell pepper
$^1/_2$ cup ($^1/_4$-inch dice) yellow bell pepper
3 tablespoons chopped fresh cilantro
3 tablespoons chopped fresh Italian flat-leaf parsley
Kosher salt and freshly ground black pepper to taste

Smoked Eggplant Salad

On delicatessen menus, you will usually see this dish listed as an appetizer, but my family likes it as a salad, and often serves it as part of a buffet spread that includes tuna salad and egg salad. Because cooked eggplant never won any beauty contests, be sure to serve it with lots of colorful garnishes. At Abigael's, I cook the eggplants in a commercial smoker, but a grill will also impart the right amount of smoky flavor. If neither is an option, just bake the eggplants on an aluminum foil–lined baking sheet in a preheated 400°F. oven until tender, about 45 minutes.

MAKES
8 TO 12
SERVINGS

2 large eggplants (about
   1½ pounds each), pierced a
   few times with a fork
1 medium onion, finely
   chopped
3 tablespoons fresh lemon juice
1 pickled hot red cherry
   pepper, finely chopped, with
   1 teaspoon pickling juice
2 garlic cloves, minced
Kosher salt and freshly ground
   black pepper to taste
Black Mediterranean olives,
   pitted and coarsely chopped,
   for garnish
Cherry tomatoes, halved, for
   garnish
Lavash or pita bread, for
   serving

1. Build a charcoal fire on one side of an outdoor grill and let it burn until the coals are covered with white ash. Or preheat a gas grill on high heat, and then turn one burner off.

2. Lightly oil the grill. Place the eggplants over the hot area of the grill. Cook, uncovered, turning occasionally as the skin darkens and the eggplant has been seared on all sides, about 7 minutes. Transfer to the cooler part of the grill. Cover and cook until the eggplant is tender and collapsed, 30 to 40 minutes.

3. Remove and discard the eggplant skin. Chop the eggplant plup with a large knife, then scrape it into a medium bowl. Stir in the onion, lemon juice, pickled pepper, pickling juice, and garlic, and season with salt and pepper. Cover and refrigerate until chilled, at least 2 hours or overnight. (The salad can be prepared up to 3 days ahead.)

4. Garnish the salad with the olives and cherry tomatoes. Serve chilled with the lavash for dipping.

Challah Panzanella Salad

MAKES
4 TO 6
SERVINGS

During a trip to Italy, I developed a taste for the famed bread salad, panzanella, which is usually made from day-old, crusty (and salt-free) Tuscan bread. I experimented with the recipe, using toasted challah instead, and the rich egg bread made a good thing better. Substitute pita bread torn into bite-sized pieces, and you'll have another great Mediterranean bread salad, fattoush. Mix the salad at least an hour ahead so the tomato juices and vinegar have time to permeate the bread, but serve it the same day it is made.

1. To make the vinaigrette, heat the oil, garlic, and red pepper flakes in a medium skillet over medium heat, stirring, until the garlic turns golden. Remove from the heat and carefully stir in the lemon juice, vinegar, and oregano, being careful of splattering. Set aside to cool.

2. Position a rack in the center of the oven and preheat the oven to 400°F. Spread the bread cubes on a large baking sheet. Bake, stirring occasionally, until the cubes are lightly toasted and crisp, about 10 minutes. Cool completely.

3. In a large bowl, mix the bread cubes, plum tomatoes, yellow tomato, onion, parsley, olives, basil, and capers. Toss with the vinaigrette. Let stand for an hour or so to combine the flavors. Season with salt and pepper before serving, but do not refrigerate.

GARLIC VINAIGRETTE
$1/2$ cup extra-virgin olive oil
3 garlic cloves, thinly sliced
$1/4$ teaspoon hot red pepper flakes
2 tablespoons fresh lemon juice
1 tablespoon balsamic vinegar
$1/2$ teaspoon dried oregano

4 cups ($3/4$-inch cubes) challah (about 6 ounces)
2 plum tomatoes, cut into $3/4$-inch cubes
1 yellow beefsteak tomato, cut into $3/4$-inch cubes
$1/2$ small red onion, sliced into thin half-moons
$1/4$ cup chopped fresh parsley
$1/4$ cup pitted and chopped black Mediterranean olives
2 tablespoons chopped fresh basil
2 tablespoons bottled nonpareil capers, rinsed
Kosher salt and freshly ground black pepper to taste

Warm Sweet Pepper Salad
with Feta Cheese

When you serve this bright salad, expect to find many Sephardic flavors on the plate, from extra-virgin olive oil to tangy feta cheese. Without the cheese, it can do double duty as a side dish for simply grilled chicken or lamb chops. The trick is to keep the pepper strips crisp—a quick sauté is all they need.

**MAKES
4
SERVINGS**

6 tablespoons extra-virgin olive
oil

2 garlic cloves, thinly sliced

2 red bell peppers, cored,
seeded, and cut into 1/4-inch
strips

1 yellow bell pepper, cored,
seeded, and cut into 1/4-inch
strips

1 green bell pepper, cored,
seeded, and cut into 1/4-inch
strips

10 ounces flat-leaf or baby
spinach, stemmed, well
washed, and dried

4 ounces feta cheese, crumbled

2 ripe plum tomatoes, chopped

1/4 cup pitted and coarsely
chopped green
Mediterranean olives

2 tablespoons pine nuts,
toasted (see page 175)

1 tablespoon nonpareil capers,
rinsed

2 tablespoons fresh lemon juice

Kosher salt and freshly ground
black pepper to taste

1. Heat 4 tablespoons of the oil and the garlic in a very large skillet over medium heat, stirring, until the garlic is golden, about 2 minutes. Increase the heat to medium-high and add the red, yellow, and green bell peppers. Cook uncovered, stirring occasionally, until the peppers are crisp-tender, about 5 minutes.

2. While the peppers are cooking, mix the spinach, feta cheese, tomatoes, olives, pine nuts, and capers in a large bowl. Add the just-cooked peppers and toss to wilt the spinach and soften the cheese. Drizzle with the lemon juice and the remaining 2 tablespoons olive oil, season with salt and pepper, and toss. Serve immediately.

PAREVE VARIATION
Omit the feta cheese.

Quinoa Tabbouli Salad

Tabbouli is a famous Middle Eastern salad made with bulgur and vegetables. My version uses quinoa, which is actually from South America. Quinoa is a nutritious and tasty grain available at most natural food stores and some supermarkets. Be sure to rinse the quinoa well before using, since it has a natural coating that becomes bitter and sticky when cooked.

1. Place the quinoa in a fine-meshed sieve and rinse well under cold running water. Drain well.

2. Heat 1 tablespoon of the oil in a medium skillet over medium heat. Add the quinoa and cook, stirring often, until the moisture evaporates and the quinoa has toasted to a light golden color, 3 to 4 minutes. Add the stock or water and bring to a boil. Cover tightly and reduce the heat to medium-low. Cook until the quinoa is tender and has absorbed the liquid, 12 to 15 minutes. Remove from the heat and fluff the quinoa with a fork. Cool, uncovered, for 15 minutes.

3. Transfer the quinoa to a medium bowl. Add the tomatoes, cucumber, onion, and currants. In a small bowl, whisk the lemon juice and remaining 4 tablespoons oil, pour over the salad, and mix. Stir in the basil, chives, and mint. Season with salt and pepper. Cover and refrigerate to chill and blend flavors, at least 2 hours or overnight. (The salad can be prepared up to 1 day ahead. Reseason with lemon juice, salt, and pepper before serving.)

4. Serve chilled or at room temperature.

$1^1/4$ cups quinoa

5 tablespoons extra-virgin olive oil

$2^1/2$ cups Vegetable Stock (page 43) or water

2 ripe plum tomatoes, seeded and cut into $^1/2$-inch cubes

$^2/3$ cup ($^1/4$-inch dice) seedless English cucumber, unpeeled

$^1/3$ cup finely chopped red onion

$^1/4$ cup dried currants, soaked in warm water for 20 minutes, drained, and patted dry

$^1/4$ cup fresh lemon juice

$^1/2$ cup chopped fresh basil

3 tablespoons finely chopped fresh chives

2 tablespoons chopped fresh mint

Kosher salt and freshly ground black pepper to taste

Potato-Fennel Salad

MAKES
6
SERVINGS

Fennel adds the faintest hint of licorice and a refreshing crunch that's especially good with grilled or poached salmon. If you like a more pronounced fennel flavor, add the chopped fennel fronds.

3 pounds small red new potatoes, scrubbed but unpeeled

1½ cups (¼-inch dice) fennel bulb (½ of a medium bulb)

3 scallions (green and white parts), chopped

½ cup finely chopped red onion

3 tablespoons chopped fennel fronds (optional)

3 tablespoons balsamic vinegar

1 tablespoon Dijon mustard

¾ cup extra-virgin olive oil

Kosher salt and freshly ground black pepper to taste

1. Place the potatoes in a large saucepan and add enough lightly salted cold water to cover. Cover and bring to a boil over high heat. Set the lid askew. Reduce the heat to medium and cook until the potatoes are tender, about 25 minutes. Drain well and allow to cool just until easy to handle (the potatoes should be dressed while they are still warm).

2. Cut the potatoes in half and transfer to a large bowl. Mix in the fennel, scallions, onion, and chopped fennel fronds, if using.

3. In a medium bowl, whisk the vinegar and mustard together. Gradually whisk in the oil until fully combined. Pour over the warm salad and toss gently. Season with salt and pepper. Cover and refrigerate until chilled, at least 1 hour or overnight. (The salad can be prepared up to 2 days ahead. Reseason with vinegar, salt, and pepper before serving.)

4. One hour before serving, remove the salad from the refrigerator. Serve at room temperature.

Smoked Trout and Orange Salad

One Passover, I decided I wanted a change from the traditional gefilte fish appetizer, and this is what I came up with. The combination of sweet oranges, smoky trout, and pleasantly bitter radicchio is so perfect that now I serve it year-round, garnished with pea shoots (which aren't kosher for Passover). Asian produce markets carry pea shoots, but you can easily substitute cilantro sprigs or celery leaves.

1. To make the vinaigrette, whisk together the orange juice, lime juice, and honey in a medium bowl. Add the cilantro and gradually whisk in the oil. Season with salt and pepper.

2. In another bowl, combine the smoked fish, orange segments, and onion. Gently mix in the orange vinaigrette. Season with salt and pepper. Cover and refrigerate until chilled, at least 1 and up to 4 hours.

3. To serve, place a radicchio cup on a plate and fill each cup with the salad. Serve immediately on a bed of the pea shoots.

ORANGE-CILANTRO
VINAIGRETTE

2 tablespoons fresh orange juice (use the juice from sectioning oranges)
1 tablespoon fresh lime juice
1$^{1}/_{2}$ teaspoons honey
1$^{1}/_{2}$ tablespoons chopped fresh cilantro
$^{1}/_{3}$ cup plus 1 tablespoon extra-virgin olive oil
Kosher salt and freshly ground black pepper to taste

6 skinless and boneless smoked trout fillets, broken into large flakes
4 large seedless oranges, supremed (see page 141)
1 small red onion, thinly sliced
8 large, cup-shaped radicchio leaves
Pea shoots, cilantro sprigs, or celery leaves, for garnish

Wild Rice Salad with Toasted
Walnuts and Sun-Dried Berries

MAKES
6 TO 8
SERVINGS

I first tasted this salad during a motorcycle trip through Nevada's Sierra Buttes mountains. The picture-perfect setting, with snow-capped mountains and a crystal-clear lake, would make anything taste better. When I got back to New York, I re-created the recipe, and was thrilled to find out that it tasted even better than I had remembered.

2 cups (12$\frac{1}{2}$ ounces) wild rice (see Note), rinsed and drained

$\frac{1}{2}$ cup strawberry or mango nectar

2 tablespoons balsamic vinegar, plus more as needed

$\frac{1}{2}$ teaspoon curry powder

$\frac{1}{4}$ teaspoon ground cumin

2 tablespoons safflower or other vegetable oil

Kosher salt and freshly ground black pepper to taste

$\frac{1}{2}$ cup dried cranberries and/or blueberries (preferably a combination), soaked in warm water for 20 minutes, drained, and patted dry

1 cup red seedless grapes, cut in half lengthwise

$\frac{1}{2}$ cup walnut pieces, toasted (see page 175)

$\frac{1}{2}$ cup finely chopped celery

$\frac{1}{4}$ cup chopped fresh cilantro

1. Place the wild rice in a medium saucepan and add enough lightly salted cold water to cover by 2 inches. Bring to a boil over high heat. Reduce the heat to low and cover tightly. Simmer until the wild rice is "puffed" and tender, 45 minutes to 1$\frac{1}{4}$ hours, depending on your particular rice. Drain well and rinse under cold running water.

2. In a small bowl, whisk the strawberry or mango nectar, balsamic vinegar, curry powder, and cumin. Gradually whisk in the oil, then season with salt and pepper. Add the berries and let stand for 5 minutes to absorb the vinaigrette's flavor.

3. In a large bowl, mix the cooked wild rice, grapes, walnuts, and celery. Pour the dressing and berries over the rice, add the cilantro, and mix gently. Cover and refrigerate until chilled, at least 2 hours. (The salad can be prepared up to 1 day ahead. Reseason with balsamic vinegar, salt, and pepper before serving.)

4. Serve chilled.

NOTE: Be flexible with wild rice cooking times. Hand-harvested wild rice is more expensive and takes longer to cook than machine-harvested brands.

Israeli Chopped Vegetable Salad

You will find this salad throughout the Middle East, but Israel's version is especially wonderful. This is a chance to use as many kinds of ripe summer tomatoes as possible— red, yellow, heirloom, cherry, or pear—whatever you can find at the local market.

1. In a medium bowl, gently mix the tomatoes, cucumber, red and green bell peppers, cilantro, and mint.

2. In a small bowl, whisk the lime juice, sugar, and oil. Pour over the vegetables and mix again. Season with salt and pepper. Cover and refrigerate until chilled, at least 2 hours. (The salad can be made up to 8 hours ahead.)

3. Serve chilled, with a slotted spoon.

1 pound ripe assorted tomatoes, seeded and cut into ³/₄-inch dice
1 large English cucumber, unpeeled, cut into ¹/₂-inch dice
1 red bell pepper, cored, seeded, and cut into ¹/₂-inch dice
1 green bell pepper, cored, seeded, and cut into ¹/₂-inch dice
2 tablespoons chopped fresh cilantro
2 tablespoons chopped fresh mint
3 tablespoons fresh lime juice
¹/₂ teaspoon sugar
¹/₄ cup extra-virgin olive oil
Kosher salt and freshly ground black pepper to taste

Meat

Here are my favorite recipes for those delicious,

hoofed, cud-chewing stars of the kosher kitchen: beef, veal, and lamb. These dishes are not just my personal faves, but recipes I have served to thousands of satisfied customers at Abigael's. Jewish dietary laws restrict meat consumption to the forequarter of the animals, cuts that usually require long, slow cooking. What these cuts lack in tenderness, they make up in flavor, as anyone who has eaten tender short ribs or brisket can attest.

I assume that most people who buy this book are already purchasing their meat at a kosher butcher. A kosher meat-processing plant butchers and salts the meat according to special laws that I won't go into here—suffice it to say that they know what they're doing.

If you buy only kosher meats, you must remember that like kosher poultry, they will already have been salted. This means a very light hand must be used when adding salt to the dish as it cooks. The thinner the cut, the more salt the meat absorbs. For example, skirt steak will absorb more salt than brisket. So if you are in the habit of automatically salting your food before tasting, break the habit.

Latin Beef Brisket with Chimichurri

MAKES
6
SERVINGS

Cilantro lovers will flip for this tender brisket inspired by the flavors of Latin America. For a company dinner, you'll want to give this herb-infused brisket the four-star treatment with a finish of sautéed bell peppers and onions, a swirl of mashed sweet potatoes, and barbecue vinaigrette. But, for family meals, you can certainly make the brisket by itself, and hope that you have leftovers for sandwiches and other meals. In either case, plan ahead to give the brisket time for the marination and slow cooking that make it so incredibly tender. For a large group, double all of the ingredients and use a 6-pound brisket.

CHIMICHURRI

7 garlic cloves

4 jalapeño peppers, seeded and coarsely chopped

7 bay leaves

1¼ cups packed flat-leaf parsley leaves

²/₃ cup packed cilantro leaves

2½ tablespoons dried oregano

1¼ cups distilled white vinegar

1¼ cups extra-virgin olive oil

Kosher salt to taste

2 cups water

One 3½-pound, first-cut beef brisket, trimmed of excess surface fat, soaked in cold water to cover for 1 hour, drained

SWEET POTATOES

2½ pounds (6 medium) sweet potatoes (also called orange yams)

Kosher salt and freshly ground black pepper to taste

1. To make the chimichurri, in a food processor fitted with the metal blade, with the machine running, drop the garlic, jalapeños, and bay leaves through the feed tube to chop them. Add the parsley, cilantro, and oregano, and pulse to chop the leaves. Then, with the machine running, add the vinegar and oil, scraping down the sides of the bowl as needed, and blend until the chimichurri is smooth. Season to taste with the salt.

2. Pour 1 cup of the chimichurri into a covered container and refrigerate. Mix the remaining chimichurri with the water in a large nonreactive (stainless-steel, ceramic, or glass) baking dish. Place the brisket in the dish and cover tightly with plastic wrap. Refrigerate, occasionally turning the brisket in the marinade, for at least 24 and up to 48 hours.

3. Position a rack in the center of the oven and preheat the oven to 350°F. Transfer the brisket and marinade to a roasting pan or nonreactive Dutch oven. Cover and bake until very tender when pierced with a meat fork, about 3½ hours. Cool slightly. Transfer the brisket to a carving board. Using two forks, pull the brisket into long shreds. Transfer to a bowl and add a few spoons of cooking liquid to keep moist. (The brisket can be prepared up to 1 day ahead, covered, and refrigerated.)

4. Meanwhile, prepare the sweet potatoes. Pierce the sweet potatoes with a fork and place on a large baking sheet. Bake on another rack in the oven with the brisket (or use a second oven, set to 350°F.) until very tender when pierced with the tip of a knife, about 1¼ hours. Protecting your hands with a towel, split the sweet potatoes lengthwise with a knife and scoop out the flesh into a food processor fitted with the metal blade. Purée and season with salt and pepper. Transfer to a heatproof bowl, cover tightly with aluminum foil, and place in a skillet of simmering water to keep warm. (The potatoes can be peeled, mashed, and cooled up to 2 hours ahead. Reheat in a covered bowl in the microwave.)

5. To make the vinaigrette, whisk the barbecue sauce and vinegar in a medium bowl. Gradually whisk in the oil to make a thick vinaigrette.

6. Heat 2 tablespoons of the oil in a 12-inch skillet over medium-high heat. Add the onion, red and green bell peppers, and jalapeño. Cook, stirring occasionally, until the vegetables are just crisp-tender, about 5 minutes. Transfer to a large platter and cover with aluminum foil to keep warm.

7. Add the remaining 2 tablespoons oil to the skillet and heat over medium-high heat. Add half of the shredded brisket and cook without stirring until the meat begins to crisp, about 3 minutes. Scrape up with a metal spatula, and continue cooking until the meat begins to crisp again, about 2 minutes. Transfer to the platter of vegetables.

8. Return the brisket and vegetables to the skillet and mix well to heat through. Stir in the cilantro and lime juice and season with salt and pepper.

9. For individual servings, transfer the mashed sweet potatoes to a pastry bag fitted with a large ½-inch star tube. For each serving, pipe a large rosette in the center of a dinner plate. Arrange the brisket and vegetables around the rosette. Drizzle the vinaigrette decoratively on the plate, and serve immediately. For family-style serving, pass the platter of meat and vegetables and the bowl of sweet potatoes. In either case, serve the reserved chimichurri as a sauce on the side. Serve with lime wedges.

BARBECUE VINAIGRETTE

1½ tablespoons store-bought barbecue sauce

1½ tablespoons balsamic vinegar

½ cup extra-virgin olive oil

4 tablespoons extra-virgin olive oil

1 medium large red onion, halved lengthwise and cut into thin half-moons

2 red bell peppers (or 1 red and 1 yellow), cored, seeded, and cut into thin strips

1 green bell pepper, cored, seeded, and cut into thin strips

1 jalapeño pepper, seeded and chopped

¼ cup chopped fresh cilantro

2 tablespoons fresh lime juice

Kosher salt and freshly ground black pepper to taste

Lime wedges, for serving

Apple Cider Brisket

MAKES
6
SERVINGS

This is one of my most famous dishes, guaranteed to get comments like, "This is the best brisket I ever tasted!" For a representative of the old-fashioned brisket school, it couldn't be simpler...or better. If the whole brisket won't fit into your pan, cut it in half. At the restaurant, I cool the brisket in the cooking liquid and refrigerate it overnight, an extra step that adds flavor and makes the beef easier to carve. But your kitchen will smell so wonderful that I won't blame you if you serve it right away.

2 tablespoons vegetable oil
One 6-pound whole beef
   brisket, outer fat trimmed
3 large onions, halved
   lengthwise and thinly sliced
   into half-moons
3 cups apple cider, as needed
$1/2$ cup unsulfured molasses
6 garlic cloves, thinly sliced
1 tablespoon chopped fresh
   rosemary or $1^{1}/2$ teaspoons
   dried rosemary
1 tablespoon chopped fresh
   thyme or $1^{1}/2$ teaspoons
   dried thyme
Kosher salt and freshly ground
   black pepper to taste

1. Position a rack in the center of the oven and preheat the oven to 325°F.

2. Heat the oil in a large Dutch oven or small roasting pan over medium-high heat. Add the brisket and cook, turning once, until browned on both sides, about 8 minutes. Transfer to a plate.

3. Add the onions to the same pot and cook, stirring occasionally, just until softened, about 5 minutes. Place the brisket on top of the onions, add the cider and molasses, and sprinkle the meat and onions with the garlic, rosemary, and thyme. If necessary, add more cider (or even water) to almost cover the brisket. Bring to a simmer, then cover tightly. Place in the oven and bake until the brisket is fork-tender, about 3 hours.

4. Uncover and let the brisket cool in the pot. Cover and refrigerate until the next day.

5. Scrape off and discard any hardened fat on the surface of the cooking liquid. Transfer the brisket to a carving board, and slice thinly against the grain.

6. Meanwhile, bring the cooking liquid to a boil over high heat. Taste, and if the flavor needs concentrating, simmer for a few minutes to evaporate excess liquid. Season with salt and pepper. Return the sliced brisket to the liquid, reduce the heat to medium-low, and simmer until heated through. Serve hot with the onions.

Harvest Beef Stew with Port Wine

Although you can now find many excellent dry kosher wines, sweetened wine has a special place in Jewish homes. Port is a fortified, sweetened red wine with an especially rich and luscious flavor that's terrific in this beef stew. The natural sugars in the root vegetables play up the port wine flavor. Cut the vegetables into relatively large chunks so they retain their shape after the long cooking. Serve with mashed potatoes or egg noodles.

4 tablespoons vegetable oil
3 pounds beef chuck, cut into
   ^{1}/2-inch chunks
1 medium onion, chopped
1 medium celery rib with
   leaves, chopped
2 large carrots, cut into
   1^1/2-inch pieces
2 medium parsnips, cut into
   1^1/2-inch pieces
2 medium turnips, cut into
   1^1/2-inch cubes
2 garlic cloves, minced
2 tablespoons all-purpose flour
1^1/2 cups tawny or ruby port
2 cups Beef Stock (page 41)
1 teaspoon dried thyme
1 bay leaf
Kosher salt and freshly ground
   black pepper to taste
2 tablespoons chopped fresh
   parsley

1. Position a rack in the center of the oven and preheat the oven to 325°F.

2. Heat 2 tablespoons of the oil in a large Dutch oven or flameproof casserole over medium-high heat. In batches without crowding, add the beef and cook, turning occasionally, until browned, about 6 minutes. Transfer to a plate.

3. Add the remaining 2 tablespoons oil to the Dutch oven. Reduce the heat to medium. Add the onion and celery and cook, stirring often, until softened, about 4 minutes. Stir in the carrots, parsnips, turnips, and garlic, and cook until the garlic is fragrant, about 1 minute. Sprinkle with the flour and mix well to coat. Add the port and stir to loosen the browned bits on the bottom of the pot. Add the browned beef, stock, thyme, and bay leaf. If needed, add enough water to barely cover the ingredients. Bring to a boil and tightly cover the pot.

4. Bake, stirring occasionally, until the meat is tender, about 1^1/2 hours.

5. Using a slotted spoon, transfer the meat and vegetables to a serving platter and cover tightly with aluminum foil to keep warm. Let the cooking liquid stand for a few minutes, then skim off and discard the fat that rises to the surface. Bring the cooking liquid to a boil over high heat and cook until slightly thickened and reduced by about one-fourth, about 5 minutes. Season the sauce with salt and pepper and pour it over the meat and vegetables. Sprinkle the stew with parsley and serve hot.

heritage recipe

Dinner in a Pot

This is another one of those heirloom recipes that require loving attention to make correctly. The first order of business is to use chicken stock to cook the meat and vegetables. If you are short on stock, you can use water to make up half the amount. Next, instead of adding everything to the pot at once (a sure way to get dry, overcooked chicken and soggy potatoes), cook the ingredients according to the time they really need. Follow these simple instructions and you'll be rewarded with a huge platter of tender meats and succulent vegetables, not to mention one heck of a soup! Don't forget the parsley sauce— it's worth the few extra minutes it takes to make it. The parsley sauce reminds me of my first "blooper" while filming New Jewish Cuisine. New show, new equipment, new food processor . . . which I did not figure out how to open ahead of time. Yup, you guessed it . . . parsley sauce all over the place! Ed McMahon would have a field day with that one!

MAKES
6 TO 8
SERVINGS

1 gallon Chicken Stock (page 40) or use half water and half stock

2½ pounds flanken (cross-cut short ribs)

Seasoning Sachet: 12 fresh parsley sprigs, 12 peppercorns, 1 teaspoon dried thyme, and 2 bay leaves, wrapped in cheesecloth and tied into a bundle

4 chicken drumsticks

4 chicken thighs

4 kosher veal or beef sausages, cut into 2-inch chunks

8 medium boiling potatoes, scrubbed but unpeeled

2 medium carrots, cut into 1-inch lengths

1. Bring the stock, flanken, and seasoning sachet to a boil in a large pot over high heat, skimming off the foam that rises to the surface. Reduce the heat to medium-low and simmer for 1½ hours.

2. Add the chicken to the pot and cook for 15 minutes. Add the sausages, potatoes, carrots, parsnips, leeks, and turnip, adding boiling water if needed to cover the vegetables. Cook until the vegetables are tender, about 45 minutes. Using a skimmer or slotted spoon, transfer the meat and vegetables to a large bowl. Add about 2 cups of the cooking liquid to the bowl and cover tightly with aluminum foil to keep it moist and warm.

3. Skim off and discard the fat from the top of the broth. Increase the heat to high and simmer to slightly reduce the liquid and intensify its flavor, about 15 minutes. Season with salt and pepper.

4. Meanwhile, make the parsley sauce. Purée the parsley, vinegar, garlic, and capers in a food processor fitted with the metal blade. With the machine running, gradually add the oil in a slow, steady stream. Season with salt and pepper. Cover and store at room temperature until ready to serve.

5. To serve, sprinkle chopped parsley over the meat and vegetables. Serve in individual bowls, adding a ladleful of hot broth to each serving. Pass the horseradish and the parsley sauce on the side.

OLD WINES AND NEW

Until very recently, Jewish wine meant sweet wine. Since wines that have been fortified with sweeteners keep longer, especially in the warm Middle Eastern climates of the ancient Jews, a dosage of sugar or honey was necessary. In addition, wine was often made from raisins rather than fresh grapes, which resulted in sweet wine as well. So it's easy to see how our ancestors got a sweet tooth when it came to wine.

When the great wave of immigration to America occurred, Jews on the eastern seaboard were forced to use the local Concord grapes. These grapes are not naturally sweet enough to ferment, so sugar was added to the grape juice. Again, sweet wine was the order of the day.

Now winemakers in California, Israel, and elsewhere are making dry kosher wines with grapes of European origin, such as Cabernet Sauvignon and Chardonnay. Like the old-fashioned kosher wines, these new wines are made under rabbinical supervision with kosher products (no animal-based soaps can be used to wash the barrels, for example). When a wine is labeled "Kosher for Passover," it means that the wine never touched bread, grain, or any leavening agents, which is important because yeast is often used to aid the fermentation process. One of my favorite winemakers, kosher or otherwise, is Baron Herzog from California.

2 medium parsnips, cut into 1-inch lengths
2 medium leeks, halved, well rinsed, and cut into 1-inch lengths
1 large turnip, peeled and cut into $1/2$-inch cubes
Kosher salt and freshly ground black pepper to taste

PARSLEY SAUCE
3 cups packed Italian flat-leaf parsley leaves
$1/4$ cup red wine vinegar
2 garlic cloves
1 tablespoon drained bottled nonpareil capers
$1/2$ cup extra-virgin olive oil
Kosher salt and freshly ground black pepper to taste

Chopped Italian flat-leaf parsley, for serving
Freshly grated horseradish, for serving

Superb Sabbath Cholent

MAKES
16 TO 20
SERVINGS

During a consulting job for King David Restaurant in Cedarhurst, Long Island, I tested and tasted until I was satisfied I had made the best cholent ever. This recipe makes a huge amount for a 10-quart flameproof casserole or Dutch oven (leftovers freeze well), but it can easily be halved for a smaller batch. Because many cooks like to make cholent in a slow cooker, I also provide directions for that option.

2 pounds dried Great Northern beans, rinsed

1 cup dried garbanzo beans (chickpeas), rinsed

2 tablespoons vegetable oil, plus more as needed

1½ pounds beef chuck, cut in 1½-inch cubes

1½ pounds cross-cut beef flanken, cut between the bones into large pieces

1½ pounds boneless and skinless turkey thighs, cut into 1½-inch cubes (see Note)

2 large onions, coarsely chopped

2 medium carrots, coarsely chopped

2 medium celery ribs, coarsely chopped

5 garlic cloves, coarsely chopped

1 cup dry white wine

3 tablespoons cider vinegar

2 tablespoons honey

1 tablespoon tomato paste

1 pound veal sausage, cut into 2-inch chunks

1. The morning before making the cholent, place the beans and chickpeas in a large bowl and add enough cold water to cover by 2 inches. Let stand for at least 4 and up to 12 hours. (Or, to reduce the soaking time, bring the beans and enough water to cover to a boil in a large pot. Cook for 1 minute, then remove from the heat, cover, and let stand for 1 hour.) Drain the beans.

2. Position a rack in the lower third of the oven and preheat the oven to 250°F.

3. Heat the oil in a 10-quart Dutch oven or deep flameproof casserole over medium-high heat. In batches, add the beef chuck cubes, flanken, and turkey thighs. Turn occasionally, adding more oil as needed, until browned, about 6 minutes per batch. Transfer the browned meat to a baking sheet.

4. Add a couple of tablespoons of oil to the pot if needed and heat. Add the onions, carrots, celery, and garlic, and cook until softened, about 5 minutes. Stir in the wine, vinegar, honey, and tomato paste, scraping up the browned bits at the bottom of the pot. Bring the mixture to a boil and return the browned meat to the pot. Stir in the drained beans, sausage, pearl barley, and the seasoning sachet. Add enough water to cover the ingredients by 1 inch.

5. Cover tightly and bake in the oven without stirring for at least 12 and up to 18 hours. Serve hot.

NOTE: If you can't find turkey thighs, use 3 turkey drumsticks sawed crosswise into 1½-inch pieces. (If not already sawed, ask the butcher to do it.) Use the meaty parts only, and save the bony parts for soup. Cook the drumstick rounds whole—don't bother to cut the meat off the bone. After cooking, tell everyone to watch out for the bones.

½ pound uncooked pearl barley
Seasoning Sachet: 12 fresh parsley sprigs, 2 teaspoons dried thyme, 10 whole black peppercorns, 2 bay leaves, wrapped in cheesecloth and tied into a bundle with kitchen twine
Kosher salt and freshly ground black pepper to taste

SLOW-COOKER VARIATION

For a 6-quart slow cooker, divide the recipe in half. For a 3½-quart slow cooker, use about one-third of the ingredients. Don't worry about exact measurements; a little more or less of something won't hurt. Brown the meat in a large skillet and place in the crockery insert. Cook the vegetables and make the cooking liquid in the same skillet, and add to the insert, along with the drained beans, sausage, pearl barley, and seasoning sachet. Add enough cold water to cover the beans by 1 inch. Cover and cook on low for at least 12 and up to 18 hours.

Short Ribs with Apricots
and Garbanzo Beans

MAKES
6 TO 8
SERVINGS

Long-simmered in wine and stock until the meat literally melts off the bone (at Abigael's we call them Melted Short Ribs), this scrumptious dish also has sweet-tangy apricots, crunchy nuts, and fragrant herbs for more layers of flavor and texture. Try to use short ribs on the bone, not the cross-cut, flanken-style ribs.

2 tablespoons vegetable oil, with more as needed

6 pounds beef short ribs, cut between the bones into whole, individual ribs

1 large white onion, chopped

2 tablespoons light brown sugar

3 garlic cloves, coarsely chopped

3 cups Beef Stock (page 41), as needed

2 cups dry white wine, such as Chardonnay

1 cup dried apricots

1/4 cup all-purpose flour

One 15- to 19-ounce can garbanzo beans (chickpeas), rinsed and drained

Kosher salt and freshly ground black pepper to taste

1. Position a rack in the center of the oven and preheat the oven to 300°F.

2. Heat the oil in a very large (at least 6-quart) Dutch oven or roasting pan over medium-high heat. In batches, without crowding, sear the short ribs on all sides, about 5 minutes, adding more oil to the pan as needed. Transfer to a platter.

3. In a very large Dutch oven or roasting pan, layer the browned ribs with the onion, brown sugar, and garlic. Pour the broth and wine over the ribs, adding additional broth or water to barely cover them. Cover tightly and bake until very tender, about 2 1/2 hours.

4. Meanwhile, soak the apricots in a small bowl with enough hot water to cover for 20 minutes. Drain, reserving 1/2 cup of the soaking liquid. Whisk the flour into the liquid until smooth, and set aside.

5. Using tongs or a slotted spoon, transfer the short ribs to a deep platter and cover tightly with aluminum foil to keep warm. Let the cooking liquid stand for 5 minutes, then skim the fat from the surface. Place the Dutch oven on top of the stove and bring the cooking liquid to a boil over high heat. Cook until the liquid has reduced by half, about 15 minutes.

6. Whisk the flour mixture into the simmering liquid and cook until thickened and no raw flour taste remains, about 5 minutes. Stir in the garbanzo beans and apricots and heat through, seasoning with salt and pepper. Return the short ribs to the pot and heat through.

7. Mix the almonds, mint, and parsley together in a salad bowl. Drizzle each serving with a spoonful of honey and sprinke with the almonds and herbs.

SHORT RIBS WITH DRIED FRUITS
Substitute $1/4$ cup each of golden raisins and dried currants for the $1/2$ cup apricots.

FOR SERVING
$1/4$ cup slivered almonds, toasted (see page 175)
3 tablespoons chopped fresh mint
3 tablespoons chopped fresh parsley
$1/4$ cup honey

Peruvian Steak
with Red Grapes and Onions

After my son's trip to Peru he brought home several rolls of film, countless souvenirs, and one comment about the food: "I couldn't stop eating the steak with cumin crust." I dug for a little more information, and came up with this version, which has an unusual grape-onion sauce. Use homemade beef stock for the sauce—beef bouillon will make it too salty after reduction. Serve this with a nice salad, such as Abigael's House Salad on page 62.

STEAKS

1/4 cup cumin seeds, coarsely ground (use a mortar or pestle or an electric spice grinder)

1 teaspoon garlic powder

1 teaspoon onion powder

1/2 teaspoon freshly ground black pepper

1/4 teaspoon kosher salt

Four 12- to 14-ounce boneless rib eye steaks

SAUCE

3 tablespoons vegetable oil

1 medium red onion, halved lengthwise and cut into thin half-moons

3/4 cup Beef Stock (page 41)

1/4 cup hearty red wine

1 cup halved seedless red grapes

Kosher salt and freshly ground black pepper to taste

1. To make the spice blend, mix the cumin, garlic and onion powders, pepper, and salt in a shallow dish. Measure and reserve 1 teaspoon of the spice blend. Dip both sides of each steak in the remaining spice blend to coat.

2. To make the sauce, heat 1 tablespoon of the oil in a 12-inch skillet over medium heat. Add the onion and cook, stirring often, until golden brown, about 5 minutes. Transfer to a bowl and set aside. Wipe out the skillet with paper towels.

3. Add the remaining 2 tablespoons oil to the skillet and heat over medium-high heat until hot but not smoking. Add the steaks and cook, turning once, until rare, about 8 minutes. (The steaks will continue to cook to medium-rare outside of the pan. Cook for a few minutes longer if you like your meat more well done.) Transfer to a plate and tent with aluminum foil to keep warm.

4. Return the skillet to medium-high heat and add the onion and the reserved teaspoon of spice blend. Stir just until the spices become fragrant, about 20 seconds. Add the stock and wine and bring to a boil, stirring up the browned bits in the skillet. Cook, stirring occasionally, until the liquid is reduced by half, about 5 minutes. Add the grapes and cook until they are heated through, about 3 minutes. Season the sauce with salt and pepper and remove from the heat.

5. Serve the steaks with the sauce spooned on the side.

Marinated Rib Eye Steak

**MAKES
4
SERVINGS**

Night after night, Abigael's sells more of this steak than any other dish on the menu. We always serve it with the Double-Cooked Honey Potatoes on page 189. A salad of thinly sliced fennel tossed with a vinaigrette makes a nice side dish.

1. To make the marinade, combine the orange and pineapple juices, olive oil, molasses, garlic and onion powders, ground chile, liquid smoke (if using), and pepper in a 1-quart zip-tight plastic bag. Add the onion and shake to blend. Add the steaks, close the bag, and refrigerate for 12 to 24 hours.

2. Build a charcoal fire in an outdoor grill and let it burn until the coals are covered in white ash. Or preheat a gas grill on high.

3. Remove the steaks from the marinade. Lightly oil the grill. Grill the steaks, turning once, until medium-rare, about 8 minutes (or longer for more well-done meat).

4. Serve immediately, with the potatoes.

MARINADE
$^3/_4$ cup fresh orange juice
$^3/_4$ cup unsweetened pineapple
  juice
$^1/_2$ cup extra-virgin olive oil
2 tablespoons unsulfured
  molasses
1 teaspoon garlic powder
1 teaspoon onion powder
1 teaspoon pure ground pasilla
  chile or chili powder
1 teaspoon liquid smoke
  (optional)
$^1/_2$ teaspoon freshly ground
  black pepper
1 medium onion, thinly sliced

Four 12- to 14-ounce boneless
  rib eye steaks
Double-Cooked Honey
  Potatoes (page 189)

Skirt Steak Salad
with Barbecue Vinaigrette

This is the perfect salad for a warm summer night when you want something substantial but not too filling. Skirt steak, which is quite tender, should be cut with the grain, unlike other steaks from not-so-tender areas of the beef. Don't be alarmed at my suggestion to soak the meat in water before cooking. Because this steak is thin, it really absorbs the salt during the koshering process, and the soaking helps remove some of the saltiness.

STEAK

1¹/₂ pounds skirt steak
3 tablespoons fresh lemon juice
1 teaspoon garlic powder
1 teaspoon onion powder
¹/₂ teaspoon freshly ground
   black pepper
²/₃ cup vegetable oil

8 ounces mixed baby greens
   (mesclun)
¹/₂ red onion, cut into thin
   half-moons
2 plum tomatoes, peeled,
   seeded, and cut into
   ¹/₂-inch dice
¹/₂ cup Barbecue Vinaigrette
   (page 79)
Guacamole (recipe follows)
Tortilla chips, for serving

1. Soak the skirt steak in cold water to cover for 1 hour to remove excess salt. Drain and pat dry with paper towels.

2. Mix the lemon juice, garlic and onion powders, and pepper in a zip-tight plastic bag, and shake to combine. If the steaks are too long to work with, cut them crosswise into two or three manageable pieces. Place the steaks in the bag and close. Refrigerate for at least 2 and up to 4 hours.

3. Build a charcoal fire in an outdoor grill and let it burn until the coals are covered with white ash. Or preheat a gas grill to high. Lightly oil the grill.

4. Grill the steaks, turning once, until medium-rare, about 6 minutes per side or longer, if desired. Let stand for a few minutes. Holding the knife at a slight diagonal, thinly slice each steak vertically along its length.

5. In a large bowl, toss the greens, onion, and tomatoes with the vinaigrette, and arrange on individual dinner plates. Top with the steak strips and garnish with dollops of guacamole and the tortilla chips.

Guacamole

PAREVE
MAKES ABOUT 2 CUPS

2 ripe avocados, peeled, pitted, and coarsely chopped
1 plum tomato, peeled, seeded, and cut into $1/4$-inch dice
2 tablespoons fresh lime juice
2 tablespoons chopped fresh cilantro
2 teaspoons seeded and minced jalapeño pepper
Kosher salt to taste

In a medium bowl, mix the avocados, tomato, lime juice, cilantro, and jalapeño, keeping the texture coarse. Season with salt. Press plastic wrap directly on the surface of the guacamole and refrigerate for at least 1 hour to let the flavors blend.

Stuffed Peppers with Creole Sauce

MAKES
6
SERVINGS

Stuffed peppers are one of the all-time great comfort foods, but there's no reason why they should taste bland. The Creole sauce and seasoning give them my "New Jewish Cuisine" twist.

6 bell peppers (preferably 2 each of red, yellow, and green peppers, or 3 each of red and green peppers)
$1/2$ cup long-grain rice
3 tablespoons extra-virgin olive oil
1 medium onion, chopped
3 garlic cloves, minced
2 scallions (white and green parts), chopped
Creole Sauce (recipe follows)
$1/3$ cup matzo meal or seasoned dried bread crumbs
1 large egg, beaten
3 tablespoons chopped fresh cilantro
2 teaspoons kosher salt
$1/2$ teaspoon freshly ground black pepper
$1/4$ teaspoon ground hot red (cayenne) pepper
$1^1/2$ pounds ground beef

1. Position a rack in the center of the oven and preheat the oven to 350°F. Lightly oil a 9×13-inch baking dish.

2. Cut the top off each bell pepper to make a lid. Reserve the top pieces with the stems intact. Remove and discard the ribs and seeds from the peppers.

3. Bring a medium saucepan with 2 quarts of lightly salted water to a boil. Add the rice and cook, uncovered, until barely tender, about 15 minutes. Drain in a sieve, rinse under cold water, then drain thoroughly.

4. Heat the oil in a large skillet over medium heat. Add the onion and garlic. Cook, stirring occasionally, until the onion is wilted, about 3 minutes. Stir in the scallions and cook until softened, about 1 minute. Transfer to a large bowl and allow to cool slightly.

5. Stir in $1/4$ cup of the Creole sauce, the cooked rice, matzo meal, beaten egg, cilantro, salt, black pepper, and cayenne. Add the ground beef and mix with your hands (oil them first, if you wish, to prevent sticking) just to combine. Do not overmix.

6. Spoon the stuffing into the peppers and replace the tops. Stand the peppers upright in the baking dish. Pour the remaining Creole sauce around the peppers. Cover the dish tightly with aluminum foil.

7. Bake for 45 minutes. Remove the foil and continue to bake until the peppers are tender and the filling is cooked through, about 15 minutes. Serve hot, with the sauce from the baking dish spooned around each pepper.

Creole Sauce

PAREVE
MAKES ABOUT 4 CUPS

Spicier and more deeply flavored than garden-variety tomato sauce, my Creole Sauce turns any recipe into a taste of New Orleans. I like the subtle flavor and gentle thickening that filé powder (ground sassafrass leaves) lends to the sauce, but you can leave it out, if you prefer.

2 tablespoons extra-virgin olive oil
1 medium onion, chopped
1 small red bell pepper, cored, seeded, and chopped
1 medium celery rib, chopped
2 garlic cloves, minced
One 28-ounce can crushed tomatoes
$1/2$ cup water
$4^1/2$ teaspoons Creole Spice (recipe follows)
1 teaspoon filé powder (optional, see Sources, page 250)
Kosher salt to taste

Heat the oil in a large saucepan over medium heat. Add the onion, red bell pepper, celery, and garlic. Cook, stirring often, until softened, about 5 minutes.

Stir in the tomatoes, water, and Creole spice. Bring to a simmer over medium heat. Reduce the heat to medium-low. Simmer, stirring often, until thickened and reduced to about 4 cups, about 30 minutes. If desired, once the sauce is removed from the heat, stir in the filé powder (do not boil after adding the filé or the sauce will become stringy). Season with salt. (The sauce can be made up to 3 days ahead, cooled, covered, and refrigerated, or frozen for up to 2 months.)

CREOLE SPICE

This not-too-hot blend of spices is great for any time a recipe needs a little zing. Try it on grilled fish and poultry, and even popcorn. You may like it so much, you'll want to make a large batch; store for up to 3 months in an airtight container in a cool, dry place. Mix 1 teaspoon each sweet Hungarian paprika and garlic powder, and ½ teaspoon each onion powder, dried oregano, dried thyme, freshly ground black pepper, and ground hot red (cayenne) pepper. Makes 4½ teaspoons.

Stuffed Cabbage Rolls with Sweet-and-Sour Cranberry Sauce

Stuffed cabbage has truly earned MVP status in the Jewish kitchen. My mom always added cranberries to the sauce for her stuffed cabbage, and with a few tweaks (sorry, Mom), this is basically her recipe. I give instructions on boiling a head of cabbage to remove whole leaves so you can make stuffed cabbage whenever the inspiration strikes. However, I usually think ahead and place the whole head of cabbage in the freezer overnight. After defrosting the leaves will soften and be floppy enough to pull from the head without boiling.

**MAKES
4 TO 6
SERVINGS**

1 large head of green cabbage, about 3¹/₂ pounds

SAUCE
2 tablespoons vegetable oil
1 large onion, chopped
One 28-ounce can crushed tomatoes
One 16-ounce can whole-berry cranberry sauce
1 cup water
¹/₂ cup sugar
¹/₂ cup ketchup
¹/₂ cup golden raisins, soaked in hot water to cover for 20 minutes, drained
¹/₄ cup dry sherry
¹/₄ cup maple pancake syrup
2 tablespoons fresh lemon juice
1 teaspoon onion powder
1 teaspoon garlic powder
¹/₂ teaspoon kosher salt
¹/₄ teaspoon freshly ground black pepper

1. Position a rack in the center of the oven and preheat the oven to 350°F. Lightly oil a 10 × 15-inch baking dish.

2. Bring a large pot of lightly salted water to a boil over high heat. Using a paring knife, cut out the cabbage core. Place the whole cabbage in the water and cover. Boil until the outer leaves begin to soften, about 5 minutes. Using two large spoons, transfer the cabbage to a bowl. Pull off the softened leaves. Return the cabbage to the water and boil again to soften and remove more leaves to get 12 large leaves. With a small sharp knife, trim the thick rib in the center of each leaf by laying each leaf, rib side up, on a cutting board and cutting parallel to the work surface, shaving off about half of the rib's thickness. Coarsely chop enough of the remaining cabbage and trimmings to make 3 cups. Discard the leftover cabbage or save for another use.

3. To make the sauce, heat the oil over medium heat in a medium saucepan. Add the onion and cook, stirring often, until golden, about 6 minutes. Stir in the crushed tomatoes, cranberry sauce, water, sugar, ketchup, raisins, sherry, pancake syrup, lemon juice, onion and garlic powders, salt, and pepper. Bring to a simmer over medium heat. Cook for about 10 minutes, stirring often, to combine the flavors.

4. Meanwhile, to make the filling, cook the rice in a medium saucepan of lightly salted boiling water over high heat until tender, about 15 minutes. Drain and rinse the rice under cold water.

5. Using oiled hands, combine the ground beef, onion, cooked rice, egg, garlic and onion powders, salt, and pepper in a large bowl. Do not overmix.

6. Spread a thin layer of the sauce in the baking dish. One at a time, place about 1/3 cup of the filling on the lower third of each cabbage leaf and shape it into a thick log. Fold in the sides of the leaf and roll it up into a cylinder. Place the cabbage rolls, seam side down, in the baking dish. Pour the remaining sauce over the rolls and sprinkle the chopped cabbage over the top. Cover the baking dish tightly with aluminum foil. Place the baking dish on a baking sheet to catch bubbling juices.

7. Bake for 45 minutes. Remove the foil and bake until the topping is beginning to brown, about 30 minutes more. Let stand a few minutes, then serve hot from the baking dish.

FILLING
$1/2$ cup long-grain rice
2 pounds ground beef
1 small onion, minced
1 large egg, lightly beaten
1 teaspoon garlic powder
1 teaspoon onion powder
$2^1/2$ teaspoons kosher salt
$1/2$ teaspoon freshly ground
    black pepper

Veal Chops Milanese
with Tomato Salad and Arugula

In Milan, you'll find golden-crusted veal chops so big they fill your plate. Before being cooked, they are pounded while still on the bone. This creates wide flaps of meat to allow for more of the crispy coating that everyone loves. A combination of matzo flour, matzo meal, and matzo farfel is my secret to creating a crunchier crust than is possible with bread crumbs alone. Using matzo also opens up the possibility of enjoying this dish right through Passover week. You will need a very large, 12- to 14-inch skillet to cook both chops at once. Of course, if you have two such skillets, you can invite a couple of friends over for dinner, doubling the amount of tomato salad.

MAKES
2
SERVINGS

TOMATO SALAD
1 tablespoon fresh lemon juice
$1/4$ cup extra-virgin olive oil
2 ripe tomatoes, preferably
   1 red and 1 yellow, seeded
   and cut into $1/2$-inch dice
1 tablespoon fresh basil, cut
   into thin ribbons
$1^1/2$ teaspoons chopped fresh
   oregano
$1/4$ teaspoon chopped fresh
   rosemary
Kosher salt and freshly ground
   black pepper to taste
Two 12-ounce bone-in veal
   chops, about 1 inch thick,
   trimmed of excess fat
$1/4$ teaspoon kosher salt
$1/8$ teaspoon freshly ground
   black pepper
$1/4$ cup matzo flour (also called
   matzo cake flour)
2 large eggs, beaten with
   2 teaspoons water

1. Position a rack in the center of the oven and preheat the oven to 400°F.

2. To make the tomato salad, whisk the lemon juice and oil in a medium bowl. Add the tomatoes, basil, oregano, and rosemary, and toss. Season with salt and pepper. Cover and let stand at room temperature, stirring occasionally, while preparing the veal.

3. Place the chops between sheets of plastic wrap or wax paper. Using a heavy mallet or rolling pin, pound the meaty part of each chop until it's about $1/2$ inch thick, to create chops with a thinner flap of meat attached to the thick rib bone. (In Milanese restaurants, the veal is pounded even thinner and wider, but at home, practicality demands that you pound the veal to a size that will still allow two chops to fit into the skillet.) Season the chops with salt and pepper.

4. Place the matzo flour in a shallow dish, the beaten eggs in a second shallow dish, and the matzo meal mixed with the matzo farfel in a third shallow dish. Coat each veal chop with the matzo flour, then the egg wash, and then the matzo meal.

5. Heat the oil in a 12-inch skillet over medium heat until hot but not smoking. Add the chops and cook, turning once, until golden brown, about 5 minutes. Place the browned chops on a large baking sheet. Bake until they feel firm when pressed in the center, 8 to 10 minutes.

6. Just before serving, add the arugula to the tomato salad and mix. For each serving, place a chop on a dinner plate, and heap the tomato salad on top. Serve immediately with a wedge of lemon.

$1/2$ cup matzo meal
$1/2$ cup matzo farfel
$1/2$ cup olive oil (regular or extra-virgin)
6 ounces arugula, washed and dried, torn into bite-sized pieces
Lemon wedges, for serving

Rack of Veal with
Wild Mushroom–Farfel Dressing

Roasts are easy to prepare and always impressive, and since veal is truly one of the most elegant meats you can serve, this dish is an extra-special treat worthy of your finest holiday menu. Order this particular cut ahead of time from the butcher—it won't be cheap, but it will be lean and delicious. Because veal isn't fatty, care must be taken not to overcook it. The matzo farfel stuffing, which is baked on the side, is a great possibility to keep in mind for your Thanksgiving turkey, too. Serve with Broccolini with Red Peppers or Acorn Squash with Ginger-Orange Glaze (see pages 182 and 180).

**MAKES
6
SERVINGS**

2 tablespoons extra-virgin olive oil, plus more for the pan

One 5-rib (3³/4-pound) first-cut rack of veal, chine bone removed

1 teaspoon kosher salt

1¹/2 teaspoons chopped fresh rosemary

1 teaspoon chopped fresh thyme

¹/2 teaspoon freshly ground black pepper

3 cups Chicken Stock (page 40)

1. To make the veal, position a rack in the center of the oven and preheat the oven to 400°F. Lightly oil a roasting pan.

2. Brush the veal with the oil. Mix the salt, 1 teaspoon of the rosemary, ¹/2 teaspoon of the thyme, and the pepper in a small bowl, and sprinkle over the veal. Place the veal, rib side down, in the pan. Roast until an instant-read thermometer inserted in the center of the roast registers 140°F., about 1¹/4 hours.

3. Meanwhile, make the dressing. Lightly oil a 9 × 13-inch casserole.

4. Heat a large skillet over medium heat. Add the farfel and heat, stirring occasionally, until lightly toasted, about 3 minutes. Transfer to a large bowl. Add the stock and let stand to soften while preparing the other ingredients.

5. Heat the oil in a large skillet over medium heat. Add the onion and cook until translucent, about 5 minutes. Stir in the sun-dried tomatoes and garlic and cook for 1 minute. Add the mushrooms and cook, stirring occasionally, until they give off their liquid, about 4 minutes. Stir the mushroom mixture into the farfel and allow to cool slightly. Stir in the arugula, beaten egg, and basil, and season with the salt and pepper. Spread in the prepared casserole and cover with aluminum foil.

6. When the veal is done, remove it from the oven, place on a carving board, and cover loosely with aluminum foil. Let stand for 20 to 30 minutes. Reduce the oven temperature to 350°F. Bake the dressing until heated through, about 30 minutes.

7. While the stuffing is baking, make a sauce. Place the roasting pan over medium-high heat. Pour in the stock and bring to a boil, scraping up the browned bits in the pan with a wooden spoon. Cook until thickened and reduced to $1^1/2$ cups, about 10 minutes. Stir in the remaining $^1/2$ teaspoon each of rosemary and thyme. Whisk enough of the dissolved potato starch into the boiling liquid to thicken it to your liking. Season the sauce with salt and pepper and pour into a sauceboat.

8. Carve the veal and serve with the dressing and sauce.

WILD MUSHROOM–FARFEL DRESSING

3 cups matzo farfel

$^3/4$ cup Chicken Stock (page 40)

2 tablespoons extra-virgin olive oil

1 medium onion, chopped

2 tablespoons plumped (see page 166) and diced sun-dried tomatoes

2 garlic cloves, minced

8 ounces assorted wild mushrooms (such as cremini and stemmed shiitake), coarsely chopped

$^1/2$ cup coarsely chopped arugula

1 large egg, beaten

2 tablespoons chopped fresh basil

$^1/2$ teaspoon kosher salt

$^1/4$ teaspoon freshly ground black pepper

2 teaspoons potato starch, dissolved in 2 tablespoons cold water

Grilled Lamb Rib Chops
with Ratatouille

Lamb rib chops are a tender treat, and grilling really brings out their flavor. Ratatouille is the perfect side dish for lamb, but I prepare it in a special way. I cut the vegetables into small dice to expose more surface area and increase flavor, then I sauté them so they remain firm (classic ratatouille is simmered until very tender, if not actually mushy). If you happen to have leftover ratatouille, all the better—it makes a great pasta sauce.

RATATOUILLE

7 tablespoons extra-virgin olive oil

1 medium eggplant, cut into $1/4$-inch dice

1 small yellow squash, cut into $1/4$-inch dice

1 small zucchini, cut into $1/4$-inch dice

1 medium onion, finely chopped

1 small red bell pepper, cored, seeded, and cut into $1/4$-inch dice

1 small green bell pepper, cored, seeded, and cut into $1/4$-inch dice

3 garlic cloves, minced

6 plum tomatoes, peeled, seeded, and cut into $1/4$-inch dice

$1/2$ cup pitted and coarsely chopped black Mediterranean olives

2 tablespoons balsamic vinegar

2 tablespoons chopped fresh basil

1. To make the ratatouille, heat 3 tablespoons of the oil in a large nonstick skillet over medium-high heat. Add the eggplant and cook, stirring occasionally, until browned and barely tender (it should hold its shape), about 5 minutes. Transfer the eggplant to a bowl.

2. Heat 2 more tablespoons oil in the skillet over medium-high heat. Add the yellow squash and zucchini and cook, stirring occasionally, until the vegetables are crisp-tender, about 4 minutes. Add them to the eggplant.

3. Heat the remaining 2 tablespoons of oil to the skillet over medium heat. Add the onion and red and green bell peppers, and cook, stirring often, until softened, about 6 minutes. Add the garlic and cook until fragrant, about 1 minute. Return the eggplant and squash to the skillet, and stir in the tomatoes, olives, balsamic vinegar, basil, rosemary, and oregano. Bring to a simmer, stirring often, until the tomatoes are heated through, about 5 minutes. Season with salt and pepper and keep warm.

4. To make the lamb chops, combine the olive oil, rosemary, salt, and pepper in a small bowl. Brush the lamb chops on both sides with the flavored oil. Let stand while preparing the grill.

5. Build a charcoal fire in an outdoor grill and let it burn until the coals are covered with white ash or preheat a gas grill on high. Lightly oil the cooking surface. Grill the chops, turning once, until medium-rare, about 4 minutes per side (or longer for more well-done meat).

6. Serve the lamb chops on individual plates with a spoonful of the ratatouille. Drizzle the syrup onto the lamb and ratatouille and serve immediately.

1 tablespoon chopped fresh rosemary
2 teaspoons chopped fresh oregano
Kosher salt and freshly ground black pepper to taste

LAMB CHOPS
2 tablespoons extra-virgin olive oil
1 tablespoon chopped fresh rosemary
1 teaspoon kosher salt
$1/2$ teaspoon freshly ground black pepper
16 lamb rib chops
Balsamic Syrup (recipe follows)

Balsamic Syrup

PAREVE
MAKES ABOUT $1/4$ CUP

A flavorful drizzle of balsamic syrup, which is nothing more than boiled-down balsamic vinegar, is a creative way to decorate compatible entrées.

1 cup moderately priced balsamic vinegar

Bring the vinegar to a boil in a medium saucepan over medium heat. Simmer until syrupy and reduced by half, about 10 minutes. Allow to cool completely. (The syrup can be prepared up to 2 weeks ahead if covered and refrigerated. Return to room temperature before using.)

Braised Lamb Chops
with Spiced Tomato Sauce

MAKES
4
SERVINGS

Home cooks usually broil lamb shoulder chops, but they can also be braised, yielding the flavor of a stew in much less time. Serve the lamb with Israeli couscous or steamed new potatoes tossed with fresh parsley and a bit of extra-virgin olive oil.

8 lamb shoulder chops, cut about 3/4 inch thick
Kosher salt and freshly ground black pepper to taste
3 tablespoons extra-virgin olive oil
2 small onions, halved lengthwise and sliced into half-moons
2 medium carrots, cut into 3/4-inch dice
6 garlic cloves, chopped
1/2 cup dry white wine
1 cup canned crushed tomatoes
1 1/2 teaspoons crumbled dried rosemary
1/2 teaspoon dried oregano
1/4 teaspoon ground cinnamon

1. Position a rack in the center of the oven and preheat the oven to 325°F. Lightly oil a large baking dish.

2. Season the lamb chops with the salt and pepper. Heat 2 tablespoons of the oil in a large skillet over medium-high heat. In batches, without crowding, add the lamb chops and cook, turning once, until browned on both sides, about 4 minutes. Transfer the browned chops to the baking dish, overlapping as needed. Pour off all but 1 tablespoon of fat in the skillet.

3. Heat the remaining tablespoon of oil in the skillet and reduce the heat to medium. Add the onions, carrots, and garlic. Cook, stirring often, just until the onions are wilted, about 3 minutes. Add the wine and stir to scrape up the browned bits in the skillet. Stir in the tomatoes, rosemary, oregano, and cinnamon, and bring to a boil. Season with salt and pepper and pour over the lamb chops. Tightly cover the baking dish with aluminum foil.

4. Bake until the lamb chops are tender, about 45 minutes. Let stand for 5 minutes, then skim off the fat on the surface. Serve immediately.

Lamb and Rice Kouresht

**MAKES
6 TO 8
SERVINGS**

Kouresht is a casserole of spiced, stewed lamb layered with rice. The rice for this dish is allowed to dry out, all the better to create a crisp, golden crust in the bottom of the casserole. The crust is my favorite part, and I bet it will be yours, too.

1. Position a rack in the center of the oven and preheat the oven to 325°F.

2. Bring 3 cups of water and the salt to a boil in a medium saucepan over high heat. Add the rice and return to a boil. Reduce the heat to low and cover. Simmer until the rice is tender, about 18 minutes. Spread the rice in a thin layer on a large baking sheet. Place in the refrigerator to cool and dry out.

3. Heat 2 tablespoons of the oil in a large Dutch oven or flameproof casserole. In batches, add the lamb and cook, turning occasionally, until browned, about 6 minutes, adding more oil as needed. Transfer the browned lamb to a plate.

4. Heat the remaining 2 tablespoons oil in the Dutch oven. Add the fennel and onions and cook, stirring often, until softened, about 5 minutes. Stir in the turmeric, cinnamon, and saffron. Add the tomatoes, stock, garbanzo beans, and lime juice. Return the lamb to the pot, stir, and bring to a simmer. Cover and bake until the lamb is tender, about 1½ hours.

5. When the lamb is done, remove the Dutch oven from the oven. Increase the oven temperature to 350°F. Let the stewed lamb stand for 10 minutes. Skim off any fat from the surface and season with salt and pepper.

6. Lightly oil a 3-quart ovenproof casserole. Spread a little more than one-third of the rice in the casserole. Top with half of the stew. Layer on one half of the remaining rice, then the rest of the stew, and finally the remaining rice. Bake, uncovered, until the rice is crusty on top, about 30 minutes. Sprinkle with the chopped parsley and serve.

1½ teaspoons kosher salt, plus more to taste

1½ cups long-grain rice

4 tablespoons extra-virgin olive oil

3 pounds boneless lamb shoulder, cut into 1½-inch cubes

1 medium fennel bulb, trimmed of fronds, cut into ½-inch dice

2 medium onions, cut into ½-inch dice

1 teaspoon ground turmeric

½ teaspoon ground cinnamon

⅛ teaspoon crumbled saffron

One 28-ounce can crushed tomatoes

2 cups Beef Stock (page 41), warmed

One 15- to 19-ounce can garbanzo beans (chickpeas), drained

¼ cup fresh lime juice

Kosher salt and freshly ground black pepper to taste

2 tablespoons chopped fresh parsley, for garnish

Poultry

To call poultry a staple of Jewish cooking is an understatement. It's understandable that many cooks concentrate on chicken in the interest of convenience, versatility, and tradition, but in my kitchen, duck and turkey are equally indispensable.

Kosher poultry is salted as part of its processing. The salting actually seasons the bird from the inside out, giving it the flavor and juiciness that cause many people to claim that kosher poultry simply tastes better. It's important, though, for the cook to take that salt into account when seasoning to reduce the risk of oversalting; it's usually best to season the dish after cooking.

Ever-popular chicken has a chameleonlike talent for picking up other flavors. I am especially fond of chicken stews, where the interplay of chicken, vegetables, and seasonings is downright magical. The only trick here is that the white meat cooks before the dark meat. However, because the breasts are larger than the drumsticks and thighs, they don't get seriously overcooked. You can certainly remove the breasts from the pot a few minutes before the dark meat, if you wish.

Please don't forget poultry's cousins: turkey and duck. Holiday meals aside, it's a great idea to roast a turkey for a weekend supper and have leftovers for sandwiches, casseroles, and soups. Turkey thighs are a fine substitute for red meat in stews, and I use them in my cholent (page 84). And I think I may be the world's number one duck fan. Roast duck makes a special meal, and once you get the hang of it, you'll be roasting ducks to use their meat in stir-fries, wraps, or salads, just like I do.

Sephardic Chicken and Meatball Fricassee

MAKES
6 TO 8
SERVINGS

This is an especially substantial chicken stew, studded with beef meatballs and dried fruits. I like to use chicken leg quarters, but those of you who prefer white meat can substitute breasts, reducing the initial baking time to 30 minutes.

SEPHARDIC CHICKEN

1/4 cup dried figs, stemmed and cut into small dice
1/4 cup dried apricots, cut into small dice
1/4 cup golden raisins
2 tablespoons brandy
Pinch of crumbled saffron threads
Pinch of ground cinnamon

MEATBALLS

2 large eggs
3 tablespoons seasoned dried bread crumbs
2 tablespoons chopped fresh parsley
1/2 teaspoon onion powder
1/2 teaspoon garlic powder
1 teaspoon kosher salt
1/4 teaspoon freshly ground black pepper
1 1/2 pounds ground beef

1. Position racks in the center and top third of the oven and preheat the oven to 350°F. Lightly oil a baking sheet.

2. In a small bowl, combine the dried figs, apricots, and raisins and cover with hot water. Combine the brandy, saffron, and cinnamon in another small bowl. Let both stand while preparing the other ingredients.

3. To make the meatballs, whisk the eggs, bread crumbs, parsley, onion and garlic powders, salt, and pepper in a large bowl to combine. Add the ground beef and stir just until combined. Do not overmix. Moisten your hands with water, form the beef mixture into 24 walnut-sized balls, and place on the baking sheet. Bake on the top rack until the meatballs are beginning to brown, about 15 minutes. Remove from the oven.

4. Meanwhile, heat the 1/4 cup oil in a large skillet over medium-high heat. Add the chicken and cook until golden on both sides, about 6 minutes. Transfer to a large baking dish.

5. Pour off all but 2 tablespoons oil from the skillet. Add the onions and cook, scraping up any browned bits on the bottom of the pan, until translucent, about 5 minutes. Add the garlic and stir until fragrant, about 1 minute.

6. Drain the fruit well. Add to the skillet, along with the tomatoes and the brandy mixture. Bring to a simmer, pour over the chicken, and cover tightly. Bake on the center rack for 45 minutes. Add the browned meatballs, cover, and cook until the chicken shows no sign of pink when pierced at the thigh bone, about 15 minutes. Season with salt and pepper and serve hot.

$1/4$ cup extra-virgin olive oil

8 chicken leg quarters (with thighs)

2 medium onions, chopped

3 garlic cloves, minced

One 28-ounce can crushed tomatoes

Kosher salt and freshly ground black pepper to taste

PLUMPING FOR FLAVOR

Drying is an ancient method of preserving fruit. Even today, dried fruits find their way into many Jewish dishes, supplying a delicious hint of sweetness. But I've learned that there's more to the process than tossing raisins into a kugel. Always plump the dried fruit (be it raisins, apricots, figs, dates, cranberries, or what have you) in hot water for at least 30 minutes before using them. The bath is not just to give the fruit a moister texture—in fact, you should always cook with fresh, moist dried fruit because the dried-up stuff will taste stale and all the soaking in the world won't improve it. Plumped fruit is filled with water and won't be able to soak up the recipe's cooking juices, so it will retain more of its character and sweetness.

Perfect Roast Chicken
with Lemon and Rosemary

To my mind (and palate), this chicken is perfect! Everyone needs a good, solid roast-chicken recipe that they can turn to, and this is the one that I proudly present. The combination of rosemary, lemon, and garlic fills the kitchen with aromas that make everyone eagerly anticipate the meal. Try this with Swiss Chard Mashed Potatoes and Broccolini with Red Peppers (pages 188 and 182) for a satisfying, comforting meal.

1 tablespoon olive oil
1 tablespoon chopped fresh
　　rosemary
Grated zest of 1 lemon
$^{1}/_{2}$ teaspoon garlic powder
$^{1}/_{4}$ teaspoon freshly ground
　　black pepper
One 4-pound chicken, rinsed
　　and patted dry
2 lemons, cut in quarters (use
　　the zested lemon)
1 teaspoon kosher salt
1 medium carrot, chopped
1 medium onion, chopped
1 celery rib, chopped
2 tablespoons all-purpose flour
$1^{1}/_{2}$ cups Chicken Stock
　　(page 40)

1. Combine the olive oil, rosemary, lemon zest, garlic powder, and pepper in a small bowl. Place the chicken on a platter and spread the mixture over the surface of the chicken. Insert the lemon quarters into the cavity of the chicken. Cover with plastic wrap and refrigerate for 3 to 4 hours.

2. Position a rack in the lower third of the oven and preheat the oven to 350°F. Lightly oil a roasting rack, preferably V-shaped (see page 109), and place in a roasting pan.

3. Season the outside of the chicken all over with the salt and place on the roasting rack. Roast for 30 minutes. Add the carrot, onion, and celery to the pan and roast until an instant-read thermometer inserted in the thickest part of the thigh reads 170°F., about 1 hour.

4. Transfer the chicken to a shallow serving dish. Cover with aluminum foil and let rest for 15 minutes before carving. Discard the ingredients in the cavity of the chicken.

5. Meanwhile, make the gravy. Using a slotted spoon, remove and discard the vegetables in the pan.

Measure the drippings—if there's less than 2 tablespoons, add some olive oil. Return the drippings to the pan.

6. Place the roasting pan over medium heat. Whisk in the flour and cook, scraping up the browned bits in the pan. Whisk in the stock and bring to a boil. Reduce the heat to medium-low and simmer until thickened and no taste of raw flour remains, about 5 minutes. Season with salt and pepper and strain the gravy into a sauceboat.

7. Carve the chicken and serve with the gravy.

HOMEMADE ROASTING RACKS

While I want to encourage you to have a well-stocked kitchen, I also don't want the lack of a roasting rack to keep you from roasting a chicken. You do need something to keep the bird from sitting in its own juices, which will make the bottom soggy and prone to falling apart when the chicken is lifted from the pan. The most efficient utensil is an adjustable V-shaped rack. However, when cooking in a kitchen lacking a pan with a rack, I create my own. Just twist a length of aluminum foil into a ring, and make a circular "nest" in the pan for the chicken.

Crispy Creole Chicken Breasts

MAKES
4
SERVINGS

There is only one way to get that delectable golden crust on fried chicken, and that is to use plenty of oil. In fact, its copious use of oil may tempt some families to put this dish on their Hanukkah recipe list. No matter when you make it, it is a fine way to bring crispy, crunchy, and spicy fried chicken to the table. Just be sure that the oil is heated until it is very hot.

1 teaspoon sweet paprika
1 teaspoon onion powder
1 teaspoon freshly ground
   black pepper
$1/2$ teaspoon garlic powder
$1/2$ teaspoon light brown sugar
$1/4$ teaspoon kosher salt
Pinch of ground hot red
   (cayenne) pepper
$1/4$ cup vegetable oil, plus more
   for frying
$1/2$ cup all-purpose flour
Four 6-ounce boneless, skinless
   chicken breasts, trimmed of
   excess fat
Barbecue Vinaigrette (page 79),
   for dipping

1. Mix the paprika, onion powder, pepper, garlic powder, brown sugar, salt, and cayenne in a small bowl. Pour the $1/4$ cup of oil into a shallow dish. Place the flour in another shallow dish. Line a baking sheet with wax paper.

2. Season both sides of the chicken with the spice mixture. Dip into the oil, then coat with the flour. Set the chicken aside on the wax paper until the coating is sticky, about 15 minutes.

3. Meanwhile, pour enough oil into a large, heavy-bottomed skillet to come 1 inch up the sides. Heat the oil over medium-high heat until very hot but not smoking (the surface of the oil will shimmer slightly, and a smidgen of the coating will sizzle immediately when dropped into the oil).

4. Coat the chicken again in the flour only. Carefully add the chicken to the skillet. Cook uncovered, turning once, until the chicken is golden brown, about 10 minutes (adjust the heat as needed so the chicken cooks without burning). Using a slotted spatula, transfer the chicken to paper towels to drain.

5. Serve hot, with ramekins of the vinaigrette passed on the side for dipping.

Syrian Lemon Chicken Stew

MAKES
4
SERVINGS

This is a stew for people who aren't satisfied by bland flavors. It practically vibrates with the tangy flavors of wine, lemon, and olives, not to mention the aromatic tastes of oregano and cumin. Serve it with a simple rice pilaf.

1. Position a rack in the center of the oven and preheat the oven to 350°F.

2. Heat the oil in a large, deep, ovenproof skillet over medium-high heat. Add the chicken and cook, turning occasionally, until golden on all sides, about 6 minutes. Set the chicken aside.

3. Pour out all but 2 tablespoons of the fat from the skillet. Add the onion and garlic, stirring up the browned bits in the skillet, and cook until lightly browned, about 6 minutes. Sprinkle with the flour, oregano, and cumin, and mix well. Stir in the stock, wine, olives, and lemon juice. Return the chicken to the skillet and bring to a simmer.

4. Bake until the chicken shows no sign of pink when pierced at the thigh bone, about 1 hour. Season with salt and pepper. Stir in the parsley and serve immediately.

3 tablespoons extra-virgin olive oil
One 3¹/₂-pound chicken, cut into 8 serving pieces
1 large onion, thinly sliced
3 garlic cloves, thinly sliced
¹/₄ cup all-purpose flour
1 tablespoon dried oregano
1 teaspoon ground cumin
3 cups Chicken Stock (page 40)
1 cup dry white wine
²/₃ cup pitted and sliced green Mediterranean olives
¹/₄ cup fresh lemon juice
Kosher salt and freshly ground black pepper to taste
¹/₄ cup chopped fresh flat-leaf parsley

Grilled Chicken Breasts
with Orange-Soy Marinade

The time I spent working in a Japanese restaurant supplied me with a world of new techniques and flavors. Here are the clean, fresh tastes of that wonderful cuisine in an easy-to-make grilled chicken dish that will become a family favorite. No grill? No problem; just use the broiler. Because of the natural sugars in the orange-soy marinade, the chicken tends to burn when cooked with the direct heat of a broiler. To get around this, broil the chicken skin up just until browned, about 5 minutes. Then turn the broiler off, set the oven to 400°F., and continue cooking until the chicken is cooked through. This is great served with steamed rice and the Snap Peas and Carrots with Ginger and Sesame (page 191).

**MAKES
4
SERVINGS**

MARINADE
1/3 cup sake or dry sherry
1/3 cup soy sauce
1/3 cup fresh orange juice
Grated zest of 1 large orange
1 tablespoon dark Asian sesame oil
1 tablespoon peeled and finely chopped fresh ginger
1 garlic clove, finely chopped
1 teaspoon honey
1/8 teaspoon hot red pepper flakes

Four 10-ounce chicken breasts with skin and bone

1. To make the marinade, shake all of the ingredients in a zip-tight plastic bag. Add the chicken and close. Refrigerate, turning occasionally, for at least 2 and up to 4 hours.

2. Meanwhile, build a charcoal fire on one side of an outdoor grill and let the fire burn until the coals are covered with white ash. Lightly oil the grill grate.

3. Remove the chicken from the marinade. Place the chicken over the coals and cover the grill. Cook, turning once, until lightly browned, about 5 minutes. Transfer to the side of the grill without coals and cover the grill. Continue cooking until the chicken shows no sign of pink when pierced in the thickest part, about 20 minutes.

4. Serve hot.

Hungarian Chicken Paprikash

Many ethnic dishes have been so altered by years of cooking in America that people in the Old Country wouldn't recognize them. For example, sour cream is not always an essential ingredient in classic Hungarian chicken paprikash, which makes it a good dish for the kosher kitchen. Please search out Hungarian paprika, easy to find at specialty stores and well-stocked supermarkets, because it has more flavor than paprika from other countries. Be sure and serve this with boiled egg noodles. Or, if you're really ambitious (or Hungarian), make the shlishkas on page 160.

**MAKES
6 TO 8
SERVINGS**

1. Position a rack in the center of the oven and preheat the oven to 350°F.

2. Heat the oil in a large skillet over medium-high heat. In batches, add the chicken, skin side down. Cook, turning once, until golden, about 6 minutes. Transfer to a heatproof casserole.

3. Add the onions and fennel to the skillet. Cook, scraping up any browned bits from the bottom of the pan and stirring occasionally, until lightly browned, about 8 minutes. Stir in the red and yellow bell peppers and the garlic. Cook, stirring frequently, until the peppers soften, about 5 minutes. Sprinkle with the paprika and mix well.

4. Add the flour and stir well. Stir in the stock, tomatoes, wine, oregano, and hot pepper sauce. Bring to a simmer and cook for 3 minutes, stirring often. Pour the mixture over the chicken.

5. Bake, uncovered, until the chicken shows no sign of pink when pierced at the thigh bone, about 50 minutes. Season with salt and pepper and serve hot.

2 tablespoons extra-virgin olive oil

Two 3½-pound chickens, each cut into 8 serving pieces

2 large onions, thinly sliced

½ of a fennel bulb, cored and thinly sliced

2 red bell peppers, seeded and cut into strips

2 yellow bell peppers, seeded and cut into strips

5 garlic cloves, minced

2 tablespoons sweet Hungarian paprika, or 1 tablespoon each sweet and hot Hungarian paprika

6 tablespoons all-purpose flour

3½ cups Chicken Stock (page 40)

3 plum tomatoes, peeled, seeded, and diced

¾ cup white wine

1½ tablespoons chopped fresh oregano

1 teaspoon hot red pepper sauce

Kosher salt and freshly ground black pepper to taste

Moroccan Chicken Tagine
with Preserved Lemons

**MAKES
6 TO 8
SERVINGS**

When I toured Morocco, I often saw stews just like this one being simmered in earthenware pots over open fires. Moroccan cooks have an amazing talent for spicing that has often inspired my own cooking. This recipe uses preserved lemons, a popular Moroccan ingredient, for authentic flavor. If you don't have them, substitute the juice and zest of 1 lemon, but the result won't be quite as exotic.

¹/₂ teaspoon ground ginger
¹/₂ teaspoon ground fennel
  seeds
¹/₂ teaspoon ground cumin
¹/₂ teaspoon ground coriander
¹/₂ teaspoon ground allspice
¹/₂ teaspoon ground cinnamon
Two 3¹/₂-pound chickens, each
  cut into quarters
¹/₂ cup all-purpose flour
¹/₄ cup extra-virgin olive oil,
  more as needed
2 medium onions, thinly sliced
2 red bell peppers, cored,
  seeded, and cut into thin
  strips
2 yellow bell peppers, cored,
  seeded, and cut into thin
  strips
2 garlic cloves, minced
8 wedges Preserved Lemons
  (recipe follows), coarsely
  chopped
¹/₂ cup Chicken Stock
  (page 40)

1. Position a rack in the center of the oven and preheat the oven to 350°F.

2. In a small bowl, combine the ginger, fennel, cumin, coriander, allspice, and cinnamon. Season the chicken with the spice mixture, dredge in the flour to coat, and shake off the excess flour.

3. Heat the oil in a large skillet over medium-high heat. In batches, add the chicken, skin side down. Cook, turning once, until golden, about 5 minutes. Transfer to a heatproof casserole.

4. If the flour has burned, wipe out the skillet, add 2 more tablespoons of oil, and heat. Add the onions and red and yellow bell peppers to the skillet. Cook until softened but not browned, 5 minutes. Add the garlic and stir until fragrant, about 1 minute. Stir in the preserved lemons, stock, wine, olives, and honey, and bring to a boil, scraping up any browned bits from the bottom of the pan.

5. Pour the mixture over the chicken. Bake, uncovered, until the chicken shows no sign of pink when pierced at the thigh bone, about 1 hour. Season with salt and pepper. Stir in the cilantro and almonds and serve immediately.

1/4 cup dry white wine
2/3 cup pitted and coarsely chopped green Mediterranean olives
1 tablespoon honey
Kosher salt and freshly ground black pepper to taste
2 tablespoons chopped fresh cilantro
2 tablespoons slivered almonds, toasted (see page 175)

Preserved Lemons

PAREVE
MAKES 1 QUART

American chefs are discovering the tangy flavor and silky texture of lemons preserved in the Moroccan style. You'll need to plan ahead to make them, since they take at least one week to cure in kosher salt and fresh lemon juice. You'll be glad you have a stash in the refrigerator, ready to add to dishes that are inspired by Mediterranean cuisines—especially those that contain olives or capers.

4 large lemons, rinsed
1 cup kosher salt
1 cup fresh lemon juice, as needed
1/3 cup extra-virgin olive oil

Cut the lemons lengthwise into sixths. Toss with the salt in a medium bowl. Pack tightly into a hot 1-quart canning jar sterilized with boiling water. Add enough lemon juice to cover the lemons.

Seal the jar with the lid and shake well. Let stand at room temperature, shaking once a day.

At the end of the week, pour the oil into the jar and shake well. Cover tightly and refrigerate until needed, up to 6 months.

Russian Chicken Pojarski

Visits to the table of my friend Elena Chumakova are too infrequent, but whenever we get together, I know that I'm in for a great meal. Elena is famous for her renditions of recipes from her Russian homeland, such as these crisp poultry patties, crunchy on the outside and juicy within. I was so bowled over by her pojarski that I put them on Abigael's menu, served with Dill Mashed Potatoes (page 188). For a substantial hors d'oeuvre, make them into bite-sized nuggets, reducing the cooking time.

**MAKES
4
SERVINGS**

¼ cup chopped fresh parsley

2 teaspoons chopped fresh
oregano

1 teaspoon chopped fresh
rosemary

2 teaspoons onion powder

2 garlic cloves, minced

1½ teaspoons kosher salt

½ teaspoon freshly ground
black pepper

1 cup fresh bread crumbs

½ cup plus 2 tablespoons
extra-virgin olive oil

2 pounds ground chicken or
turkey

1 cup panko (Japanese bread
crumbs; see page 173)

1. Position a rack in the center of the oven and preheat the oven to 200°F. Line a baking sheet with paper towels.

2. In a small bowl, combine the parsley, oregano, rosemary, onion powder, garlic, salt, and pepper. Stir in the bread crumbs and ¼ cup of the oil. Add the ground chicken and mix just until combined (do not overmix). Form into eight 4-inch-wide patties.

3. Heat the remaining 6 tablespoons oil in a large skillet over medium heat. Coat the patties on both sides with the panko. In batches, without crowding, add the patties to the pan and cook, turning occasionally, until golden on both sides, about 12 minutes. Adjust the heat as needed so the patties cook steadily without browning too quickly. Use a slotted spatula to transfer them to the baking sheet and keep warm in the oven while cooking the remaining pojarski.

NOTE: To make fresh bread crumbs, whirl day-old bread, crusts and all, in a food processor or blender. If you wish, freeze in an airtight container for up to 1 month. Thaw frozen bread crumbs at room temperature for about 1 hour before using.

Yemenite Chicken
in Spiced Tomato Sauce

Twelve cloves of garlic are not too much for this dish—the Yemenite Jews like their food extravagantly spiced. For those of you who might be a bit tired of serving chicken, this intriguing recipe will change your opinion. Serve it with Israeli couscous.

1. Position a rack in the center of the oven and preheat the oven to 350° F.

2. Mix the cumin, cardamom, 1 teaspoon salt, pepper, turmeric, and coriander in a small bowl. Season the chicken all over with the spice blend.

3. Heat the oil in a Dutch oven or flameproof casserole over medium-high heat. In batches, add the chicken to the oil and cook, turning occasionally, until browned on all sides, about 8 minutes. Transfer to a platter.

4. Pour out all but 2 tablespoons of the fat in the pot. Add the onions and garlic and reduce the heat to medium. Cook, stirring often, until the onions are softened, about 5 minutes. Stir in the tomatoes with their juices and the wine. Return the chicken to the pot and bring to a boil.

5. Cover tightly and bake until the chicken shows no sign of pink when pierced with the tip of a knife, about 50 minutes. Let stand 5 minutes, then skim off the fat on the surface. Season with salt and serve hot.

3 tablespoons ground cumin

1 1/4 teaspoons ground cardamom

1 teaspoon kosher salt, plus more for seasoning

3/4 teaspoon freshly ground black pepper

3/4 teaspoon ground turmeric

1/4 teaspoon ground coriander

Two 3 1/2-pound chickens, each cut into 8 serving pieces

2 tablespoons extra-virgin olive oil

2 medium red onions, finely chopped

12 garlic cloves, finely chopped

Three 14 1/2-ounce cans tomatoes in juice (juices reserved), coarsely chopped

1 cup dry white wine

Roast Turkey with Apple, Walnut, and Challah Dressing

When it comes to turkey, I rely on the advice of my buddy Rick Rodgers. He's not Jewish, but as the author of three books on turkey and Thanksgiving, he knows his stuff(ing). This recipe incorporates my favorite seasonings with his roasting method. For most holidays, you'll want to use his challah, apple, and walnut stuffing. For Passover, make a double batch of the Wild Mushroom–Farfel Dressing on page 98. You can stuff the bird or not, but an unstuffed bird cooks in much less time.

ROAST TURKEY

One 14-pound fresh turkey, rinsed and patted dry with paper towels

1/4 cup extra-virgin olive oil, plus more if needed

2 tablespoons melted pareve margarine

4 garlic cloves, minced

1 tablespoon chopped fresh sage

1 teaspoon chopped fresh rosemary

1/2 teaspoon garlic powder

1/2 teaspoon onion powder

1 teaspoon kosher salt

1/2 teaspoon freshly ground black pepper

1 medium carrot, coarsely chopped

1 large onion, coarsely chopped

1 medium celery rib, coarsely chopped

5 cups Chicken or Turkey Stock (page 40), as needed

2/3 cup all-purpose flour

Kosher salt and freshly ground black pepper to taste

1. Position a rack in the lower third of the oven and preheat the oven to 325°F. Tie the drumsticks together and the wings to the body with kitchen twine.

2. Combine the olive oil, melted margarine, garlic, sage, rosemary, garlic and onion powders, salt, and pepper in a small bowl. Schmear all over the turkey.

3. Place the turkey on a rack in a roasting pan (or use the aluminum foil ring on page 109). Cover the breast area of the turkey, but not the wings, with aluminum foil. Don't just tent the breast with foil—really cover it. Roast, basting every 20 minutes with the pan juices (lift up the foil to reach the breast area), for 3 hours. Discard the foil and add the carrot, onion, and celery pieces to the pan. Continue roasting, basting occasionally, until a meat thermometer inserted deep into the thigh, but not touching the bone, reads 180°F., 1½ to 2 hours. (Estimate about 15 minutes per pound for a small turkey up to 14 pounds, and about 20 minutes per pound for turkeys larger than 14 pounds; if you prefer to stuff the bird, add approximately 5 minutes per pound.)

4. While the turkey is roasting, prepare the stuffing. In a large skillet, heat the schmaltz over medium-high heat. Add the onion and celery and cook, stirring often, until the vegetables are tender, about 15 minutes.

5. Mix the onion and celery, challah, walnuts, dried apples, parsley, and poultry seasoning in a large bowl. Gradually stir in enough of the broth to moisten the dressing evenly without making it soggy. Spoon into a lightly greased 10 × 15-inch baking dish and cover it with aluminum foil. (The dressing can be made up to 8 hours in advance. Refrigerate if not baking within 1 hour.)

6. Remove the turkey from the oven. Place the dressing in the oven and increase the temperature to 375°F. Bake until heated through, about 30 minutes, a bit longer if refrigerated.

7. Transfer the turkey to a serving platter and let stand for 30 minutes. (Don't ignore this advice—the rest allows the juices to soak into the meat, and makes for a moister bird.) Meanwhile, make the gravy. Strain the pan juices into a large glass measuring cup, discarding the vegetables. Let stand 5 minutes. Skim off and reserve the fat that rises to the top. You should have ²/3 cup of fat; add some olive oil, if needed. Add enough of the chicken stock to the skimmed pan juices to measure 5 cups.

8. Place the roasting pan over two burners on medium heat. Pour in the fat. Whisk in the flour and cook until bubbling. Whisk in the stock mixture and bring to a simmer, scraping up the browned bits in the pan. Reduce the heat to medium-low and cook, whisking often, until thickened and no raw flour taste remains, about 10 minutes. Season with salt and pepper. Keep warm.

9. Carve the turkey. Strain the gravy into a sauceboat. Serve the turkey with the dressing and gravy.

APPLE-CHALLAH STUFFING

¹/2 cup schmaltz (see page 165) or pareve margarine
1 large onion, chopped
3 celery ribs with leaves, chopped
10 cups (1-inch cubes) day-old challah
1¹/2 cups walnuts, toasted (see page 175) and coarsely chopped
1¹/2 cups coarsely chopped dried apples
2 tablespoons chopped fresh parsley
1 tablespoon poultry seasoning
1¹/2 cups Turkey or Chicken Stock (page 40), as needed

Turkey and Sausage Barley Jambalaya

MAKES
8
SERVINGS

When people ask me to illustrate what's new in Jewish cooking, I like to give them this recipe. Barley is a familiar grain to Ashkenazic cooks, since the climate in Eastern Europe was perfect for its cultivation. Traditional jambalaya is made from rice and nonkosher meats, but my equally flavorful version shows that barley, turkey, and pastrami can cook up into a pretty mean jambalaya, too.

4 tablespoons extra-virgin
  olive oil
1½ pounds bone-in turkey
  thighs (see Note), cut into
  1-inch pieces
8 ounces veal sausage, cut into
  ½-inch pieces
8 ounces thickly sliced,
  coarsely chopped pastrami
2 medium onions, chopped
1 large green bell pepper,
  cored, seeded, and chopped
3 medium celery ribs, chopped
2 garlic cloves, minced
1 tablespoon sweet Hungarian
  paprika
2 teaspoons dried thyme
1 teaspoon dried oregano
1 teaspoon garlic powder
1 teaspoon kosher salt
¼ teaspoon freshly ground
  black pepper
¼ teaspoon ground hot red
  (cayenne) pepper
1½ cups pearl barley
3 cups Chicken Stock (page
  40), plus more as needed
One 28-ounce can tomatoes in
  purée, tomatoes chopped
  and purée reserved

1. Position a rack in the center of the oven and preheat the oven to 350°F.

2. Heat 2 tablespoons of the olive oil in a Dutch oven or flameproof casserole over medium-high heat. Add the turkey pieces and cook until lightly golden, about 3 minutes. Transfer to a bowl.

3. Heat the remaining 2 tablespoons oil in the Dutch oven. Add the veal sausage and pastrami and cook, stirring occasionally, until the sausage begins to brown, about 5 minutes. Stir in the onions, green bell pepper, celery, and garlic. Cook until the vegetables soften, about 5 minutes. Stir in the paprika, thyme, oregano, garlic powder, salt, pepper, and cayenne, and cook until fragrant, about 30 seconds.

4. Add the barley and stir to coat well. Add the turkey, stock, and tomatoes with the purée. Bring to a boil over high heat and cover tightly.

5. Bake until the barley and turkey are tender, about 1 hour, adding more stock to the casserole if the barley absorbs all of the liquid before it is tender. Let stand 5 minutes before serving.

NOTE: To bone turkey thighs, pull off the skin. Then, using a sharp knife, cut down both sides of the thigh bone to end up with two large chunks of meat. Cut the meat into 1-inch cubes.

Asian Duck Stir-Fry

I think that duck is every bit as versatile as chicken. In my cooking classes, I often roast up a few ducks and illustrate how many ways you can use the delicious, moist meat. One of my favorite duck recipes is this Asian stir-fry. You can use either bok choy or napa cabbage, but a combination gives double the flavor and texture. Stir-fry the leftover bok choy with ginger and garlic as a side dish for another meal, and use the remaining napa cabbage for Asian Two-Cabbage Slaw (page 66).

1. Heat the peanut oil in a large skillet over high heat. Add the duck meat and cook, stirring frequently, until crisped around the edges, about 2 minutes. Stir in the garlic and ginger and cook, stirring frequently, until fragrant, about 30 seconds.

2. Add the red bell pepper, apple, pineapple, and cashews, and stir-fry until the red pepper is crisp-tender, about 2 minutes. Add the bok choy, cabbage, teriyaki sauce, and hoisin sauce. Stir well to combine, then remove from the heat and mix in the sesame oil. Serve with the rice.

NOTE: This is the equivalent of the meat from one 5-pound roast duck. Follow the instructions on roasting duck from the recipe for Roast Duck with Apple–Golden Raisin Sauce on page 122. If you wish, substitute the dark meat of roast chicken (about half of a 3¹/₂-pound chicken, roasted).

1 tablespoon peanut or vegetable oil

3 cups roasted, thinly sliced duck meat (see Note)

3 garlic cloves, minced

2 teaspoons peeled and minced fresh ginger

1 small red bell pepper, cored, seeded, and cut into ¹/₄-inch strips

²/₃ cup (¹/₂-inch dice) chopped peeled Granny Smith apple

²/₃ cup (¹/₂-inch dice) fresh pineapple chunks

¹/₃ cup roasted unsalted cashews

2 large leaves and stems bok choy, cut into ¹/₄-inch strips

2 large leaves napa cabbage, shredded

3 tablespoons bottled teriyaki sauce

2 tablespoons hoisin sauce

2 teaspoons dark Asian sesame oil

Cooked white rice, for serving

Roast Duck with Apple–Golden Raisin Sauce

Roasting a duck is not as daunting as it may seem. This recipe uses a double-cooking technique that allows the home cook to make roast duck that is every bit as tasty as those prepared at Abigael's. We roast and cool the duck well, which allows for easy removal of most of the bones that make for difficult carving. The duck is then reheated in a very hot oven, a step that guarantees a crispy skin and moist meat.

> MAKES
> 4
> SERVINGS

When I prepared this recipe on New Jewish Cuisine, *I knew it was a hit! The kitchen crew, camera operators, and lighting technicians all gathered around to watch me bone it. I wonder, was it my knife skills or the succulent scraps they were interested in?*

ROAST DUCK

1 Granny Smith apple, unpeeled, cut into quarters

1 seedless orange, cut into quarters

Two 5-pound ducklings, rinsed and patted dry

$^1/_2$ teaspoon coarsely cracked (butcher-grind) black pepper

APPLE-RAISIN SAUCE

$^1/_4$ cup cider vinegar

$^1/_4$ cup sugar

1 whole star anise pod

2 Granny Smith apples, peeled, cored, and chopped into $^1/_2$-inch dice

$^1/_2$ cup apple cider

$^1/_4$ cup golden raisins

$^1/_8$ teaspoon ground cinnamon

$^1/_4$ cup brandy

1 teaspoon cornstarch

1. Position a rack in the center of the oven and preheat the oven to 450°F.

2. Stuff 2 each of the apple and orange quarters in the cavity of each duck. Season the duck with the pepper. Using the upturned tines of a meat fork, prick the duck skin all over, especially in the fatty thigh and breast areas, being careful not to pierce the flesh. Place them, breast side up, on a large roasting rack set in a large roasting pan (if you don't have a rack large enough, fashion a rack from foil—see page 109).

3. Roast the ducks for 1 hour. Reduce the heat to 400°F. and roast until the ducks are deep golden brown and an instant-read thermometer inserted in the thickest part of the thigh reads 180°F., about 30 minutes. Remove the pan from the oven, being careful not to spill the rendered fat in the pan, and allow to cool completely.

4. Using poultry shears, cut each duck in half lengthwise. Pull off and discard the carcass and thigh bone from each duck, leaving four semiboneless duck halves with the wings attached. (It's amazing how flexible the duck is and how easily this is accomplished. Your hands will get a little greasy, but that's the only drawback.) Cover and refrigerate for up to 1 day.

5. To make the sauce, combine the vinegar, sugar, and star anise in a small saucepan. Cook over medium heat, swirling the pan occasionally by the handle to combine the ingredients until they melt into a syrup and it turns golden brown, about 3 minutes. Stir in the apples, cider, raisins, and cinnamon. Bring to a simmer. Cook until the apples are tender but hold their shape, about 10 minutes. Pour the brandy into a small bowl, sprinkle the cornstarch over it, and whisk to dissolve. Whisk the mixture into the simmering sauce to thicken, and cover to keep warm.

6. When ready to serve, heat the oven to 450°F. Place the duck halves, skin side up, on a baking sheet with sides. Add 1 cup hot water to the pan (this is just enough to create some steam). Bake until the skin is crisp and sizzling and the meat is heated through, about 15 minutes.

7. Serve the duck with the sauce passed on the side.

Fish

Any fish with fins and scales is considered kosher.

This means that you can choose from practically every variety you'll find at the neighborhood fish market. Of course, shellfish, mollusks, and squid are not kosher. Imitation shrimp meat is available, but be careful of surimi (sometimes labeled imitation crabmeat), which is not always kosher.

Fish plays a huge role in holiday meals. For Passover, gefilte fish (preferably in the form of my Gefilte Fish Terrine with Carrot and Beet Salads on page 22) is a must, and for other holidays, you'd better have some smoked fish to offer for a nosh (at least in my house). At Rosh Hashanah (which means "head of the year" in Hebrew), a fish course is often served with the head still attached to play up the turn of phrase—Brook Trout with Lime Brown Butter, Mangoes, and Cashews on page 139 would be a good choice. There are many other recipes in this chapter that are designed for extra-special meals, holidays or not.

What about everyday meals? There are plenty of ways to cook fish—broiled, grilled, sautéed, and braised—and each method gives the flesh a different character. While I like each of these techniques, I am partial to sautéing, which gives fish a delicate crispness. Sautéing is also a very quick cooking method that gives me time to prepare an incredible sauce or a wonderful spiced crust. A proper fish spatula (with a thin, slightly curved blade to improve manipulation) will help you turn the fillets in the skillet without breaking them.

In order to sauté four servings without crowding, you need a very large skillet. Every cook should have a twelve- to fourteen-inch skillet, anyway. Once you have this kind of skillet, it will become a workhorse in your kitchen. Not only will it fit four to six servings of fish fillets (depending on the fish and

the size of the fillet), but it will come in handy when you want to cook a whole chicken or four lamb chops, too. Choose a top-of-the-line brand with a heavy bottom and keep it out of the dishwasher; you will never have to buy another one again. It doesn't matter if you get a nonstick or uncoated interior, but the nonstick is slightly more versatile and allows you to use less oil for some recipes. However, to get the really crisp exterior that everyone loves, don't skimp on the oil.

Sea Bass Vera Cruz

This Mexican-style recipe is actually a one-pot dish. Make the zesty sauce in a large skillet, add the fish fillets, and bake. You can serve it directly from the skillet for a family meal, or plate the fillets and sauce for a more formal presentation. No matter how you serve it, it tastes great. Consider serving it with the New Mexican Rice Pilaf on page 176 and a cool, crisp salad.

2 tablespoons extra-virgin olive oil

2 garlic cloves, thinly sliced

1 medium onion, chopped

1 jalapeño pepper, seeded and minced

1^{1}/2 pounds (^{3}/4-inch dice) peeled and seeded plum or Roma tomatoes (4 cups)

^{1}/2 cup dry white wine

^{1}/4 cup pitted and coarsely chopped green Mediterranean olives

2 tablespoons chopped fresh cilantro, plus more for garnish

Six 6-ounce sea bass fillets

^{1}/2 teaspoon kosher salt, plus more to taste

^{1}/4 teaspoon freshly ground black pepper, plus more to taste

1. Position a rack in the center of the oven and preheat the oven to 350°F.

2. Heat the oil in a 12- to 14-inch ovenproof skillet over medium heat. Add the garlic and cook until golden, about 1 minute. Add the onion and jalapeño and cook, stirring occasionally, until the onion is translucent, about 5 minutes. Stir in the tomatoes and the wine, and bring to a boil over high heat. Reduce the heat to medium and cook at a brisk simmer, stirring often, until thickened into a sauce, about 20 minutes. Stir in the olives and cilantro.

3. Season the fillets with the salt and pepper. Fold each fillet in half crosswise, to double its thickness, and place in the sauce. Bake until the fish is barely opaque when prodded in the thickest part with the tip of a sharp knife, about 15 minutes.

4. Season the sauce with salt and pepper. Sprinkle cilantro over the top. Serve directly from the skillet.

Mediterranean-Style Halibut with Linguine

Halibut is a mild, versatile fish, and this method gives the fillets a crispy topping with flavorful, wine-infused flesh. (It's also great with grouper or sea bass.) The timing is important—the pasta should be cooked and ready to drain just as the fish comes out of the oven. If the fish needs more time, just toss the linguine in the warm cooking pot with the tomato-olive sauce and spinach and cover tightly; the pasta will stay hot for 5 minutes or so. For a simpler meal, skip the pasta, and serve the crusted fish and lemon-butter sauce with your favorite sautéed vegetables.

**MAKES
4
SERVINGS**

HALIBUT

$1/2$ cup Italian-style seasoned
    dried bread crumbs
2 tablespoons freshly grated
    Parmesan cheese
2 tablespoons finely chopped
    fresh parsley
2 garlic cloves, minced
1 teaspoon dried basil
1 teaspoon dried oregano
$1/4$ teaspoon kosher salt
$1/8$ teaspoon freshly ground
    black pepper
3 tablespoons extra-virgin
    olive oil
Six 8-ounce (1-inch-thick)
    halibut fillets (see Note)
$1/2$ cup dry white wine
1 tablespoon fresh lemon juice

1. Position a rack in the top third of the oven and preheat the oven to 350°F. Lightly oil a 10×15-inch baking dish. Bring a large pot of lightly salted water to a boil.

2. To prepare the halibut, mix the bread crumbs, cheese, parsley, garlic, basil, oregano, salt, and pepper in a small bowl. Add 2 tablespoons of the oil and mix with your hands to give the mixture the consistency of wet sand.

3. Arrange the fish fillets in a single layer in the baking dish. Pat an even layer of the bread-crumb mixture on top of each fillet. Drizzle the remaining 1 tablespoon oil over the topping. (The fish can be prepared up to this point 4 hours ahead, covered, and refrigerated.)

4. Pour the wine and lemon juice around, not over, the fish. Bake until the crust is golden brown and the fish is opaque, about 20 minutes.

5. For the pasta sauce, heat the oil, garlic, and red pepper flakes in a large skillet over medium heat until the garlic begins to color, about 2 minutes. Add the onion and cook, stirring often, until softened, about

3 minutes. Stir in the tomatoes, olives, and lemon juice, and cook just to heat the tomatoes through, about 2 minutes. Remove from the heat.

6. Meanwhile, cook the pasta in the boiling water until al dente, about 9 minutes. Drain the pasta and return to the pot. Add the sauce and mix well. Stir in the spinach and season with salt and pepper. Cover tightly to keep warm.

7. To serve, divide equal amounts of the pasta on one side of warmed dinner plates. Using a slotted spatula, place a fish fillet next to the pasta. Add the butter, one slice at a time, to the cooking liquid in the baking dish, and whisk until the butter is melted and the sauce is lightly thickened. Ladle the sauce around the fish and pasta and serve immediately.

NOTE: Halibut is a flatfish and resembles a huge sole or flounder. Because the halibut's body is thick in the center and tapers down toward the tail, the thickness of the fillets can vary enormously. If you can't get thick halibut fillets, use the thin ones, and simply fold them in half to make them thicker.

PASTA SAUCE

$1/3$ cup extra-virgin olive oil

2 garlic cloves, chopped

$1/2$ teaspoon hot red pepper flakes

$1/2$ small red onion, chopped

4 plum or Roma tomatoes, peeled, seeded, and cut into $3/4$-inch cubes

$1/3$ cup pitted and coarsely chopped black olives

2 tablespoons fresh lemon juice

1 cup packed thinly sliced spinach leaves

Kosher salt and freshly ground black pepper to taste

3 tablespoons unsalted butter, thinly sliced and chilled

1 pound linguine

Salmon Confit with Gazpacho Relish and Dill Oil

In classic French culinary terminology, confit is meat or poultry cooked in its own fat (duck and goose are the most popular types, and are even available canned in France). Cooking salmon in olive oil confit-style infuses it with flavor and gives it a luscious silky texture. Look for a source from which to buy the extra-virgin oil in bulk so it won't be prohibitively expensive. When cooking the salmon, don't overheat the oil— the idea is to poach the fish gently, not deep-fry it. Any leftover dill oil is great as a condiment for steamed new potatoes or grilled fish or poultry. The oil won't keep forever, even in the refrigerator, so make it in small batches.

MAKES
6
SERVINGS

DILL OIL

1/2 cup packed fresh dill, stalks and fronds
3/4 cup extra-virgin olive oil

SALMON CONFIT

3 cups extra-virgin olive oil, plus more as needed
6 whole black peppercorns
2 garlic cloves, peeled and smashed under a heavy knife
1 bay leaf
Six 6-ounce salmon fillets

1. To make the dill oil, bring 1 quart of lightly salted water to a boil in a large saucepan. Plunge the entire bunch of dill into the boiling water and cook for 5 seconds, just to set the color. Drain and rinse under cold water. Blot the dill dry with paper towels. Purée the dill and oil in a blender until smooth and transfer to an airtight container. (The oil can be made up to 5 days ahead, covered, and refrigerated. Return to room temperature before using.)

2. To make the confit, combine the oil, peppercorns, garlic, and bay leaf in a 12- to 14-inch skillet. Place the salmon in the oil, being sure the fillets are barely covered with the oil; add more oil as needed. Turn the heat to medium. As soon as the oil begins to bubble around the edges of the salmon and the surface of the salmon turns opaque, remove the skillet from the heat.

3. Cool the salmon in the oil, where it will continue to cook. Using a slotted spatula, transfer the salmon to a platter and cover tightly with plastic wrap. Refrigerate until chilled, at least 2 hours or up to 1 day.

4. To make the relish, combine the grapefruit pieces, red and yellow tomatoes, cucumber, green, red, and yellow peppers, onion, and jalapeño in a medium bowl. Toss with the 3 tablespoons of olive oil and season with salt and pepper. Cover with plastic wrap and refrigerate until chilled, at least 30 minutes and up to 6 hours.

5. To serve, place a mound of greens in the center of 6 plates. Top each with a salmon fillet. Spoon about $^1/_3$ cup of the gazpacho relish on each fillet, allowing some to drip down the sides. Drizzle the salmon and greens, as well as the plate, with a tablespoon or two of dill oil. Serve chilled or at room temperature.

SPICING IT UP WITH CHILES

When I cook with chiles in my cooking classes, I prepare myself to calm down the students who are terrified that I am going to make the food too hot. Well, those people don't know their chiles, but I'm happy to teach them.

There are many, many chiles out there. They are available fresh, dried, ground, and sometimes canned. Sure, some of them are very hot and spicy, but others are much milder. For example, ancho and New Mexican chiles have a sweet, almost fruity accent, and are much less hot than habanero (a real killer) or even jalapeño peppers. I often blend different chiles to get a specific flavor that isn't possible with just one variety.

When I say chile powder, I usually mean pure ground dried chile of one variety. Chili powder, found in almost every American kitchen, is a blend of mild ground chiles mixed with garlic powder, cumin, and other seasonings, and is meant as a seasoning for Texas-style meat chili. I suppose you could substitute boring old chili powder for ground chiles if you really need to (use more chili powder because it is milder), but I do encourage you to add a little spice to your life and try the unadulterated version.

GAZPACHO RELISH
$^1/_2$ cup yellow grapefruit supremes (see page 141)
$^1/_2$ cup ($^1/_4$-inch dice) peeled and seeded red plum tomatoes
$^1/_2$ cup ($^1/_4$-inch dice) seeded yellow tomatoes, or more plum tomatoes
$^1/_4$ cup ($^1/_4$-inch dice) seedless English cucumber
$^1/_4$ cup ($^1/_4$-inch dice) green bell pepper
$^1/_4$ cup ($^1/_4$-inch dice) red bell pepper
$^1/_4$ cup ($^1/_4$-inch dice) yellow bell pepper
$^1/_4$ cup ($^1/_4$-inch dice) red onion
2 teaspoons seeded and minced jalapeño pepper
3 tablespoons extra-virgin olive oil
Kosher salt and freshly ground black pepper to taste

8 ounces mixed baby greens (mesclun), washed and dried

Falafel-Crusted Salmon with Jerusalem Dressing

Seeing one dish evolve into another is always a big thrill for a chef. Occasionally I serve falafel (the crispy garbanzo cakes) with the salmon cakes on page 24. I pushed, prodded, and played around with the combination of falafel and salmon until I was happy with the results—a salmon fillet in a savory garbanzo bean-and-spice crust. The creamy dressing brings even more Middle Eastern flavor to the plate. Note that the garbanzo beans need to be soaked for at least 12 hours to be soft enough for grinding into the paste that becomes the crust.

**MAKES
4
SERVINGS**

JERUSALEM DRESSING
2 tablespoons fresh lemon juice
1¹/₂ teaspoons pure ground
   pasilla chile (see page 131) or
   chili powder
¹/₂ teaspoon onion powder
¹/₄ teaspoon ground cumin
¹/₄ teaspoon ground coriander
¹/₄ teaspoon kosher salt
¹/₄ teaspoon freshly ground
   black pepper
¹/₈ teaspoon ground hot red
   (cayenne) pepper
¹/₃ cup sour cream
¹/₄ cup mayonnaise
1 tablespoon chopped fresh
   cilantro

LEMON VINAIGRETTE
2 tablespoons fresh lemon juice
¹/₃ cup plus 1 tablespoon extra-
   virgin olive oil
Kosher salt and freshly ground
   black pepper to taste

1. To make the dressing, whisk the lemon juice, ground chile, onion powder, cumin, coriander, salt, pepper, and cayenne. (If the mixture appears too thick, add a teaspoon or two of water.) Fold in the sour cream and mayonnaise. (The dressing can be prepared up to 1 day ahead, covered, and refrigerated.)

2. To make the vinaigrette, place the lemon juice in a small bowl and gradually whisk in the oil. Season with salt and pepper. (The vinaigrette can be made 4 hours ahead, covered, and refrigerated. Whisk again before using.)

3. To make the falafel crust, with the machine running, drop the garlic into a food processor fitted with the metal blade to mince. Add the drained garbanzo beans and the onion and process, stopping occasionally to scrape down the bowl, until the beans are ground into a thick paste, about 2 minutes. Add the cilantro, parsley, cumin, coriander, salt, pepper, and cayenne, and pulse to combine. Press about ¹/₄ cup of the bean mixture in a thick layer on the flesh side of each fillet. (The fillets can be prepared up to 4 hours ahead, covered tightly with plastic wrap, and refrigerated.)

4. Position a rack in the top third of the oven and preheat the oven to 350°F.

5. Heat the oil in a 12- to 14-inch ovenproof non-stick skillet over medium-high heat. Add the salmon, crust side down, and cook until the crust is golden, about 2 minutes. Turn and cook for 1 minute. Bake for 4 minutes for medium-rare salmon, or longer if you prefer.

6. Toss the greens, onion, tomato, cucumber, and olives with the lemon vinaigrette in a large bowl. Divide the salad among 4 serving plates. Stir the cilantro into the Jerusalem dressing. Top each salad with a salmon fillet and drizzle with the Jerusalem dressing. Serve immediately, garnished with the pita bread.

PAREVE VARIATION

Substitute additional mayonnaise for the sour cream.

MEDITERRANEAN OLIVES

Why do I specify Mediterranean olives in my recipes? There are three answers: Flavor, flavor, and flavor. These olives are often available in bulk at delicatessens, or you might find them in jars. If they don't come pitted, it's an easy chore. Just crush the olives, one at a time, under a heavy, medium saucepan, to expose the pit. Pick out the pit (don't worry that the flesh isn't intact) and chop the flesh.

FALAFEL-CRUSTED SALMON

2 garlic cloves

1 cup dried garbanzo beans (chickpeas), refrigerated for 12 to 24 hours in cold water to cover

1/3 cup chopped onion

1 tablespoon chopped fresh cilantro

1 teaspoon chopped fresh parsley

1/2 teaspoon ground cumin

1/4 teaspoon ground coriander

1/4 teaspoon kosher salt

1/4 teaspoon freshly ground black pepper

1/4 teaspoon ground hot red (cayenne) pepper

Four 8-ounce skinless salmon fillets

1/4 cup extra-virgin olive oil

7 ounces mixed baby greens (mesclun), rinsed and dried

1 small red onion, halved lengthwise and sliced into thin half-moons

1 beefsteak tomato, seeded and cut into 1/2-inch cubes

1 cup thinly sliced seedless English cucumber

1/2 cup pitted and coarsely chopped black Mediterranean olives

2 pieces of Syrian Pita (page 208) or store-bought pita, cut into wedges

Porcini-Crusted Striped Bass with Smoked Trout and Scallion Mashed Potatoes and Port Wine Syrup

MAKES
4
SERVINGS

An Abigael's classic, this harmonious dish combines delicate sea bass and robust porcini for a juxtaposition of flavors that is a joy to eat. The earthiness of the smoked trout mashed potatoes is beautifully balanced by the port wine syrup.

PORT WINE SYRUP

2 cups plus 2 tablespoons
   tawny port
2 tablespoons red currant jelly
1 tablespoon balsamic vinegar
1 whole star anise
1 teaspoon cornstarch

BROCCOLI RABE

2 tablespoons extra-virgin olive
   oil
2 garlic cloves, thinly sliced
Pinch of hot red pepper flakes
1 bunch broccoli rabe, well
   rinsed

1. To make the port wine syrup, bring 2 cups of the port, the currant jelly, balsamic vinegar, and star anise to a boil in a medium saucepan over medium heat. Cook, stirring occasionally, until syrupy and reduced to $3/4$ cup, about 20 minutes. Sprinkle the cornstarch over the remaining 2 tablespoons port in a small bowl and stir to dissolve. Whisk into the simmering syrup to thicken the syrup. (The syrup can be prepared up to 2 hours ahead if stored uncovered at room temperature.)

2. Position a rack in the top third of the oven and preheat the oven to 400°F.

3. To prepare the broccoli rabe, heat the oil, garlic, and red pepper flakes in a large skillet over medium heat until the garlic turns light gold, about 2 minutes. Add the broccoli rabe and $1/4$ cup water. Cover tightly and cook until the broccoli rabe is barely tender, about 5 minutes. Remove from the heat and keep warm.

4. Combine the porcini powder, salt, and pepper in a small bowl. Dip the flesh side only of each fillet into the porcini mixture.

5. Heat the oil in a large ovenproof skillet over medium-high heat. Add the fillets, porcini side up, and cook until the underside is lightly browned, about 2 minutes. Turn the fillets over and place the skillet in the oven. Bake until the fish is barely opaque in the thickest part, about 5 minutes.

6. Spoon a mound of mashed potatoes in the centers of 4 plates. Lean a fillet next to each mound. Drizzle the port syrup around each fillet. Place a tangle of broccoli rabe on each plate and serve immediately.

NOTE: Wild porcini mushrooms are renowned for their earthy flavor. I use them in my Wild Mushroom and Barley Soup (page 56) to make an attention-getting version of this Jewish cooking standard. Though many have tried, porcini seem impossible to cultivate, so the vast majority of them in this country are dried. You can make your own mushroom powder by grinding whole dried porcini in an electric coffee grinder. International Spice (see Sources, page 250) carries kosher porcini, both whole and ground.

BASS

$1/4$ cup dried porcini mushroom powder (see Note)

1 teaspoon kosher salt

$1/4$ teaspoon freshly ground black pepper

2 tablespoons extra-virgin olive oil

Four 6-ounce skinless striped bass fillets

1 recipe Smoked Trout and Scallion Mashed Potatoes (page 187)

Moroccan Sea Bass with Israeli Couscous and Red Pepper Vinaigrette

**MAKES
6
SERVINGS**

The spices of Morocco enliven the sea bass, and accent the red pepper vinaigrette and couscous salad. If you make the vinaigrette and salad well before serving, this dish will come together in no time flat.

RED PEPPER AND TOMATO VINAIGRETTE

2 tablespoons extra-virgin olive oil

1/4 cup (1/4-inch dice) red bell pepper

1/4 cup (1/4-inch dice) green bell pepper

1/4 cup (1/4-inch dice) yellow bell pepper

2 plum tomatoes, coarsely chopped

1/2 cup chopped yellow tomato, or substitute more plum tomatoes

1 teaspoon seeded and minced jalapeño pepper

1 tablespoon fresh lemon juice

1 tablespoon fresh lime juice

2 tablespoons chopped fresh cilantro

1/2 cup extra-virgin olive oil

Kosher salt and freshly ground black pepper to taste

1/4 cup pitted and finely chopped black Mediterranean olives

1. To make the vinaigrette, heat the oil in a large skillet over medium-high heat. Add the red, yellow, and green bell peppers and cook, stirring occasionally, until browned around the edges, about 5 minutes.

2. Pulse the cooked peppers, plum and yellow tomatoes, and jalapeño in a food processor to coarsely chop. Add the lemon and lime juices and pulse to combine. Add the cilantro and pulse again. With the machine running, gradually add the oil to make a thick vinaigrette. Season with salt and pepper. Stir in the olives. (The vinaigrette can be prepared up to 4 hours ahead, covered, and stored at room temperature.)

3. To make the sea bass, combine the ginger, fennel, cumin, salt, coriander, allspice, cinnamon, and pepper in a small bowl. Season both sides of the fish with the spice mixture.

4. Position a rack in the center of the oven and preheat the oven to 375°F. Heat the olive oil in a 12- to 14-inch ovenproof skillet over medium-high heat. Sear the fillets on both sides, starting with the skin side first, until golden brown, about 2 minutes per side. Transfer the skillet to the oven and cook the fish until it is barely opaque in the thickest part, about 8 minutes.

5. To assemble, place a portion of couscous salad on each of 6 serving plates. Place a bass fillet on top and drizzle with the vinaigrette. Serve immediately.

ISRAELI COUSCOUS

While Moroccan couscous consists of tiny golden pellets of dried semolina pasta, the Israeli version is larger white balls that resemble uncooked pearl tapioca. Like its North African cousin, Israeli couscous is meant for soaking up the savory juices from stews, ragouts, pot roasts—you name it.

Israeli couscous is cooked like pasta in boiling water, with one important difference: The couscous is toasted first in a little oil to intensify the wheat flavor, and to help keep the pellets separate. Don't overdo this step—you only want a very light toasting. You can't undo overtoasted couscous.

SEA BASS

$^3/_4$ teaspoon ground ginger

$^3/_4$ teaspoon fennel seed, ground in a mortar or coffee grinder

$^1/_2$ teaspoon ground cumin

$^1/_2$ teaspoon kosher salt

$^1/_2$ teaspoon ground coriander

$^1/_4$ teaspoon ground allspice

$^1/_4$ teaspoon ground cinnamon

$^1/_4$ teaspoon freshly ground black pepper

Six 8-ounce sea bass fillets, skin on

2 tablespoons extra-virgin olive oil

1 recipe Israeli Couscous Salad with Summer Vegetables and Lime Vinaigrette (page 67)

Jamaican Jerk Salmon
with Guava Vinaigrette

MAKES
6
SERVINGS

Whenever my family and I visit Jamaica, our first stop is Rita's Roadside, where we are greeted with a warm smile and tight hugs from her strong arms. When I finally got up the nerve to ask for this recipe, Rita happily obliged. The meaty richness of salmon stands up to Rita's jerk spice blend, which is usually used as a seasoning on grilled pork or chicken that is "jerked" apart into servings.

1. To make the vinaigrette, combine the guava nectar, lime juice, honey, and curry powder in a blender. With the machine on, gradually pour in the oil to make a thick dressing. Season with salt. (The dressing can be prepared up to 1 day ahead, covered, and refrigerated. Whisk well before serving.)

2. Position a rack in the top third of the oven and preheat the oven to 350°F. Lightly oil a baking sheet.

3. In a small bowl, mix the onion powder, allspice, thyme, cinnamon, black pepper, cayenne, sugar, and nutmeg. Cut each salmon steak in half lengthwise to make a total of 6 long, thick strips. Brush both sides of the salmon with the oil. Season one side of each piece with the spice mixture. Arrange the fish on the baking sheet, spiced side up.

4. Bake without turning the fish until the meat looks barely opaque with a rosy center when prodded with the tip of a knife in the thickest part, about 12 minutes.

5. Toss the salad greens with $3/4$ cup of the vinaigrette. Heap equal portions of the salad on 6 dinner plates and top with the salmon. Drizzle the remaining vinaigrette around the salad. Serve immediately.

GUAVA VINAIGRETTE
$1/4$ cup canned guava nectar
2 tablespoons fresh lime juice
2 teaspoons honey
$1/2$ teaspoon curry powder
$2/3$ cup vegetable oil
Kosher salt to taste

1 teaspoon onion powder
1 teaspoon ground allspice
$3/4$ teaspoon dried thyme
$3/4$ teaspoon ground cinnamon
$1/4$ teaspoon freshly ground
    black pepper
$1/4$ teaspoon ground hot red
    (cayenne) pepper
$1/4$ teaspoon sugar
$1/8$ teaspoon freshly grated
    nutmeg
Three 14- to 16-ounce (1-inch-
    thick) salmon steaks
1 tablespoon vegetable oil
9 ounces baby mixed greens
    (mesclun), rinsed and dried

Brook Trout with Lime Brown Butter, Mangoes, and Cashews

This dish is simplicity itself. The sauce has a terrific interplay of flavors and textures, from sweet mango to crunchy cashews (try it on grilled mahimahi fillets, too). Don't save this for times when you want to fire up a grill, because the trout is also great cooked in the broiler. If you grill the trout, don't worry if the skin sticks to the grid—most people remove it before eating anyway. The best precautions are oiling the grid and the fish well, and cooking the fish over indirect heat.

**MAKES
4
SERVINGS**

1. Build a charcoal fire on one side of an outdoor grill and let it burn until the coals are covered with white ash. Or preheat a gas grill on high, then turn one burner off. Oil the grill well.

2. Brush the trout well with the oil and season them with the salt and pepper. Grill the fish over the hot area, turning once, just to make grill marks on both sides, about 2 minutes. Move to the cooler area of the grill and cover. Continue cooking just until opaque when prodded in the thickest part with the tip of a sharp knife, 8 to 10 minutes. Transfer the fish to a platter and tent with aluminum foil to keep warm.

3. While the fish is cooking, melt the butter in a medium skillet over medium heat. When the butter begins to sizzle, swirl the pan continually until the butter begins to turn a caramel brown color. Stir in the mango, cashews, scallion, and mint, and toss to combine. Gently stir in the lime juice and season with salt and pepper.

4. Serve the trout with the sauce spooned over the top.

4 brook trout (10 to 12 ounces each)

2 tablespoons extra-virgin olive oil

1 teaspoon kosher salt, plus more to taste

1/2 teaspoon freshly ground black pepper, plus more to taste

1/2 cup (1 stick) unsalted butter

1 ripe mango, pitted, peeled, and cut into 3/4-inch dice

1/2 cup coarsely chopped salted cashew halves

1 scallion (green and white parts), chopped

2 tablespoons chopped fresh mint

1/4 cup fresh lime juice

NOTE: To broil the trout, position a broiler rack 6 inches from the heat source, and preheat the broiler. Oil the grilling rack. Broil the trout, turning once, until opaque when prodded in the center, 10 to 12 minutes.

Fennel-Crusted Snapper
with Grapefruit-Cilantro Sauce

The sauce for these snapper fillets is a killer! So you can savor every drop, serve the vegetables and any starch as side dishes. I recommend the Snap Peas and Carrots with Ginger and Sesame on page 191, and some creamy mashed potatoes.

GRAPEFRUIT-CILANTRO SAUCE

2 pink medium grapefruits
1½ cups dry white wine
2½ tablespoons mirin (see Note)
2 tablespoons fresh orange juice
2 tablespoons heavy cream
1 tablespoon rice vinegar
7 tablespoons unsalted butter, 1 tablespoon softened and 6 tablespoons chilled and cut into 6 slices
1 tablespoon all-purpose flour
3 tablespoons chopped fresh cilantro
Kosher salt and freshly ground black pepper to taste

1. To make the sauce, grate 1 teaspoon of zest from 1 grapefruit and set aside. Section 1 grapefruit according to the instructions on page 141, and set 8 grapefruit supremes aside, reserving the remaining grapefruit for another use. Squeeze the juice from the other grapefruit. Measure ²/₃ cup juice and save or drink the rest.

2. Bring the wine, grapefruit juice, mirin, orange juice, heavy cream, and vinegar to a boil in a large saucepan over high heat. (The cream will curdle at first, but it will smooth out as it boils.) In a small bowl, mash the softened butter and flour together with a rubber spatula to make a paste. Whisk about ¹/₃ cup of the hot liquid into the paste to thin it, then whisk the mixture into the saucepan. Reduce the heat to medium and cook at a brisk simmer until the sauce is reduced to ³/₄ cup, about 20 minutes. Stir in the reserved zest. (The sauce can be prepared up to this point 2 hours ahead. Cover and store at room temperature.)

3. To prepare the snapper, mix the fennel, flour, salt, and pepper in a shallow dish. Dip the flesh side only of the fillets into the fennel mixture to coat.

4. Heat the oil in a 12- to 14-inch skillet over medium-high heat. Add the fillets, flesh side down. Cook until the undersides are lightly browned, about

3 minutes. Turn and cook until the fish is barely opaque when prodded in the center with the tip of a knife, about 2 minutes. Remove from the heat and cover to keep warm.

5. To finish the sauce, bring it to a simmer over medium heat. Remove from the heat and whisk in the chilled butter, 1 tablespoon at a time. Stir in the cilantro and season with salt and pepper.

6. For each serving, place a fillet in the center of a dinner plate, and spoon the sauce around it. Top each fillet with 2 grapefruit sections. Serve immediately.

SNAPPER
$1/4$ cup fennel seeds, toasted (see page 66) and coarsely ground
$1/4$ cup all-purpose flour
$1/2$ teaspoon kosher salt
$1/4$ teaspoon freshly ground black pepper
Four 6- to 7-ounce skinless red snapper fillets
2 tablespoons vegetable oil

NOTE: Mirin is a Japanese sweet rice wine, available in a kosher version at Kosher Depot (see Sources, page 250). You can also substitute sweet white wine.

THE CITRUS SECTION

I love cooking with citrus juices—their bright flavor complements so many dishes. Rather than adding more salt, I find that a squeeze of lemon or lime juice often gives a dish the balance it needs. (This trick is especially helpful for people on salt-restricted diets.) Be sure to have an efficient juicer in your kitchen. It doesn't matter if yours is an inexpensive electric juicer or a reamer-type manual model, as long as it works well enough that you won't consider juicing a chore.

While we rarely eat the flesh of lemons and limes, oranges give both delicious fruit and zesty juice. But in order to serve the orange flesh without the thick membrane and seeds, the orange segments must be sectioned out from the undesirable parts. Some chefs call each tender orange section a "supreme." When you "supreme" an orange, you also release a few tablespoons of fresh juice that should be collected, just in case the recipe uses it (and it usually does).

To supreme an orange, trim the top and bottom off a large seedless orange so that it stands on the work counter. Using a serrated knife, cut off the thick peel where it meets the flesh so you end up with a skinless orange sphere. Working over a medium bowl to catch the juices, hold the orange in one hand and cut between the thin membranes to release the segments, letting them fall into the bowl. Squeeze the juices from the membranes into the bowl. Drain the segments and reserve the juice.

Fish Tacos San Pedro

This dish is responsible for one of my most vivid food memories. My wife and I were in Southern California working on my television show, and ended up at a very humble restaurant in the San Pedro harbor area. Their specialty was a fish taco, served with a chunky sauté of onions, peppers, and potatoes.

VEGETABLES

2 tablespoons extra-virgin olive oil

1 medium onion, chopped

1 small red bell pepper, cored, seeded, and chopped

1 small green bell pepper, cored, seeded, and chopped

1 jalapeño pepper, seeded and minced

2 garlic cloves, minced

2 medium baked potatoes, cooled and cut into ³/₄-inch cubes

Kosher salt and freshly ground black pepper to taste

¹/₂ teaspoon pure ground pasilla chile (see page 131) or chili powder

¹/₂ teaspoon ground cumin

¹/₂ teaspoon dried oregano

¹/₂ teaspoon kosher salt

Six 8-ounce tilapia fillets, cut in half on the diagonal

2 tablespoons extra-virgin olive oil

Warmed flour tortillas

Lime wedges

Guacamole (page 91)

Tomato Salsa (page 155)

1. To prepare the vegetables, heat the oil in a large skillet over medium heat. Add the onion, red and green bell peppers, jalapeño, and garlic, and cook, stirring often, until tender, about 10 minutes. Stir in the potatoes and cook until heated through, about 5 minutes. Season with salt and pepper. Transfer to a bowl and cover to keep warm.

2. Meanwhile, in a small bowl, mix the ground chile, cumin, oregano, and salt. Season the fillets with the chile mixture. Heat the oil in a 12- to 14-inch skillet over medium-high heat. Add the fish and cook, turning once, until opaque, about 8 minutes (the thinner pieces of fish will cook more quickly and can be removed as soon as they cook, if you wish). Place the fillets on a platter.

3. Serve immediately with the vegetables, tortillas, lime wedges, guacamole, and salsa in separate bowls, so that your guests can make their own tacos.

Tuna au Poivre
on Tomato-Onion Salad

For a meal that is so classy, this sure is easy. Tuna has a meaty quality that made me think that it would stand up to a peppercorn coating, and I was right. Instead of crushing peppercorns in your kitchen, you can purchase kosher cracked peppercorns from Spice House International (see Sources, page 250). In my opinion, tuna cooked past medium-rare is not worth eating. If you are a well-done tuna kind of person, I suggest you open up a can, chop the celery, and grab the mayo.

**MAKES
4
SERVINGS**

1. To make the salad, whisk the vinegar and oregano in a medium bowl. Gradually whisk in the oil. Add the tomatoes and onions and toss, seasoning with the salt and pepper. Cover and refrigerate until chilled, at least 1 hour.

2. Season the tuna steaks on both sides with the salt and pepper. Pour the cracked black pepper in a shallow dish or on a sheet of wax paper. Press one side of the tuna into the pepper to coat.

3. Heat the oil in a large skillet over medium-high heat. Add the tuna, peppered side down. Cook, turning once, until the tuna is seared on the outside but rare within, about 4 minutes. If you like your tuna more well done (don't go past medium doneness!), cover the pan and cook for 2 to 4 minutes longer. Slice each steak against the grain into $^{1}/_{4}$-inch slices.

4. Heap equal amounts of arugula on each of 4 dinner plates. Top with the tomato salad. Arrange the tuna slices decoratively around the salad.

TOMATO-ONION SALAD

$1^{1}/_{2}$ tablespoons balsamic
 vinegar
1 teaspoon dried oregano
$^{1}/_{3}$ cup extra-virgin olive oil
3 large, ripe beefsteak tomatoes,
 cut into 1-inch cubes
2 small red onions, thinly
 sliced
Kosher salt and freshly ground
 black pepper to taste

Two 8-ounce center-cut tuna
 steaks
1 teaspoon kosher salt
$^{1}/_{4}$ teaspoon freshly ground
 black pepper
$^{1}/_{4}$ cup coarsely cracked black
 peppercorns (crush in a
 mortar or under a heavy
 saucepan)
2 tablespoons extra-virgin
 olive oil
$^{1}/_{2}$ pound arugula, well washed
 and trimmed

Vegetable
MAIN COURSES

All Jewish cooks should have a substantial

collection of vegetarian main course recipes up their sleeves. Of course, vegetable dishes are a good source of vitamins and fiber and help balance the diet. But most important, they sidestep the issues of separating meat from dairy. For the most part, these vegetable main dishes are pareve. Just add a salad, and dinner is served!

Until recently, vegetarian cooking got a bad rap for being bland and stodgy. Those days are over. With the creative use of herbs and spices, an appreciation for international dishes, and an increased selection of fresh vegetables (I remember when portobello mushrooms were considered exotic, and it wasn't that long ago!), even a nonvegetarian cook can make a satisfying meatless main course. Just don't announce that the meal is vegetarian, especially to guys who think that eating meat and potatoes is a sign of virility. If they *really* like potatoes, wait until they try Ray's Potato and Vegetable Pie on page 158.

You will also find meatless main courses in the pasta chapter, but in the recipes that follow, the vegetables are the cream of the crop.

Scarlet Fire Vegetarian Chili

Chili is often made with meat, but this vegetarian version is so packed with veggies that you'll never miss the beef. This recipe has been in my collection for a long time, and was created by my good friend Jay Minzer. Pure ground New Mexican chile gives a mild kick—use a hotter chile, such as mulato, if you want more heat. Depending on the garnishes you use, this dish can be pareve, dairy, or meat.

$^1/_2$ cup vegetable oil

1 medium onion, cut into
$^1/_2$-inch dice

1 red bell pepper, cored,
seeded, and cut into
$^1/_2$-inch dice

1 yellow bell pepper, cored,
seeded, and cut into $^1/_2$-inch
dice

3 garlic cloves, minced

1 tablespoon pure ground mild
New Mexican chile

10 ounces white button
mushrooms, sliced

1 tablespoon ground cumin

2 teaspoons onion powder

2 teaspoons garlic powder

$2^1/_4$ teaspoons dried oregano

One 28-ounce can tomatoes in
juice, drained and chopped,
juice reserved

3 cups fresh or thawed frozen
corn kernels

One 15- to 19-ounce can
garbanzo beans (chickpeas),
drained

One 15- to 19-ounce can
kidney beans, drained

1. Heat the oil in a large, heavy-bottomed soup pot over medium-high heat. Add the onion, red and yellow bell peppers, and garlic. Cook, stirring occasionally, until the onions are softened, about 10 minutes. Add the ground chile and stir until fragrant, about 1 minute. Add the mushrooms and cook, stirring often, until they give off their juices, about 5 minutes.

2. Stir in the cumin, onion powder, garlic powder, and oregano, then the tomatoes and their juice. Bring to a simmer and reduce the heat to medium-low. Simmer, stirring frequently, until slightly thickened, about 15 minutes.

3. Stir in the corn, garbanzos, kidney beans, and Great Northern beans and return to a simmer. Stir well and cook until heated through, about 10 minutes. Stir in the molasses. Season with salt to taste.

4. Ladle into bowls and serve hot with the garnishes of your choice.

DAIRY VARIATION

Top with shredded Cheddar cheese, chopped scallions, chopped onions, and/or sour cream

MEAT VARIATION

Top with crisp sautéed pastrami cracklings (see page 55), chopped scallions, and/or chopped onions

One 15- to 19-ounce can Great Northern white beans, drained
1 tablespoon unsulfured (light) molasses
Kosher salt to taste

Israeli Couscous
with Curried Vegetables

MAKES
4 TO 6
SERVINGS

This dish shows just how hearty and flavorful vegetarian cooking can be. And it looks great, too! For a more classic presentation, toss the cooked couscous with a dash of olive oil, then the cilantro and scallions. Mound the couscous on each serving plate, then top with the vegetables.

3 tablespoons extra-virgin olive oil

1¹/₂ cups Israeli couscous

4 cups water

1 teaspoon salt, plus more to taste

2 medium carrots, cut into ¹/₄-inch dice

1 small zucchini, cut into ¹/₂-inch dice

1 small yellow squash, cut into ¹/₂-inch dice

1 red bell pepper, cored, seeded, and cut into ¹/₂-inch dice

One 15-ounce can garbanzo beans (chickpeas), drained and rinsed

1 cup halved cherry tomatoes

1 tablespoon curry powder

2 teaspoons ground cumin

2 scallions (white and green parts), chopped

¹/₄ cup chopped fresh cilantro

Kosher salt and freshly ground black pepper to taste

1. Heat 1 tablespoon of the oil in a medium saucepan. Add the couscous and cook, stirring often, until lightly toasted, about 2 minutes. Add the water and 1 teaspoon salt. Bring to a boil over high heat, then reduce the heat to medium-low. Cover and simmer until the couscous is tender, about 10 minutes. Drain.

2. Meanwhile, heat the remaining 2 tablespoons oil in a large skillet over medium-high heat. Add the carrots and cover. Cook for 1 minute. Stir in the zucchini, yellow squash, and red bell pepper. Cook uncovered, stirring occasionally, until crisp-tender, about 5 minutes. Stir in the garbanzo beans and cook for 1 minute. Add the cherry tomatoes and cook until heated through, about 2 minutes. Stir in the curry powder and cumin and mix well.

3. Stir in the drained couscous, scallions, and cilantro. Season with salt and pepper and serve hot.

Mediterranean Eggplant and Egg Casserole

I devised this quick recipe when I was preparing a show on Persian cooking, but versions of it are actually prepared all over the Mediterranean. The turmeric deepens the color of the eggs, giving the dish a striking golden hue. For an Italian touch, substitute 3 tablespoons chopped fresh basil or even 1 teaspoon dried oregano for the turmeric. Serve it with a cool salad and pita bread for a simple but satisfying meal.

1. Position a rack in the center of the oven and preheat the oven to 350°F. Place the eggplant cubes on an oiled baking sheet. Bake, stirring occasionally, until tender and lightly browned, about 45 minutes.

2. Heat the oil in a large skillet over medium heat. Add the onions and cook, stirring often, until the onions are golden, about 8 minutes. Add the garlic and cook until golden, about 2 minutes. Mix in the cooked eggplant and tomatoes, and cook until the tomatoes are heated through, about 3 minutes. Add the turmeric and mix well.

3. Beat the eggs with the salt and pepper and pour over the vegetables. Cook just until the eggs begin to solidify, about 1½ minutes. Stir the mixture to combine, and cook until the eggs are done to your preference. Transfer to a serving bowl, sprinkle with parsley, and serve hot.

2 medium (1½ pounds each) eggplants, cut into 1-inch cubes

2 tablespoons extra-virgin olive oil

2 medium red onions, chopped

6 garlic cloves, chopped

2 ripe plum or Roma tomatoes, coarsely chopped

1 teaspoon ground turmeric

5 large eggs

1 teaspoon kosher salt

¼ teaspoon freshly ground black pepper

Chopped fresh parsley, for garnish

Savory Hamantaschen
with Vegetable-Cheese Stuffing

MAKES
4 TO 6
SERVINGS

I love sweet hamantaschen as much as the next guy, but my "inner chef" kept wanting to turn them into something savory. This is what I came up with, a kind of open-faced calzone that would send any pizza shop cook reeling.

VEGETABLE-CHEESE FILLING

2 tablespoons extra-virgin olive oil

1 medium onion, chopped

2 small zucchini, trimmed and chopped into $1/2$-inch dice

$1/2$ cup cored, seeded, and chopped green bell pepper

$1/2$ cup cored, seeded, and chopped red bell pepper

3 garlic cloves, finely chopped

$1/2$ cup coarsely chopped pitted black Mediterranean olives

3 tablespoons chopped fresh basil

2 tablespoons chopped fresh oregano

2 large eggs, beaten

1 cup farmer's cheese or ricotta cheese

1 cup shredded Havarti cheese

$1/2$ teaspoon kosher salt

$1/4$ teaspoon freshly ground black pepper

1. To make the filling, heat the oil in a large skillet over medium heat. Add the onion and cook until softened, about 3 minutes. Add the zucchini, green and red bell peppers, and garlic. Cook, stirring often, until the vegetables are tender, about 10 minutes. Stir in the olives and herbs. Remove from the heat and allow to cool.

2. In a large bowl, combine the eggs with the farmer's cheese and Havarti. Add the cooled vegetables, salt, and pepper and mix just to combine. Refrigerate the filling until ready to make the hamantaschen.

3. Position racks in the top third and center of the oven and preheat the oven to 450°F. Sprinkle two large baking sheets with cornmeal.

4. On an unfloured work surface, roll out half of the dough into an 11-inch round about $1/2$ inch thick. Spread half of the filling on the center of the round, leaving a 2-inch border. Shape the dough into a large triangle: Fold the right and left sides over, and fold the bottom of the round up, partially covering the filling and leaving the center exposed. Pinch the corners to seal. Slide the bottom of a tart pan or a rimless baking sheet under the triangle and transfer to a cornmeal-dusted baking sheet. Brush the dough with oil. Repeat with the remaining dough and filling.

5. Bake until the crust is golden brown and the filling is set, about 25 minutes. If the crust is browning too much, tent with aluminum foil. The hamantaschen on the center rack may take a few minutes longer to bake. Let stand for 5 minutes before serving.

Yellow cornmeal, for
    sprinkling on baking sheets
Pizza Dough (page 210)
Olive oil, for brushing

WHEN DAIRY ISN'T KOSHER AFTER ALL . . .

Even though most cooks don't consider cheese a meat product, the kosher cook must take a different outlook. Rennet, the ingredient that coagulates most cheese, is an animal product. You must be aware of the cheeses that contain rennet and those that don't (or use another kind of binding agent). When my recipe calls for cheese, I assume you will purchase a kosher brand. Most yogurts aren't kosher, either, because they often contain gelatin, another animal by-product, so look carefully at the label to ascertain if a vegetable-based rennet is used.

heritage recipe

Grandma's Latkes with Sour Cream and Ginger Applesauce

Here's my favorite latke recipe, ready to serve for brunch, as a side dish, or as the star of Hanukkah dinner. Be sure to use enough oil in the skillet—not just to celebrate the miracle of the oil, but to give the latkes the crispiness that we all love. Serve these with the Apple Cider Brisket on page 80, and you'll have a holiday meal that your family will want to eat for eight days! Or make them into silver dollar–sized pancakes, top with sour cream, caviar, or smoked salmon and chives, and serve as hors d'oeuvres. For a meat meal, simply omit the sour cream.

> **MAKES ABOUT 12 PANCAKES**

2¹/₂ pounds baking potatoes (russet or Burbank), peeled
1 medium onion, shredded
¹/₂ cup matzo meal
3 large eggs, lightly beaten
¹/₄ cup finely chopped fresh chives
¹/₂ teaspoon onion powder (optional)
2 teaspoons kosher salt
¹/₄ teaspoon freshly ground black pepper
Vegetable oil, for frying
Sour cream, at room temperature, for serving (optional)
Ginger Applesauce (recipe follows), for serving

1. Position a rack in the center of the oven and preheat the oven to 200°F. Line a baking sheet with paper towels. Using the large holes of a box grater or the grating disk of a food processor, alternately grate the potatoes and onion into a large bowl (this provides better distribution of the onions). Using your hands, squeeze out as much moisture as you can from the potato mixture.

2. In a small bowl, mix the matzo meal, eggs, chives, onion powder (if using), salt, and pepper. Stir into the potatoes.

3. Add enough oil to a large, deep skillet to come ¹/₂ inch up the sides. Do not skimp! Heat over medium-high heat until very hot but not smoking. In batches without crowding, using about ¹/₃ cup of the potato mixture for each pancake, carefully add the mixture to the oil, spreading it with a spoon to make 3- to 4-inch pancakes. Fry, turning once, until deep golden brown on both sides, about 6 minutes. Use a slotted spatula to transfer to the baking sheet. Serve immediately or keep warm in the oven while making the remaining pancakes. Drain off any excess liquid that forms in the bowl as you make subsequent batches. (To freeze, completely cool the cooked latkes and wrap individually in aluminum foil. To reheat, thaw the latkes, then bake in a preheated 400°F. oven until heated through, about 10 minutes.)

4. Serve hot with the sour cream and applesauce.

Ginger Applesauce

PAREVE
MAKES ABOUT 3½ CUPS

If you like an old-fashioned, mildly spiced applesauce, simply leave out the ginger and star anise. But I bet if you leave them in, you'll be glad you did. Use a cooking apple that tends to fall apart during cooking, such as McIntosh, Golden Delicious, or Jonathan, or a combination.

1 (3-inch) cinnamon stick
4 whole cloves
1 whole star anise, broken into points
⅓ cup sugar
⅓ cup water
1 tablespoon fresh lemon juice
2 tablespoons peeled and minced fresh ginger
1½ pounds cooking apples, peeled, cored, and cut into quarters

Tie the cinnamon stick, cloves, and star anise in a piece of cheesecloth to make a sachet. Bring the sugar, water, lemon juice, ginger, and spice sachet to a simmer over low heat in a large saucepan.

Stir in the apples. Increase the heat to high and bring to a boil. Cover and reduce the heat to low. Simmer, stirring often, until the apples are soft, about 15 minutes.

Discard the spice sachet. Mash the apples in the saucepan until chunky. Taste and add more sugar if needed. Serve warm or chilled. (The applesauce can be made up to 5 days ahead, covered, and refrigerated.)

Portobello Fajita

MAKES
6
SERVINGS

Meaty portobello mushrooms are tasty to begin with, but marinating and roasting them adds two more levels of flavor. Tuck them into flour tortillas to make fajitas, or use corn tortillas and call them soft tacos! To turn these into a great-looking first course, cut each rolled fajita on the diagonal to make a pinwheel, overlap in a large circle on a dinner plate, and heap a green salad in the center.

2 tablespoons extra-virgin
   olive oil
1 large onion, halved
   lengthwise and cut into thin
   half-moons
1 small green bell pepper,
   cored, seeded, and cut into
   $1/4$-inch strips
Roasted Portobello Mushrooms
   (page 164), cut into $3/4$-inch
   slices
2 ripe Hass avocados, pitted,
   peeled, and cut into $1/2$-inch
   dice
2 tablespoons fresh lime juice
Kosher salt and freshly ground
   black pepper to taste

Six 10-inch flour tortillas,
   warmed
Tomato Salsa (recipe follows)

1. Heat the oil in a large skillet over medium-high heat. Add the onion and pepper and cook, stirring occasionally, until tender, about 6 minutes. Add the sliced mushrooms and mix. Cool completely.

2. In a small bowl, mash the avocados and lime juice with a fork to make a chunky spread and season with salt and pepper.

3. For each fajita, top a tortilla with portions of the mushroom mixture, salsa, and avocado mixture. Starting at the bottom, fold the tortilla up about one-quarter of the way. Fold the left and right sides to the center, and continue rolling. Cut in half on a sharp diagonal, and place the two halves on a plate. Serve immediately.

DAIRY VARIATION
Serve the fajitas with sour cream.

Tomato Salsa

PAREVE
MAKES ABOUT 3 CUPS

5 ripe plum or Roma tomatoes, cut into $1/2$-inch dice
$1/2$ cup finely chopped red onion
2 tablespoons chopped fresh cilantro
2 tablespoons fresh lime juice
1 tablespoon extra-virgin olive oil
1 garlic clove, minced
1 jalapeño pepper, seeded and minced
Kosher salt to taste

Combine all of the ingredients in a medium bowl. The salsa is best served the day it is made, at room temperature. If necessary, cover and refrigerate for up to 1 day.

Wild Mushroom Kugel

MAKES
10 TO 12
SERVINGS

Kugel is one of the most beloved foods of Jewish cooking. It can also be one of the most maligned. When a kugel is good, everyone at the table goes nuts. When a kugel is not so good, everyone eats it anyway, but there is plenty of complaining after the party—or simply a lot of leftovers. My New Jewish Cuisine version of this favorite is made with a medley of wild mushrooms, cheeses, and sour cream. No one will fault this kugel for being too dry (and I doubt you'll have any leftovers).

12 ounces medium-width egg
  noodles
10 tablespoons unsalted butter
1 small red onion, halved
  lengthwise and cut into thin
  half-moons
1 large leek, white part only,
  well rinsed and chopped
3 garlic cloves, minced
1 pound assorted mushrooms
  (such as white button,
  cremini, portobello, and
  stemmed shiitake), thinly
  sliced
2 tablespoons chopped fresh
  basil
1 teaspoon chopped fresh
  rosemary
2 cups ricotta cheese or cottage
  cheese (preferably 1 cup of
  each)
1 cup sour cream
5 large eggs, lightly beaten
1 teaspoon kosher salt
1/2 teaspoon freshly ground
  black pepper
1/2 cup fresh bread crumbs,
  made from firm white bread
  or challah

1. Position a rack in the center of the oven and preheat the oven to 325°F. Lightly oil a 15 × 10-inch casserole dish.

2. Bring a large pot of lightly salted water to a boil. Add the egg noodles and cook just until tender, about 8 minutes. Drain well.

3. Meanwhile, heat 2 tablespoons of the butter in a large skillet over medium heat. Add the onion, leek, and garlic. Cook, stirring occasionally, until the onion is lightly golden, about 5 minutes. Stir in the mushrooms and cook, stirring occasionally, until the mushrooms are tender, about 6 minutes. Stir in the basil and rosemary.

4. Whisk the ricotta cheese, sour cream, and eggs in a large bowl. Mix in the drained noodles, the mushroom mixture, and the salt and pepper. Spread in the baking dish. Top with the bread crumbs. Melt the remaining 1/2 cup butter in a small saucepan (or use a microwave oven). Drizzle the melted butter over the noodles.

5. Bake, uncovered, until the top is golden brown and the center feels set, 45 to 50 minutes. Let stand at room temperature for 5 minutes. Serve hot.

Spaghetti Squash
with Pine Nuts and Arugula

Spaghetti squash is a deceptive-looking vegetable. Its smooth yellow exterior gives no hint of the delicious strings of flesh inside. Those "strings" look very much like spaghetti, and many cooks go for the obvious and toss them with tomato sauce. I do, too (see the variation that follows), but I really prefer it with this elegant, creamy sauce.

1. Position a rack in the center of the oven and preheat the oven to 350°F. Place the squash in a roasting pan and bake until it can be pierced with a meat fork, about 1 hour. Cool until easy to handle. Protecting your hands with a kitchen towel, split the squash lengthwise. Use a large spoon to remove and discard the seeds. Working over a large warmed bowl, use a fork to scrape the flesh from the skin along the length of the squash to keep the strands as long as possible. Cover tightly with aluminum foil to keep warm.

2. Melt 1 tablespoon of the butter in a medium skillet. Add the onion and cook, stirring occasionally, until golden, about 5 minutes. Stir into the squash.

3. Melt the remaining 5 tablespoons butter in the same skillet over medium heat. Add to the squash, along with the cheese, arugula, pine nuts, basil, nutmeg, and cayenne. Toss gently, breaking as few squash strands as possible. Season with salt and pepper.

4. To serve, heap the squash on 4 plates. Serve immediately with additional cheese passed on the side.

1 large spaghetti squash
   (2$\frac{1}{2}$ pounds)
6 tablespoons ($\frac{3}{4}$ stick)
   unsalted butter
1 small red onion, chopped
$\frac{1}{2}$ cup freshly grated Parmesan
   cheese, plus more for
   serving
2 ounces arugula, rinsed, stems
   removed, and cut into thin
   strips (1 packed cup)
$\frac{1}{3}$ cup pine nuts, toasted (see
   page 175)
2 tablespoons chopped fresh
   basil
$\frac{1}{8}$ teaspoon freshly grated
   nutmeg
$\frac{1}{8}$ teaspoon ground hot red
   (cayenne) pepper
Kosher salt and freshly ground
   black pepper to taste

SPAGHETTI SQUASH CASSEROLE MARINARA

Spread the tossed squash in a buttered 8-inch square baking dish, then top with 2 cups Marinara Sauce (page 167). Sprinkle with an additional $\frac{1}{4}$ cup grated Parmesan cheese. Bake in a preheated 350°F. oven until heated through, about 20 minutes.

Ray's Potato and Vegetable Pie

You've all heard about how great dishes are often discovered by accident. This potato dish, which can be served as a main course as well as a side dish for a special dinner, was created from leftovers by one of my chefs, Ramón (Ray) Mercedes. You can use steamed or sautéed vegetables, though I lean toward the sautéed veggies because they have a bit more flavor. If you have a collection of fresh herbs, reduce the basil to 1 tablespoon, and add 1 teaspoon each chopped fresh rosemary and thyme.

3 pounds baking (Burbank or russet) potatoes, peeled and cut in half

2 tablespoons extra-virgin olive oil, plus more for the pan

1 large onion, finely chopped

1 red bell pepper, finely chopped

3 garlic cloves, minced

1/4 cup liquid nondairy creamer

3 tablespoons pareve margarine

1/4 cup chopped fresh parsley

2 tablespoons chopped fresh basil

1 teaspoon kosher salt

1/4 teaspoon freshly ground black pepper

5 large eggs, beaten

3 cups cooked, coarsely chopped vegetables, such as spinach, broccoli florets, thinly sliced zucchini or yellow squash, or a combination

1. Place the potatoes in a large saucepan and add enough lightly salted water to cover. Bring to a boil over high heat. Cook until the potatoes are tender, about 25 minutes.

2. Meanwhile, heat the oil in a large skillet over medium heat. Add the onion, red bell pepper, and garlic and cook, stirring occasionally, until the onion is translucent, about 6 minutes.

3. Drain the potatoes well. Transfer to a large bowl. Add the creamer and margarine, and mash with a hand masher or hand-held electric mixer. Mix in the onion–bell pepper mixture, parsley, basil, salt, and pepper. Gradually fold in the eggs, then the vegetables.

4. Position a rack in the center of the oven and preheat the oven to 375°F. Lightly oil a 9-inch deep-dish pie pan. Beginning with a thick layer of potatoes, spread three layers of potatoes and two layers of vegetables in the pan. Place the pan in a larger roasting pan.

5. Slide the rack halfway out of the oven. Place the roasting pan on the rack and add enough hot water to the pan to come halfway up the sides of the pie pan. Slide the rack back into the oven. Bake until the pie feels firm in the center, about 30 minutes. Let stand for 5 minutes. To serve, spoon out of the pan.

DAIRY VARIATION

Substitute heavy cream and butter for the nondairy creamer and margarine. Add $1/2$ cup freshly grated Parmesan cheese to the mashed potatoes. Sprinkle $1/4$ cup shredded mozzarella cheese on each vegetable layer.

Potato Dumplings
with Provençale Sauce

Shlishkas (Hungarian potato dumplings) are members of the gnocchi family. Or are gnocchi related to shlishkas? The answer to this "chicken or egg" question depends on whether you get the recipe from an Ashkenazic or Sephardic cook! The classic way to serve shlishkas is tossed with toasted bread crumbs. I like this jazzier version, with a fresh tomato sauce, and they're also great served with marinara sauce.

The first secret of tender shlishkas is to use starchy baking potatoes. Be sure to let some of the steam escape from the cooked potatoes, which removes excess moisture and reduces the amount of flour needed to make the dough. Be flexible with the amount of flour, as it varies according the relative starchiness of the potatoes, the moisture content, and even the weather. And don't crowd the dumplings in the boiling water—if you add too many, the water won't return to the boil quickly, and the dumplings won't firm up as well.

> **MAKES
> 6 TO 8
> SERVINGS**

SHLISHKAS

4 large baking (russet) potatoes,
  peeled
1¹/₂ cups all-purpose flour,
  more as needed
1 large egg, beaten
1 tablespoon extra-virgin olive
  oil
1 tablespoon kosher salt
¹/₄ teaspoon freshly ground
  black pepper
Pinch of freshly grated nutmeg

1. Boil the whole potatoes in a large saucepan of lightly salted water over high heat until tender, about 25 minutes. Drain and let stand for 5 minutes.

2. Pass the hot potatoes through a ricer into a large bowl. Make a well in the center and add 1¹/₂ cups of flour, egg, oil, salt, pepper, and nutmeg to the well. Fold repeatedly with a large spatula or spoon until the mixture forms a firm but not sticky dough. Do not overwork. If needed, add flour, 1 tablespoon at a time.

3. Line two large baking sheets with parchment or paper and dust with flour. Working with about one-sixth of the dough at a time, place the dough on a lightly floured work surface. Roll under the palms of your hands into a ³/₄-inch-thick rope. Cut into 1-inch lengths. If you wish, pick up each shlishka and press one side against the tines of a large dinner fork to create grooves. Place the shlishkas on the prepared baking sheets. (The shlishkas can be made up to 8 hours ahead, covered with plastic wrap, and refrigerated. Or freeze the shlishkas on the baking sheets until solid. Transfer the frozen shlishkas to zip-tight freezer bags and seal. Freeze for up to 2 months. Cook the frozen shlishkas without thawing.)

4. Bring a large pot of lightly salted water to a boil over high heat. In batches, without crowding, drop the shlishkas into water. Stir gently to dislodge any shlishkas on the bottom of the pot. Cook, stirring occasionally, until the shlishkas rise to the surface of the water, then cook until tender, 2 to 3 minutes longer. Using a large skimmer or wire-mesh sieve, transfer the shlishkas to a large bowl of cold water. When all of the shlishkas are cooked, drain well. Spread on a lightly oiled baking sheet. (The shlishkas may be made ahead up to 1 day ahead, tossed with oil, covered with plastic wrap, and refrigerated. Or freeze uncovered until solid, transfer to freezer bags, and freeze for up to 1 month. Thaw completely before using.)

SAUCE

2 tablespoons extra-virgin olive oil

2 garlic cloves, sliced

1 medium red onion, halved lengthwise and thinly sliced into half-moons

2 pounds ripe beefsteak tomatoes (preferably a combination of red and yellow tomatoes), seeded and cut into $1/2$-inch cubes

$1/4$ teaspoon fennel seeds

$1/4$ teaspoon hot red pepper flakes

Kosher salt and freshly ground black pepper to taste

2 tablespoons chopped fresh basil

2 tablespoons chopped fresh oregano

5. To make the sauce, heat the oil in a 12-inch skillet over medium heat. Add the garlic and cook just until golden, about 2 minutes. Add the onion and cook, stirring occasionally, until softened, about 5 minutes. Add the tomatoes, fennel, and red pepper flakes. Cook, stirring occasionally, just until heated through, about 5 minutes. Season with salt and pepper.

6. Add the shlishkas to the skillet. Stir gently to coat with the sauce. Mix in the basil and oregano. Serve immediately.

DAIRY VARIATION

When the sauce is finished, stir in 4 tablespoons unsalted butter until melted. Serve the shlishkas with grated Parmesan cheese.

Pasta
AND
Grains

In old Jewish kitchens, pasta meant noodles.

Without noodles, there could be no kugel or kasha varnishkes; not even lokshen to garnish your soup. Egg barley is another very Jewish member of the noodle family that many people may not know much about—which is really too bad.

In my kitchen, pasta certainly means noodles, but it also means spaghetti, linguine, orecchiette, lo mein, Israeli couscous, and more. I don't care where the pasta comes from—I love cooking it and eating it. You can find kosher versions of just about any pasta (see Mail-Order Sources, page 250). Don't forget to stock the kitchen shelves with rice, kasha, and other grains, too, as they can be every bit as delicious and versatile as pasta.

One of the reasons I love pasta and grains is because they are so easy to keep on hand, stashed in the cupboard, just hanging out and waiting for me to decide how to cook them. Pasta and grains are the backbone of a well-stocked pantry, along with such staples as olives, capers, pine nuts, anchovies, lemons, onions, garlic, and bread crumbs. I also keep a reserve of homemade marinara sauce in the freezer and a hunk of Parmesan cheese in the fridge. With these ingredients ready to rock and roll, all I need to do is stop off at the market and get a fresh ingredient or two. And anytime I can buy groceries for dinner in the express lane it's okay with me.

Egg Barley with Roasted Portobello Mushrooms and Balsamic Drizzle

Egg barley vies with egg noodles as the classic Jewish-American pasta. Most people think of it as "Grandma" food—tasty and made with love, but not usually served in any distinguished manner. Here, egg barley gets the upscale treatment with roasted mushrooms and a splash of reduced balsamic vinegar. You may wonder why I suggest using schmaltz combined with margarine as an option for all-chicken fat. Well, some cooks shy away from animal fats in cooking. Since I don't like the flavor of margarine by itself this is my compromise.

**MAKES
6
SERVINGS**

ROASTED PORTOBELLO MUSHROOMS

1/4 cup balsamic vinegar
1/4 cup extra-virgin olive oil
4 garlic cloves, chopped
1 teaspoon chopped fresh thyme
1/2 teaspoon chopped fresh rosemary
1/2 teaspoon kosher salt
1/4 teaspoon freshly ground black pepper
6 large portobello mushrooms

1. To prepare the mushrooms, whisk the vinegar, olive oil, garlic, thyme, rosemary, salt, and pepper in a glass baking dish. Add the mushrooms and turn to coat. Marinate at room temperature, turning occasionally, for 30 minutes.

2. Position a rack in the top third of the oven and preheat the oven to 350°F. Lightly coat a baking sheet with oil. Lift the mushrooms out of the marinade and place on the baking sheet. Roast until tender, about 20 minutes.

3. Heat the oil in a wide, medium skillet over medium-high heat. Add the egg barley and cook, stirring frequently, until lightly toasted, 2 to 3 minutes. Add the boiling water and salt. Bring to a boil and cook until the egg barley is tender, about 10 minutes. Drain well.

4. Meanwhile, melt the schmaltz in a large skillet over medium heat. Add the onion and cook, stirring occasionally, until golden, about 5 minutes. Add the sliced button mushrooms and cook, stirring occasionally, until they are tender and juicy, about 5 minutes. Stir in the drained egg barley, rosemary, and thyme. Season with salt and pepper.

5. Slice the cooked portobello mushrooms into ¹/₂-inch-thick slices. Heap equal amounts of the egg barley on 6 plates, top with the portobello slices, and a sprinkling of chives. Drizzle 1 teaspoon of the balsamic syrup onto each plate, and serve immediately.

PAREVE VARIATION

Substitute pareve margarine for the schmaltz.

SCHMALTZ

Schmaltz, rendered chicken fat, is one of the glories of the Jewish kitchen. Like other saturated fats, it has an undeniably wonderful flavor. Back in the old days, chicken fat and skin were much easier to purchase from the butcher, so many cooks rendered their own schmaltz at home, slowly simmering the chopped fat until it melted into a golden pool. (One of the benefits of homemade schmaltz is gribenes, the crisp strips of poultry skin left in the pan after all the fat has been rendered, which are great as a salad garnish or as a snack.)

To make schmaltz, coarsely chop 1 pound chicken fat and skin (available at kosher butchers and markets) by hand with a large knife, or pulse in a food processor. Mix with ½ cup water in a heavy-bottomed, ovenproof saucepan. Bring to a boil over medium heat, stirring often. Cover and bake in a preheated 300°F. oven until the fat has rendered into a golden liquid with pieces of golden brown solids, about 1½ hours. Do not let the schmaltz get too brown. Strain through a fine sieve into a covered container, reserving the gribenes (solids), if you wish.

While that is the traditional way to render schmaltz, my mom taught me a much easier way. Whenever you make chicken stock, and I hope you make it a lot, chill the cooled stock overnight. The rendered fat will rise to the surface and harden. Simply scrape the firm, pale yellow fat off the stock. To store, melt the schmaltz in a small saucepan. Strain through a fine sieve into a covered container. Schmaltz can be stored in the refrigerator for up to 2 weeks, or frozen for up to 3 months.

EGG BARLEY

1 tablespoon extra-virgin olive oil
1 cup egg barley
6 cups boiling water
¹/₂ teaspoon kosher salt
2 tablespoons schmaltz (see Box) or 1 tablespoon pareve margarine and 1 tablespoon schmaltz
1 medium onion, chopped
1 pound white button mushrooms, thinly sliced
1 teaspoon chopped fresh rosemary
1 teaspoon chopped fresh thyme
Kosher salt and freshly ground black pepper, for garnish

Chopped fresh chives, for garnish
6 teaspoons Balsamic Syrup (page 101)

Fettuccine with Cremini
and Roasted Peppers

MAKES
4 TO 6
SERVINGS

With marinara sauce on hand, you can throw this pasta together in no time. In fact, it's a good argument in favor of keeping some sauce in the freezer. Another time, substitute sliced zucchini and yellow squash for the mushrooms.

3 tablespoons extra-virgin
  olive oil
2 garlic cloves, minced
1 pound cremini mushrooms,
  sliced
1 batch Marinara Sauce (recipe
  follows)
2 red bell peppers, roasted (see
  page 27), skinned, seeded,
  and coarsely chopped
1/3 cup sun-dried tomatoes,
  plumped and diced (see
  Note)
2 teaspoons chopped fresh
  rosemary
Kosher salt and freshly ground
  black pepper to taste
1 pound dried fettuccine

1. Heat the olive oil and garlic in a large saucepan over medium heat until the garlic begins to color, about 2 minutes. Add the mushrooms and cook until they give off their juices, about 5 minutes. Stir in the marinara sauce, roasted peppers, sun-dried tomatoes, and rosemary, and bring to a simmer. Reduce the heat to medium-low and simmer for 10 minutes. Season with salt and pepper. Keep the sauce warm.

2. Meanwhile, bring a large pot of lightly salted water to a boil over high heat. Add the pasta and cook, stirring occasionally, until barely tender, about 9 minutes. Drain and return to the pot.

3. Add the sauce to the pasta and mix well. Serve immediately.

NOTE: Tomatoes that are sun-dried but not soaked in oil are increasingly available in bulk. They are easy to rehydrate. Cover the sun-dried tomatoes with very hot tap water in a medium bowl. Add a splash of red or white distilled vinegar to the water (this heightens the tomato flavor) and let stand until the tomatoes are plumped, about 30 minutes. Drain well and pat completely dry with paper towels. Use immediately. To store, pack rehydrated sun-dried tomatoes in a covered container and add enough olive oil to cover them completely. The oil-packed tomatoes will keep for at least 6 months. When you need them, let the jar stand at room temperature until the oil softens, then remove the required amount of tomatoes and replenish the jar with additional oil.

Marinara Sauce

PAREVE

MAKES ABOUT 3½ CUPS

Here's a solid, basic recipe for this standard tomato sauce. Why not make a large batch and freeze to have handy for pasta dishes?

2 tablespoons extra-virgin olive oil
2 garlic cloves, crushed
One 28-ounce can crushed tomatoes with purée
1 teaspoon dried basil
1 teaspoon dried oregano
Kosher salt and freshly ground black pepper to taste

Heat the oil in a medium saucepan over medium heat. Add the garlic and stir until golden, about 2 minutes. Stir in the tomatoes, basil, and oregano, and bring to a boil. Reduce the heat to medium-low and simmer, stirring often, until slightly thickened, about 20 minutes. Season with salt and pepper. (The sauce can be made up to 3 days ahead, cooled, covered, and refrigerated, or frozen for up to 3 months.)

Hungarian Noodles with Caramelized Cabbage, Onions, and Fennel

This Hungarian dish is a shining example of how to coax lots of flavor from humble ingredients. The slow cooking of the cabbage, fennel, and onions melds them together while turning them golden. Only Hungarians would combine cabbage with red bell peppers like this.

4 tablespoons (¹/2 stick)
   unsalted butter
¹/2 cup extra-virgin olive oil
1 small head of cabbage, thinly
   sliced
1 large onion, halved
   lengthwise and thinly sliced
   into half-moons
2 cups thinly sliced fennel
1 tablespoon chopped fresh
   thyme or 1 teaspoon dried
   thyme
Kosher salt and freshly ground
   black pepper to taste
1 pound medium egg noodles
1 pound pot cheese or small-
   curd cottage cheese, at room
   temperature.
2 medium red bell peppers,
   roasted (see page 27),
   skinned, seeded, and
   coarsely chopped
¹/4 cup chopped fresh parsley
Hot or sweet Hungarian
   paprika, for garnish

1. Melt the butter in the oil in a very large skillet over medium heat. In batches, stir in the cabbage, cooking each batch until it wilts to make room for more. Stir in the onion and fennel. Cover and cook, stirring often, until the vegetables are tender and golden, 20 to 30 minutes. Stir in the thyme and season with salt and pepper.

2. Meanwhile, bring a large pot of lightly salted water to a boil over high heat. Add the noodles and cook until tender, about 8 minutes. Drain well.

3. Return the noodles to the empty cooking pot. Add the cabbage, pot cheese, and red bell peppers and mix gently. Serve immediately, topped with parsley and a sprinkle of paprika.

PAREVE VARIATION
Substitute pareve margarine for the butter and omit the cheese.

Fettuccine with Seafood Puttanesca

MAKES
4 TO 6
SERVINGS

When you need a quick dinner entrée, look no further than this seafood pasta. It's a cousin to the famous spaghetti puttanesca, redolent with garlic and anchovies, and spicy with chiles.

1. Bring a large pot of lightly salted water to a boil over high heat.

2. Meanwhile, heat 3 tablespoons of the oil in a 12-inch nonstick skillet over medium-high heat until very hot but not smoking. Add the fish and cook, turning once, until golden brown on both sides, about 5 minutes. Using a slotted spoon, transfer to a plate.

3. Add the remaining 2 tablespoons oil to the skillet with the garlic, anchovies, and red pepper flakes. Cook just until the garlic begins to color, about 1 minute (it will happen quickly, as the skillet is hot). Add the wine and stock, then stir in the tomatoes, basil, and oregano. Bring to a simmer and reduce the heat to low. Simmer until slightly thickened, about 20 minutes. During the last minute or so, stir in the fish, olives, and capers. Season with salt and pepper.

4. Meanwhile, cook the pasta in the boiling water until al dente, about 9 minutes. Drain and return to the pot.

5. Add the sauce to the pasta and mix well. Serve immediately.

5 tablespoons extra-virgin olive oil

1^{1}/$_{2}$ pounds firm-fleshed fish fillets (such as cod, haddock, or scrod), cut into 1^{1}/$_{2}$-inch chunks

3 garlic cloves, minced

6 anchovy fillets packed in oil, drained and chopped

^{1}/$_{2}$ teaspoon hot red pepper flakes

^{1}/$_{2}$ cup dry white wine

^{1}/$_{2}$ cup Fish Stock (page 42) or additional wine

One 28-ounce can crushed tomatoes with added purée

1 teaspoon dried basil

1 teaspoon dried oregano

^{1}/$_{2}$ cup pitted and coarsely chopped green olives

3 tablespoons capers, drained and rinsed

Kosher salt and freshly ground black pepper to taste

1 pound dried fettuccine

Orecchiette with Sardines

In Sicily, this dish is called pasta con le sarde. *It's so popular that Sicilian markets even stock sardine and raisin "sauce" in cans. The original calls for wild fennel, not exactly the kind of thing you find at the local grocery store, but everything else will be found in a well-stocked pantry—raisins, olive oil, pasta, pine nuts, olives, and of course, canned sardines. Spinach adds color, but isn't absolutely necessary. If you wish, substitute another ever-present pantry item, sun-dried tomatoes, for the fresh ones.*

MAKES 4 TO 6 SERVINGS

1/4 cup dry Marsala
1/4 cup raisins
Pinch of crumbled saffron
1/3 cup plus 2 tablespoons olive oil
1 cup fresh bread crumbs (see Note, page 116)
2 garlic cloves, minced
Pinch of hot red pepper flakes
1 small onion, chopped
2 ripe plum tomatoes, diced
1/4 cup pitted and coarsely chopped black Mediterranean olives
1/4 cup pine nuts
Two 4-ounce tins sardines in olive oil, drained and filleted
2 tablespoons fresh lemon juice
1 pound orecchiette pasta
1 cup spinach leaves, cut into thin strips
Kosher salt and freshly ground black pepper to taste

1. Mix the Marsala, raisins, and saffron in a small bowl and let soak while preparing the other ingredients. Bring a large pot of lightly salted water to a boil over high heat.

2. Meanwhile, heat 2 tablespoons of the olive oil in a large skillet over medium heat. Add the bread crumbs and cook, stirring often, until toasted, about 3 minutes. Transfer to a plate and wipe out the skillet.

3. Heat the remaining 1/3 cup oil with the garlic and red pepper flakes in the same skillet over medium heat. Cook until the garlic is golden, about 2 minutes. Stir in the onion and cook until it is translucent, about 3 minutes. Stir in the tomatoes, olives, and pine nuts and cook, stirring occasionally, until heated through, about 2 minutes. Add the sardines and the raisins with their Marsala. Cook, stirring frequently, until the sardines are heated through, about 3 minutes. Stir in the lemon juice. Keep warm.

4. Add the pasta to the boiling water and cook until al dente, about 8 minutes. Drain and return to the pot.

5. Add the sardine sauce and spinach to the pasta and toss well. Season with salt and pepper. Transfer to a serving dish and top with the bread crumbs. Serve hot.

Thai Noodles with Peanut Sauce
and Asian Vegetables

These noodles are inspired by the kind of food you might be served on the streets of Bangkok—noodles tossed with a peanut sauce and stir-fried vegetables. I refuse to tell you exactly what vegetables to stir-fry; just use your favorites and enjoy. Unlike most peanut sauces, which use unsweetened coconut milk, this one is made with the sweeter, richer cream of coconut—like what you'd use in a piña colada.

1. To make the sauce, whisk the peanut butter, cream of coconut, water, soy sauce, orange juice, honey, rice vinegar, and sesame oil in a large bowl until smooth. Add the ginger and chiles. Set aside.

2. Bring a large pot of lightly salted water to a boil over high heat. Add the linguine and cook until tender, about 9 minutes.

3. Meanwhile, heat the oil in a large skillet over medium-high heat. Add the vegetables and stir-fry, stirring almost constantly, until heated through, about 3 minutes. Add the bean sprouts and stir-fry just to heat through, about 1 minute.

4. Drain the pasta and return it to the cooking pot. Add the peanut sauce and vegetables and mix well. Transfer to a serving bowl and top with the peanuts and cilantro. Serve hot, or cool and serve at room temperature.

PEANUT SAUCE

1 cup creamy peanut butter
$1/4$ cup sweetened cream of
coconut (Coco Lopez)
$1/4$ cup water
$1/4$ cup soy sauce
$1/4$ cup orange juice
3 tablespoons honey
3 tablespoons rice vinegar
1 tablespoon dark sesame oil
2 tablespoons peeled and
coarse-grated fresh ginger
2 Thai chiles or 1 jalapeño
pepper, seeded and minced

1 pound linguine, spaghettini, lo
mein, or other thin noodles
2 tablespoons vegetable oil
4 cups assorted fresh vegetables
(such as broccoli florets,
trimmed snow peas, thinly
sliced carrots, red pepper
strips, or sliced shiitake caps)
2 cups fresh bean sprouts
$1/3$ cup roasted peanuts, coarsely
chopped, for garnish
3 tablespoons chopped fresh
cilantro, for garnish

Spicy Macaroni and Cheese Kugel
with Three Peppers

My kids love their dad's Tex-Mex mac' and cheese, but don't look for elbow macaroni here. Like all good kugels, this one is made with flat egg noodles. If your family is chile-challenged, you can leave out the jalapeño and still have one great dish. And I've been known to make it with just Cheddar cheese, too.

12 ounces medium egg noodles

2 tablespoons extra-virgin olive oil

1 medium red onion, chopped

1 medium red bell pepper, cored, seeded, and chopped

1 medium green bell pepper, cored, seeded, and chopped

1 jalapeño pepper, seeded and finely chopped

4 tablespoons (^{1}/$_2$ stick) unsalted butter

^{1}/$_4$ cup all-purpose flour

4 cups milk, heated

1 cup (4 ounces) shredded extra-sharp Cheddar cheese

1 cup (4 ounces) shredded Monterey Jack cheese

1 cup (4 ounces) shredded mozzarella cheese

^{1}/$_2$ teaspoon pure ground ancho chile powder or regular chili powder

^{1}/$_2$ teaspoon sweet or hot Hungarian paprika

1. Position a rack in the center of the oven and preheat the oven to 350°F. Lightly butter a 13×9-inch baking dish.

2. Bring a large pot of lightly salted water to a boil over high heat. Add the noodles and cook just until barely cooked (they will cook further in the oven), about 6 minutes. Drain well.

3. Meanwhile, heat the oil in a large skillet over medium-high heat. Add the onion, red and green bell peppers, and jalapeño. Cook, stirring occasionally, until the vegetables are tender, about 6 minutes.

4. Melt the butter in the empty noodle pot over medium heat. Whisk in the flour, reduce the heat to low, and let the mixture bubble without browning for 2 minutes. Gradually whisk in the milk and bring to a simmer over medium heat. Reduce the heat to medium-low and simmer until the sauce loses any raw flour taste, about 5 minutes. Remove from the heat, add the Cheddar, Monterey Jack, and mozzarella, and whisk until smooth. Whisk in the chile power, paprika, and cayenne, and season with the salt and pepper and additional cayenne, if you wish. Stir in the noodles. Spread evenly in the baking dish.

5. To make the topping, mix the corn flakes, panko, and Parmesan cheese in a small bowl. Stir in the melted butter. Distribute evenly over the top of the noodles.

6. Bake until the topping is crispy and the kugel is bubbling around the edges, about 30 minutes. Let stand at room temperature for 10 minutes. Cut into squares and serve.

NOTE: Panko, a Japanese product, are flaky, fluffy dried bread crumbs. They add a special crispiness to recipes and, unfortunately, there is no real substitute. But they keep for a few months at room temperature in a sealed zip-tight plastic bag, and you will find lots of ways to use them as a breading and topping. For a kosher product, order from Kosher Depot (see Sources, page 250).

$1/4$ teaspoon ground hot red (cayenne) pepper, or more to taste

Kosher salt and freshly ground black pepper to taste

TOPPING

$1/2$ cup crushed corn flakes

$1/2$ cup panko (Japanese bread crumbs) or more corn flakes

$1/3$ cup freshly grated Parmesan cheese

4 tablespoons ($1/2$ stick) unsalted butter, melted

Pumpkin and Pine Nut Risotto

This risotto has autumn written all over it. For a few weeks each fall, many farmer's markets and supermarkets carry cooking pumpkins, which are much less watery than the huge ones used for jack-o'-lanterns. If you can't find them, simply use butternut squash. And be sure to use arborio rice, which has the proper starch content to lend the risotto its classic texture.

MAKES 6 SERVINGS

2 tablespoons extra-virgin olive oil, plus more for oiling the foil

One 1³/₄-pound cooking (sugar or pie) pumpkin or butternut squash, split in half, seeds removed

6 cups Vegetable Stock (page 43)

2 tablespoons unsalted butter

1 small onion, chopped

2 cups arborio rice

¹/₂ cup dry white wine

¹/₂ cup thinly sliced, stemmed Swiss chard leaves

Pinch of freshly grated nutmeg

¹/₂ cup heavy cream

¹/₂ cup grated Parmesan cheese, plus more for serving

¹/₄ cup pine nuts, toasted (see page 175)

¹/₄ cup minced chives

Kosher salt and freshly ground black pepper to taste

1. Position a rack in the top third of the oven and preheat the oven to 400°F. Lightly oil an aluminum foil–lined baking sheet.

2. Place the pumpkin, cut side down, on the baking sheet. Bake just until tender when pierced with a fork, about 40 minutes, depending on the size of the pumpkin. Set aside until cool enough to handle. Pare the pumpkin, discarding the skin. Cut the flesh into 1-inch cubes.

3. Bring the stock to a boil in a medium saucepan over high heat. Turn off the heat but leave the saucepan on the stove.

4. Heat 2 tablespoons olive oil and 1 tablespoon of the butter in a heavy-bottomed Dutch oven or flame-proof casserole over medium heat. Add the onion and cook until softened and golden, about 4 minutes. Add the rice and cook, stirring often, until it turns opaque (do not brown), about 2 minutes. Add the wine and cook until almost evaporated, about 30 seconds.

5. About 1 cup at a time, stir the hot stock into the rice. Cook, stirring almost constantly, until the rice absorbs almost all of the stock, about 3 minutes. Stir in another cup of stock, and stir until it is almost absorbed. Repeat, adjusting the heat to keep the risotto at a steady simmer and adding more stock as it is absorbed, until you use all of the stock and the rice is barely tender, about 20 minutes total. If you run out of stock and the rice isn't tender, use hot water.

6. Stir in the cubed pumpkin, chard, and nutmeg, and cook until the pumpkin is heated through, about 1 minute. Stir in the heavy cream, Parmesan, pine nuts, and 2 tablespoons of the chives. If desired, loosen the consistency of the risotto with additional stock. Season with salt and pepper. Spoon into bowls and serve immediately, sprinkled with the remaining chives. Pass additional cheese on the side.

TOASTING NUTS

With just a little effort, you can really enhance nuts like walnuts, almonds, and pine nuts. Toasting brings out their deepest flavor and gives them great crunch.

To toast walnuts and almonds, spread them on a baking sheet. Bake in a preheated 350°F. oven, stirring occasionally, until toasted and fragrant, about 10 minutes. Allow the nuts to cool completely on the sheet.

To toast pine nuts, heat a small skillet over medium heat until hot. Add the pine nuts and cook, stirring almost constantly, until the pine nuts are lightly toasted, about 2 minutes. Immediately transfer the nuts to a plate and cool completely.

New Mexican Rice Pilaf

MAKES
6 TO 8
SERVINGS

You can serve this chile-kissed rice pilaf as a side dish, but I think it has so much going for it that it deserves main-course status. To turn the pilaf into a meat dish, use chicken stock, and you could also stir in some chopped cooked chicken.

2 tablespoons extra-virgin olive oil
1¹/₂ cups fresh or frozen corn kernels
2 cups long-grain rice
1 medium red onion, finely chopped
1 red bell pepper, cored, seeded, and cut in ¹/₄-inch dice
1 green bell pepper, cored, seeded, and cut in ¹/₄-inch dice
2 jalapeño peppers, seeded and minced
1 teaspoon ground cumin
1 teaspoon pure ground New Mexican chile powder (see page 131)
1 teaspoon pure ground chipotle chile powder (see page 131)
4 cups Vegetable Stock or Chicken Stock (pages 43 and 40)
1 teaspoon kosher salt
3 scallions (green and white parts), thinly sliced
¹/₄ cup chopped fresh cilantro
2 tablespoons fresh lime juice
Lime wedges, for garnish

1. Heat the oil in a large saucepan over low heat. Add the corn and cook, stirring occasionally, until lightly browned (frozen corn won't brown), about 5 minutes. Add the rice and cook, stirring often, until it turns opaque, about 2 minutes. Stir in the onion, red and green bell peppers, jalapeños, cumin, and New Mexican and chipotle ground chile powders. Add the stock and salt, increase the heat to medium-high, and bring to a boil.

2. Reduce the heat to low and cover. Simmer until the rice is tender and the liquid has been absorbed, about 20 minutes. Remove from the heat and let stand 5 minutes.

3. Fluff with a fork, and mix in the scallions, cilantro, and lime juice. Serve hot with the lime wedges.

Kasha with Bow-Tie Pasta
and Bitter Greens

At its most basic, kasha varnishkes is a pot of kasha with some bow-tie noodles mixed in. No one will ever accuse this version of being mundane. Bitter greens interplay with the robust flavor of kasha to make this a memorable dish. I make this with arugula and chicory, but you can choose one or the other as you wish.

1. Bring a large pot of lightly salted water to a boil over high heat. While the water is heating, prepare the rest of the ingredients.

2. Heat the butter in a large skillet over medium heat until lightly browned. Add the onion and cook, stirring often, until golden, about 5 minutes. Add the mushrooms and cook, stirring often, until the mushrooms are tender, about 4 minutes. Set aside.

3. Heat the oil in a medium saucepan over medium heat. Beat the egg white in a medium bowl until foamy. Add the kasha and stir to coat. Pour into the saucepan and cook, stirring often, until the egg coating is dry and set, about 2 minutes. Stir in the mushroom mixture, the stock, 1/2 teaspoon salt, and 1/4 teaspoon pepper. Bring to a boil and cover tightly. Reduce the heat to low and simmer until the liquid is absorbed, about 3 minutes. Remove from the heat and keep covered to retain the heat.

4. Meanwhile, add the pasta to the boiling water and cook until tender, about 10 minutes. Drain well. Return to the cooking pot. Fluff the kasha with a fork. Stir the kasha and greens into the pasta. Season with salt and pepper. Serve hot.

2 tablespoons unsalted butter
1 small white onion, chopped
8 ounces assorted wild mushrooms (such as cremini, stemmed shiitake, and portobello), finely chopped
1 tablespoon extra-virgin olive oil
1 large egg white
1 cup kasha
2 cups Vegetable Stock (page 43)
1/2 teaspoon salt, plus more to taste
1/4 teaspoon freshly ground black pepper, plus more to taste
1 pound bow-tie pasta
2 cups arugula or chicory (preferably 1 cup of each), cut into thin ribbons

PAREVE VARIATION
Substitute olive oil for the butter.

Side Dishes

Granted, side dishes were created to fill out a menu, but, in some circumstances, they are essential. Haroset and tzimmes, icons of Jewish cooking, are obvious examples. What is the point of a seder without haroset, which signifies so much to Jews? Tzimmes is more than something sweet to enjoy with the Rosh Hashanah feast—it celebrates autumn's bounty and sets the stage for a sweet year.

Side dishes run the gamut from simple to fancy. Not every side dish needs to be a quick and easy sauté, although I've offered plenty of them here. Often, with a simply prepared main course (say, roast chicken or grilled lamb chops), you have time to get a little fancy with the side dish. With just a bit more effort, you can serve Swiss Chard Mashed Potatoes (page 188) with that roast chicken.

In most cases in this book, when a restaurant-style recipe has components that I consider integral to the success of the dish, I include them. Some of them, such as the ratatouille with the grilled lamb chops on page 100, could certainly be served as side dishes for other entrées, so feel free to mix and match.

Acorn Squash
with Ginger-Orange Glaze

This is one of the best side dishes you can serve when there's a chill in the air. Try it with roast chicken. The orange and ginger essence gives this underutilized vegetable a flavor that is incredible.

²/₃ cup orange marmalade

2 tablespoons peeled and minced fresh ginger

1 tablespoon dry white wine

1 tablespoon fresh lemon juice

¹/₈ teaspoon freshly grated nutmeg

Two 1¹/₂-pound acorn squashes, cut in half lengthwise, seeds removed, flesh pierced well with a fork

3 tablespoons unsweetened coconut flakes, toasted (see Note)

1. Position a rack in the center of the oven and preheat the oven to 350°F. Lightly oil an aluminum foil–lined baking sheet.

2. Bring the marmalade, ginger, wine, lemon juice, and nutmeg to a boil over medium heat, stirring often. Brush the cut side of the squash with a light coating of the glaze, reserving the remaining glaze. Place the squash, glazed side down, on the baking sheet. Bake until the squash is tender when pierced with a meat fork, 40 to 45 minutes.

3. Cut each squash in half lengthwise to make two wedges. Return the squash to the baking sheet, cut sides up. Brush generously with the remaining glaze. Bake to set the glaze, about 5 minutes.

4. Transfer to a serving platter and sprinkle with the toasted coconut. Serve hot.

NOTE: To toast unsweetened coconut flakes, spread on a baking sheet and bake in a preheated 350°F. oven, stirring often, until toasted, 3 to 5 minutes. Unsweetened flakes are smaller than the sweetened variety, and tend to brown very quickly, so keep an eye on them.

Broccoli Rabe and Garlic Sauté

MAKES
4
SERVINGS

I learned to love broccoli rabe when I was a kid growing up in an Italian neighborhood in Queens, and now it is one of my favorite vegetables—especially in the winter when tomatoes and other warm-weather produce aren't at their best. I remember how I would heap the broccoli rabe onto crusty bread, drizzle it with olive oil, and dig in. (You don't have to be a kid to do that!) These greens have plenty of flavor on their own, but I can't resist beefing them up with a bit of sausage. Leave the sausage out, if you prefer.

1. Heat the oil in a large skillet over medium-high heat. Add the sausage and cook until lightly browned, about 5 minutes. Add the garlic and red pepper flakes. Cook until the garlic begins to turn golden, about 2 minutes.

2. Stir in the broccoli rabe, then add the water and cover. Cook, stirring occasionally, until the broccoli rabe is tender, about 15 minutes. Season with salt. Serve hot.

4 tablespoons extra-virgin olive oil
$1/2$ pound veal sausage, cut into $1/2$-inch rounds
2 garlic cloves, thinly sliced
$1/4$ teaspoon hot red pepper flakes
One $1\frac{1}{2}$-pound bunch broccoli rabe, coarsely chopped
$1/4$ cup water
Kosher salt to taste

DAIRY VARIATION

Omit the veal sausage and finish with a generous sprinkling of grated Parmesan cheese.

PAREVE VARIATION

Omit the sausage and do not add cheese.

CUTTING UP WITH GARLIC

Garlic, for all of its strength, is actually very sensitive. Depending on how it is handled, garlic can be loud and pushy or calm and mellow (if not totally subdued).

Every time you cut a clove of garlic, you expose more of it to the air. The more exposed surfaces, the stronger its flavor. Therefore, sliced garlic has a gentler flavor than chopped, minced is stronger still, and garlic crushed through a press the strongest of all. Roasting garlic allows a lot of the harsh aroma and flavor to evaporate. That doesn't mean you should prefer one method over the other, but that you should pick and choose, depending on the desired result. With the broccoli rabe, I ask for sliced garlic . . . for a reason.

Broccolini with Red Peppers

Broccolini is one of the most recent additions to the produce stand. It looks like thinner, longer stems of broccoli rabe, but it is much less bitter. Best of all you can eat the whole thing without a lot of trimming. Here's a colorful, easy way to cook it.

2 bunches (about 9 ounces each) broccolini, ends trimmed
2 tablespoons extra-virgin olive oil
1 red bell pepper, cored, seeded, and cut into $1/4$-inch strips
2 garlic cloves, thinly sliced
Kosher salt and freshly ground black pepper to taste

1. Bring a large pot of lightly salted water to a boil over high heat. Add the broccolini and cook just until the stems are crisp-tender, about 3 minutes. Drain and rinse under cold running water.

2. Heat the oil in a large skillet over medium heat. Add the red bell pepper and cook, stirring often, until softened, about 4 minutes. Add the garlic and stir until fragrant, about 1 minute.

3. Add the broccolini to the skillet and cook, stirring often, until heated through, about 3 minutes. Season with salt and pepper. Serve hot.

Red Cabbage with Apples

MAKES
8 TO 12
SERVINGS

There's no secret to making red cabbage, as long as you don't rush it. Let the ingredients simmer slowly so they can melt into a soothing mingle of sweet and sour flavors. For a meat main course, bury some veal sausages in the pot to cook along with the cabbage. Serve them with latkes, and invite me over for dinner!

1. Heat the oil in a large saucepan over medium-high heat. Add the onion and cook, stirring often, until softened, about 3 minutes. In batches, stir in the cabbage, covering each batch and letting it wilt before adding more. Stir in the apples, vinegar, and sugar, mixing well to coat the cabbage with the vinegar. Bring to a boil and cover.

2. Reduce the heat to medium-low. Cook, stirring occasionally, just until the cabbage is tender, about 25 minutes. Uncover and increase the heat to high. Cook, stirring often, until the liquid evaporates, about 5 minutes. Season with salt and pepper and serve hot.

3 tablespoons vegetable oil
1 large onion, halved
    lengthwise and thinly sliced
    into half-moons
One 2$^{1}/_{2}$-pound red cabbage,
    cored and thinly sliced
2 Granny Smith apples, peeled,
    cored, and cut into $^{1}/_{2}$-inch
    cubes
$^{1}/_{2}$ cup red wine vinegar
$^{1}/_{4}$ cup sugar
Kosher salt and freshly ground
    black pepper to taste

Moroccan Eggplant, Fennel, and Sweet Peppers Sauté

MAKES
6 TO 8
SERVINGS

This side dish is so full-flavored that it could be served with rice as a main course. Otherwise, serve it with a whole grilled fish or lamb chops.

3/4 teaspoon ground cumin
3/4 teaspoon ground turmeric
1/2 teaspoon ground ginger
1/4 teaspoon ground cinnamon
5 tablespoons extra-virgin olive oil
1 medium fennel bulb, trimmed and cut into thin sticks
1 red bell pepper, cored, seeded, and cut into thin sticks
1 yellow bell pepper, cored, seeded, and cut into thin sticks
1 green bell pepper, cored, seeded, and cut into thin sticks
2 garlic cloves, minced
1 medium eggplant, trimmed and cut into 4 × 3/4-inch sticks
1/4 cup water
1 tablespoon honey
Kosher salt and freshly ground black pepper to taste

1. Mix the cumin, turmeric, ginger, and cinnamon in a small bowl; set aside. Heat 2 tablespoons of the oil in a 12-inch nonstick skillet over medium-high heat. Add the fennel and the red, yellow, and green bell peppers. Cook uncovered, stirring often, until tender, about 8 minutes. Stir in the garlic and cook until fragrant, about 1 minute. Add the spice mixture and stir for 30 seconds. Transfer to a large bowl.

2. Wipe out the skillet with paper towels. Return the skillet to the stove, add the remaining 3 tablespoons oil, and heat over medium-high heat. Add the eggplant and cook, stirring occasionally, until lightly browned and softened, about 5 minutes. Add the water and cook, uncovered, until the eggplant is tender and the water evaporates, about 3 minutes.

3. Stir the fennel and bell peppers back into the skillet and mix well. Stir in the honey and season with salt and pepper. Serve hot.

Mango-Date Haroset

On the Passover plate, haroset may represent the mortar and bricks the Hebrews used to build the Egyptian pyramids, but this doesn't mean it should look like mud! My haroset has a bright golden color (thank you, mangoes) and an intriguing exotic flavor that everyone at the table will enjoy—even those picky eaters who have been spreading the same haroset on their matzo for the last few decades.

1. Roughly chop the walnuts, pecans, and cinnamon in a food processor along with the sugar and ginger. Transfer the chopped-nut mixture to a medium bowl.

2. Stir in the mangoes, grapes, and dates. Gently stir in the wine and lemon juice. Cover with plastic wrap and refrigerate to blend the flavors, about 2 hours. (The haroset can be made up to 1 day ahead.)

¹/₂ cup walnut pieces

¹/₃ cup pecan halves

1 teaspoon ground cinnamon

3 tablespoons sugar

1 teaspoon peeled, shredded, and minced fresh ginger (use the large holes on a box grater)

2 ripe mangoes, peeled, seeded, and cut into ¹/₄-inch dice

²/₃ cup seedless red grapes, quartered

¹/₂ cup pitted dates, cut into ¹/₄-inch dice

¹/₂ cup sweet white wine

2 teaspoons fresh lemon juice

Sweet Noodle and Fruit Kugel

There's no getting around the fact that every Jewish cook needs a really great recipe for sweet noodle kugel. This one is enhanced with dried fruits, generous spicing, and a crisp topping. Save room for seconds. For an over-the-top variation, substitute two 15¼-ounce cans fruit cocktail in syrup, drained, for all the dried fruits, except the raisins, just the way it is served at my friends Bob and Frances Ross's King David Delicatessen in Cedarhurst, Long Island.

³/₄ cup assorted dried fruit,
　　such as cranberries,
　　blueberries, cherries, and
　　strawberries
³/₄ cup golden raisins
2 pounds medium egg noodles
4 large eggs, lightly beaten
1³/₄ cups sugar, divided
1¹/₂ teaspoons vanilla extract
2 tablespoons vegetable oil
2 teaspoons ground cinnamon
³/₄ teaspoon freshly grated
　　nutmeg
1 teaspoon kosher salt
2 cups corn flake crumbs

1. Position a rack in the center of the oven and preheat the oven to 325°F. Lightly oil a 15×10-inch baking pan.

2. Place the dried fruit and raisins in a large bowl and add enough hot water to cover. Let stand while preparing the rest of the ingredients.

3. Bring a large soup pot of lightly salted water to a boil. Add the noodles and cook until barely tender, about 8 minutes. Drain well.

4. Drain the fruit well. Whisk the eggs, 1¹/₂ cups of the sugar, and vanilla to combine. Add the noodles, soaked fruit, oil, 1¹/₂ teaspoons of the cinnamon, nutmeg, and salt. Spread in the baking pan.

5. Mix the corn flake crumbs and the remaining ¹/₄ cup sugar and ¹/₂ teaspoon cinnamon. Sprinkle over the noodles. Cover tightly with aluminum foil.

6. Bake, covered, for 30 minutes. Uncover and bake until the kugel feels firm in the center, about 20 minutes. Let stand at room temperature for 5 minutes. Serve warm or at room temperature.

Smoked Trout and Scallion Mashed Potatoes

MAKES
6
SERVINGS

I originally developed these pareve mashed potatoes as a side dish for my Porcini-Crusted Striped Bass and Port Wine Syrup (page 134), but I get requests to serve it as a side for other dishes, too. I could eat a bowl of it by itself! The smoky trout is unexpected, but incredibly delicious with the mashed potatoes. Try it with any sautéed fish fillets.

1. Place the potatoes in a large saucepan and add enough lightly salted water to cover. Bring to a boil over high heat. Cook until the potatoes are tender, about 20 minutes.

2. While the potatoes are cooking, heat the vegetable oil in a medium skillet over medium-high heat. Add the chopped scallions and cook, stirring often, until the scallions are heated through but still hold their shape, about 1 minute. Stir in the smoked trout and cook just to heat through, about 30 seconds. Set aside.

3. Drain the potatoes and return to the pot. Using a potato masher or hand-held electric mixer, mash the potatoes with the margarine and nondairy creamer. Fold in the smoked trout mixture. Season with salt and pepper. To keep warm for up to 10 minutes, transfer to a stainless-steel bowl and place over a pot of simmering water. Serve hot.

DAIRY VARIATION
Substitute butter and heavy cream for the margarine and nondairy creamer.

3 pounds baking (Burbank or russet) potatoes, peeled and cut into 2-inch chunks
2 tablespoons vegetable oil
4 scallions (white and green parts), chopped
1 cup (4 ounces) flaked skinless and boneless smoked trout fillet
4 tablespoons margarine, melted
$1/2$ cup liquid nondairy creamer, warmed
Kosher salt and freshly ground black pepper

Swiss Chard Mashed Potatoes

MAKES
6
SERVINGS

When making dairy mashed potatoes, use a generous hand with the cream, butter, and sour cream. For this recipe, the fresh flavor of Swiss chard calls out for olive oil, too, so I'm happy to oblige. For fluffier potatoes, add a few more tablespoons of butter and whip at high speed for a few seconds just before transferring to the serving bowl. I won't tell anyone.

1 pound green Swiss chard
3 pounds baking (Burbank or russet) potatoes, peeled and cut into 2-inch chunks
1/4 cup heavy cream
1/4 cup extra-virgin olive oil
4 tablespoons (1/2 stick) unsalted butter
1/4 cup sour cream, at room temperature
Kosher salt and freshly ground black pepper to taste

1. Wash the chard well to remove all grit. Pull off the leaves from the stalks. Stack the leaves and cut into thin slices. Finely chop the stalks.

2. Bring the potatoes and enough lightly salted water to cover to a boil in a large saucepan over high heat. Cook for 15 minutes. Add the chard leaves and stalks, and cook until the potatoes are tender, about 5 minutes.

3. Bring the heavy cream, olive oil, and butter to a simmer in a small saucepan over low heat (or use a microwave). Keep warm. (Using warm liquids keeps the mashed potatoes piping hot and discourages lumps.)

4. Drain the potato-chard mixture well. Return to the cooking pot. Using a hand-held electric mixer on medium speed (or use a potato masher), mash the potatoes, gradually adding the warm cream mixture. Blend in the sour cream and season with salt and pepper. Serve hot.

DILL MASHED POTATOES

Omit the Swiss chard. Mash the potatoes as usual, but add 3 tablespoons chopped fresh dill. Or substitute Dill Oil (page 130) for the olive oil.

PAREVE VARIATION

Substitute margarine and liquid nondairy creamer for the butter, and omit the sour cream.

Double-Cooked Honey Potatoes

I usually serve these golden cubes as a side dish to the Marinated Rib Eye Steak on page 89, but they're too good to keep under wraps for just one dish. First they're baked until tender, then deep-fried for crunch. Temperature is a key element here. The potatoes should be chilled before they are cut into cubes, then allowed to stand at room temperature for an hour or so before deep-frying. Ice-cold potatoes dropped into hot oil will dramatically drop the cooking temperature, causing the cubes to turn out soggy instead of crisp.

1. At least 4 hours before serving, bake the potatoes. Position a rack in the center of the oven and preheat the oven to 400°F.

2. Place the potatoes on a baking sheet. Bake until tender when pierced with a fork, about 1 hour. Cool to room temperature. Refrigerate, uncovered, until chilled, at least 4 hours. (The potatoes can be baked up to 1 day ahead.)

3. Cut the chilled, unpeeled potatoes into 3/4-inch cubes. Let stand at room temperature to lose their chill, 1 to 2 hours.

4. Position a rack in the center of the oven and preheat the oven to 200°F. Line a large baking sheet with paper towels.

5. Pour enough oil into a deep saucepan to come halfway up the sides, and heat over high heat to 365°F. In batches, without crowding, deep-fry the potatoes until golden brown on all sides. Use a large skimmer or slotted spoon to transfer the potatoes to the paper towels. Keep warm in the oven while deep-frying the remaining potatoes.

6. Heat the honey and margarine in a small saucepan until the margarine melts. In a large bowl, toss the potatoes and honey mixture. Season with salt and pepper and serve immediately.

4 medium baking (Burbank or russet) potatoes, scrubbed but unpeeled
Vegetable oil, for deep-frying
3 tablespoons honey
1 tablespoon pareve margarine
Kosher salt and freshly ground black pepper to taste

Yemenite Curry Rice

MAKES
4 TO 6
SERVINGS

The Yemenite Jews date their community back to the ninth century B.C., *when the Bible reports how Sheba rocked Solomon's world. Their frugal way of cooking is always well spiced, as shown by this simple, fragrant rice.*

2 tablespoons extra-virgin
  olive oil
1 small onion, chopped
1¹/₂ cups basmati rice
1 teaspoon curry powder
¹/₄ teaspoon ground turmeric
2 cups Chicken Stock
  (page 40)
1 teaspoon kosher salt
1 scallion (green and white
  parts), chopped
2 tablespoons dried currants,
  plumped in hot water to
  cover for 20 minutes, then
  drained
2 tablespoons pine nuts,
  toasted (see page 175)
1¹/₂ teaspoons zahtar (see page
  207) or 1 teaspoon dried
  marjoram and ¹/₂ teaspoon
  sesame seeds

1. Heat the oil in a medium saucepan over medium heat. Add the onion and cook, stirring occasionally, until it is translucent, about 3 minutes. Add the rice and cook, stirring frequently, until it turns opaque, about 3 minutes. Stir in the curry powder and turmeric and stir for 30 seconds.

2. Stir in the stock and salt and bring to a boil. Cover tightly and reduce the heat to low. Cook until the liquid is absorbed and the rice is tender, about 17 minutes.

3. Remove from the heat and let stand for 5 minutes. Fluff with a fork, and stir in the scallion, currants, pine nuts, and zahtar. Serve hot.

PAREVE VARIATION
Substitute Vegetable Stock (page 43) for the chicken stock.

Snap Peas and Carrots
with Ginger and Sesame

This is a colorful, fresh-tasting side dish. If you wish, you can substitute 6 ounces of trimmed snow peas for the snap peas, but with the following changes: Cook the carrots, covered, until they are almost done, about 6 minutes. Add the snow peas, uncover, and stir-fry until the snow peas are tender and the water evaporates, about 2 minutes.

1. Place the sesame seeds in a large skillet over medium heat. Cook, stirring almost constantly, until toasted, about 2 minutes. Transfer to a plate and set aside.

2. Add the oil and ginger to the skillet and stir for 30 seconds. Add the carrots and the water. Cover and cook for 2 minutes. Add the snap peas. Cook, covered, until the snap peas are crisp-tender, about 7 minutes. Uncover and cook until the water evaporates.

3. Stir in the soy sauce, then the sesame oil. Season with the pepper. Sprinkle with the sesame seeds and serve hot.

2 teaspoons sesame seeds

2 tablespoons vegetable or peanut oil

$1^{1}/_{2}$ teaspoons peeled and minced fresh ginger

2 medium carrots, cut into thin sticks

$^{1}/_{3}$ cup water

12 ounces snap peas, trimmed

2 tablespoons soy sauce

2 teaspoons dark Asian sesame oil

Freshly ground black pepper to taste

String Beans Puttanesca

MAKES
4 TO 6
SERVINGS

Here's a way to serve green beans that's a huge improvement on the boring old "aman-dine." Toss them with a quick sauté of tomatoes, garlic, anchovies, and olives, and they'll enliven main courses with simple flavors.

1 pound green beans, trimmed
    and cut into 1¹/₂-inch lengths
¹/₃ cup extra-virgin olive oil
1 small onion, chopped
2 garlic cloves, minced
4 anchovy fillets, finely
    chopped
¹/₄ teaspoon hot red pepper
    flakes
4 plum tomatoes, cut into
    ¹/₄-inch dice
1 teaspoon dried basil
1 teaspoon dried oregano
¹/₂ cup pitted and coarsely
    chopped black
    Mediterranean olives, such
    as Gaeta
Kosher salt to taste

1. Bring a large pot of lightly salted water to a boil over high heat. Add the green beans and cook until the beans are bright green and still firm to the bite, about 3 minutes. Drain and rinse under cold running water. Drain again.

2. Heat the olive oil in a large skillet over medium-high heat. Add the onion and cook, stirring occasionally, until the onion is translucent, about 3 minutes. Add the garlic, anchovies, and red pepper flakes. Cook, stirring often, until the garlic is golden, about 2 minutes.

3. Stir in the tomatoes, basil, and oregano. Cook until the tomatoes give off their juices, about 3 minutes. Stir in the green beans and olives. Cook, stirring often, until the green beans are heated through and coated with the sauce, about 3 minutes. Season with the salt. Serve hot.

Sweet Potato and Apple Casserole

More than a Rosh Hashanah casserole, this dish could happily grace your Thanksgiving table, too. I like the savory addition of the onions—it makes this much less cloying than other versions.

1. Position a rack in the center of the oven and preheat the oven to 350°F. Grease a 13 × 9-inch baking dish with margarine.

2. Bring a large pot of lightly salted water to a boil over high heat. Add the sweet potatoes, return to the boil, and parcook the sweet potatoes just until slightly softened (they will remain pretty crisp and must retain their shape), about 2 minutes. Drain and rinse under cold water. Drain well.

3. Meanwhile, heat the oil in a medium skillet over medium heat. Add the onions and cook, stirring occasionally, until it is golden, about 5 minutes. Heat the syrup, cider, margarine, honey, cinnamon, ginger, and nutmeg in a small saucepan over low heat until the margarine melts.

4. Layer the sweet potatoes slices in the baking dish, tucking in apple slices at regular intervals. Sprinkle with the onion, and pour the syrup mixture over all. Mix the corn flakes and granola in a small bowl, and sprinkle evenly over the top.

5. Cover tightly with aluminum foil. Bake for 30 minutes. Uncover and bake until the sweet potatoes are tender, about 20 minutes. Serve hot.

4 large sweet potatoes, peeled, halved lengthwise, and cut into $1/4$-inch-thick half-moons

1 tablespoon olive oil

1 medium onion, finely chopped

$1/2$ cup maple-flavored pancake syrup

$1/2$ cup apple cider

$1/4$ cup ($1/2$ stick) pareve margarine

$1/4$ cup honey

$1/4$ teaspoon ground cinnamon

$1/4$ teaspoon ground ginger

$1/4$ teaspoon freshly grated nutmeg

3 Granny Smith apples, unpeeled, halved lengthwise, cored, and cut into $1/4$-inch half-moons

1 cup corn flake crumbs

$1/2$ cup granola

Root Vegetable Tzimmes

MAKES
8
SERVINGS

In the Old Country, tzimmes meant a meat and vegetable stew that combined both sweet and savory flavors. Over the years, it has evolved into a sweet side dish that is especially popular as part of the Rosh Hashanah menu. Here, the combination of root vegetables, dried fruits, and spices makes this a tzimmes well out of the ordinary.

2 tablespoons margarine

1 medium onion, chopped

1 pound sweet potatoes, peeled and cut into ³/4-inch dice

4 medium carrots, sliced into ¹/2-inch rounds

2 medium parsnips, sliced into ¹/2-inch rounds

³/4 cup (¹/2-inch dice) dried apricots

³/4 cup (¹/2-inch dice) pitted dried plums (prunes)

2 cups fresh orange juice

¹/3 cup honey

Grated zest of ¹/2 orange

Grated zest of ¹/2 lemon

1 teaspoon kosher salt

¹/2 teaspoon ground cinnamon

¹/2 teaspoon freshly grated nutmeg

¹/4 teaspoon ground allspice

¹/4 teaspoon freshly ground black pepper

1. Melt the margarine in a large saucepan over medium heat. Add the onion and cook, stirring occasionally, until golden, about 5 minutes. Stir in the sweet potatoes, carrots, parsnips, apricots, prunes, orange juice, honey, orange and lemon zests, salt, cinnamon, nutmeg, allspice, and pepper, and bring to a boil.

2. Cover and reduce the heat to medium-low. Simmer, stirring frequently, until the vegetables are tender, about 30 minutes. If necessary, uncover and cook until the orange juice has evaporated, about 3 minutes.

3. Transfer to a bowl and serve immediately. (The tzimmes can be made up to 2 days ahead, cooled, covered, and refrigerated. Reheat gently before serving.)

Parsnip Oven Fries

MAKES
4 TO 6
SERVINGS

I love these! Golden brown and sweet as sugar (almost), these roasted parsnip "fries" are just the ticket to serve with a simple roast chicken. Parsnips of the same size are very difficult to find. Don't get obsessive and simply try to cut them in relatively equal pieces.

1. Position a rack in the center of the oven and preheat to 400°F.

2. Peel the parsnips. Some parsnips are thin, and some are thick, so don't expect perfectly even pieces—go for a rough "steak fry" look with pieces 2 to 3 inches long and about 1 inch square. If a parsnip has an elongated end, cut it off where the root begins to widen, and consider that one fry. Cut the bulbous part of the root in half lengthwise, and then into quarters or sixths. Spread the parsnip fries on a large baking sheet. Drizzle the fries with the oil and toss with your hands to coat evenly.

3. Bake, turning the fries occasionally with a metal spatula (useful for scraping up fries that stick to the sheet), until tender and golden brown, about 50 minutes. If desired, remove the thinner fries when tender, and return to the sheet to reheat with the thicker fries just before serving.

4. Season with salt and pepper and serve hot.

2 pounds parsnips
3 tablespoons extra-virgin
  olive oil
Kosher salt and freshly ground
  black pepper, to taste

Breads
AND BRUNCH DISHES

In Jewish cooking, breads are touchstones of

cultural identity. In the Jewish world, you'll find braided challah, bialies (represented here by my bialy loaf), bagels (for which I don't include a recipe because they are easy to buy and not especially home baker–friendly), and rye bread. Sephardic cooks have their pita breads, skillet breads, and focaccia.

I worked for a time with one of New York's great bakers, Amy Scherber of Amy's Breads. What I learned from that woman could fill a book, but I have to restrict it to just one chapter! Here are a few pointers for the home baker.

■ In bread baking, the type of flour used is very important. Unbleached and bread flours have high gluten contents and are best for yeast-based baking. Bleached all-purpose flour has a moderate gluten content, and should be reserved for cakes, cookies, and pastry.

■ Professional bakers, out of necessity, are used to making dough with machines. I use a standing heavy-duty electric mixer to make dough at home (KitchenAid is a familiar brand), which can make easy work out of kneading. One word of advice: If you are new to breadmaking, mix the dough into a mass *with the paddle blade* first, *then* switch to the dough hook. After you become adept at using the mixer and are familiar with the consistency of the dough, you can simply use the dough hook for the entire procedure, from mixing to kneading, if you wish.

■ If you want to make the dough by hand, no problem. Mix all of the liquid ingredients (except the dissolved yeast) in a large bowl, then add the dissolved yeast. Gradually stir in enough of the flour to make a stiff dough. Turn the dough out onto a lightly floured work surface and knead by hand, working in the remaining flour as you go. Continue kneading until the dough is smooth and supple, about 10 minutes.

■ There are a lot of variables to take into account when baking bread, as the flour can retain atmospheric humidity, which makes it absorb more or less water. That is why the amount of flour is always approximated in a bread recipe. You'll know when you've added enough flour by feeling the dough—it should feel like a baby's tush. Bread dough made with a high proportion of whole-grain flour, such as whole wheat or rye, is an exception, and it will always feel slightly tacky no matter how much white flour is added.

■ The longer the rising period (called "fermenting" by professionals), the better the flavor of the bread, so don't rush it. Most recipes (these included) suggest letting the dough rise in a warm place, but the best temperature for fermenting dough is 78°F. Keep this in mind when you choose that "warm spot." We're really talking about "the ambient temperature of the average warm kitchen with a turned-on oven" here, but "warm spot" sounds much less intimidating.

■ Refrigerating the dough not only gives the baker more leeway with the time, it improves the flavor of the bread. Cover the dough airtight and refrigerate for up to twenty-four hours, punching down the dough if it rises too high. Bring the dough to room temperature (this will take a couple of hours in the average kitchen), shape, and let rise again before baking.

So heat up the oven and let's get baking.

Bialy Loaf

MAKES
2 MEDIUM
LOAVES

The bialy is the much-loved cousin to the bagel, but once you're out of Brooklyn, you won't see bialies too often. Usually round, with a fried onion topping in the center, they are always welcome at any party with bagels and lox on the menu. The following recipe combines the flavors of the bialy in a sliceable loaf.

2 cups warm (105° to 115°F.) water

Two ¼-ounce packages (or 5 teaspoons) active dry yeast

1½ tablespoons sugar

1 teaspoon kosher salt

4½ cups unbleached flour, as needed

Yellow cornmeal, for sprinkling

2 tablespoons vegetable oil

2 cups chopped onions

1. Pour the water into the bowl of a heavy-duty electric mixer and sprinkle in the yeast. Let stand for 3 minutes, then stir to dissolve.

2. Add the sugar and salt. Attach the bowl to the mixer and fit with the paddle blade. On low speed, gradually add enough of the flour to make a dough that cleans the sides of the bowl. Change to the dough hook. Knead on medium speed until the dough is smooth and supple, about 8 minutes.

3. Lightly oil a large bowl. Gather the dough into a ball. Place in the bowl and turn to coat on all sides with the oil. Cover tightly with plastic wrap and let stand in a warm place until doubled in volume, about 1½ hours.

4. Lightly dust two large baking sheets with cornmeal. Turn out the dough onto a lightly floured surface and knead briefly to expel the air. Cut into 2 equal pieces. Pat out 1 piece of dough into an 8×6-inch rectangle. Roll up lengthwise into a tight cylinder, and pinch the seams closed. Fit into an 8×4-inch loaf pan. Repeat with the remaining dough. Cover each pan loosely with plastic wrap and let stand at room temperature until the loaves barely rise above the tops of the pans, about 45 minutes.

5. Meanwhile, heat the oil in a large skillet over medium heat. Add the onions and cook, stirring often, just until softened, about 4 minutes. Do not let the onions turn golden—they will cook further in the oven. Cool completely.

6. Position a rack in the center of the oven and preheat the oven to 400°F. Using your fingertips, make ¼-inch-deep indentations in the tops of the loaves. Fill the indentations with the onions. Bake the loaves until golden brown and the bottoms sound hollow when rapped with your knuckles (remove a loaf from the pan, protecting your hands with kitchen towels), about 25 minutes. Cool in the pan on a wire rack for at least 30 minutes before slicing.

Brooklyn Breadsticks

MAKES ABOUT 16 BREAD-STICKS

This recipe is from a show we did on the breads of Brooklyn. If one had to choose only two of the many ethnic groups that have made their mark on that great borough, plenty of votes would come in for the Italians and the Jews. While we don't think of breadsticks as particularly Jewish, it should be remembered that there are plenty of Jews in Rome, as a visit to one of the fine restaurants in that city's Jewish Quarter will illustrate.

$1/4$ cup warm (105° to 115°F.) water
1 tablespoon malt syrup (available at bakery suppliers and natural food stores) or unsulfured molasses
$1^3/4$ teaspoons active dry yeast
1 cup cool water
2 tablespoons extra-virgin olive oil, plus more for brushing
$1^1/2$ teaspoons kosher salt
4 cups unbleached flour, as needed
Yellow cornmeal, for sprinkling
2 tablespoons poppy seeds

1. Mix the warm water and malt syrup in the bowl of a heavy-duty electric mixer. Sprinkle in the yeast and let stand until the mixture looks foamy, about 5 minutes.

2. Add the cool water, 2 tablespoons of oil, and salt. Attach the bowl to the mixer and fit with the paddle blade. Mix on low speed to dissolve the salt. Gradually add enough flour to make a soft dough that pulls away from the sides of the bowl. Change to the dough hook and knead on medium speed until the dough is smooth and supple (if the dough climbs up the hook, just scrape it down), about 5 minutes. Transfer the dough to a lightly floured surface and form into a ball. It should be quite soft and almost sticky.

3. Lightly oil a medium bowl. Place the dough in the bowl and turn to coat on all sides with the oil. Cover tightly with plastic wrap. Let stand in a warm place until doubled in volume, about $1^1/4$ hours.

4. Position racks in the top third and center of the oven and preheat the oven to 450°F. Sprinkle two 18×12-inch baking sheets with cornmeal.

5. Punch down the dough. Sprinkle a work surface with cornmeal. Pat and stretch out the dough into a 12×9-inch rectangle. Brush the top of the dough with oil and sprinkle with the poppy seeds. Using a pizza wheel or sharp knife, cut the dough lengthwise into $1/2$-inch strips. Place the strips about $1/2$ inch apart on the baking sheets. Try to keep the seeds facing up, but don't be concerned if the breadsticks twist a little.

6. Bake immediately, switching the position of the racks from top to bottom after 6 minutes, until the breadsticks are golden brown, 8 to 10 minutes. Cool completely.

Herb and Onion Focaccia

**MAKES
1 LARGE
FOCACCIA**

Most focaccias have toppings, but I prefer my flavorings right in the bread. Try this exceptional version of the famous Italian flatbread, and I bet you'll agree.

1. Heat 1 tablespoon of the oil in a large skillet over medium heat. Add the onion and cook, stirring often, until translucent, about 3 minutes. Add the garlic and cook until the mixture is very fragrant, about 2 minutes. Cool completely. Stir in the herbs.

2. Mix the warm water and sugar in the bowl of a heavy-duty electric mixer. Sprinkle in the yeast and let stand for 3 minutes.

3. Add the cool water, the cooked onion mixture, ¼ cup of the oil, and 2 teaspoons of the salt. Attach the bowl to the mixer and fit with the paddle blade. Mix on low speed to dissolve the yeast. Gradually add enough of the flour to make a soft dough that just cleans the sides of the bowl. Change to the dough hook. Knead on medium-low speed until the dough is smooth and supple, about 8 minutes.

¼ cup plus 3 tablespoons extra-virgin olive oil
½ cup chopped onion
2 tablespoons finely chopped garlic
¼ cup chopped fresh herbs, such as rosemary, thyme, basil, oregano, and marjoram
¼ cup warm (105° to 115°F.) water
2 tablespoons sugar
One ¼-ounce package (or 2½ teaspoons) active dry yeast
1 cup cool water
2½ teaspoons kosher salt, divided
4 cups unbleached flour

4. Lightly oil a large bowl. Gather the dough into a ball. Place in the bowl and turn to coat on all sides with the oil. Cover tightly with plastic wrap. Let stand in a warm place until the dough has doubled in volume, about 1 hour.

5. Lightly oil a 17 × 12 × 1-inch jelly roll pan. Punch the dough down. Stretch and pat the dough to fit the pan. (If the dough retracts, cover loosely with plastic wrap, let stand for 5 minutes and try again.) Cover again, and let stand until the dough looks puffy, about 30 minutes.

6. Position a rack in the center of the oven and preheat the oven to 450°F. Using your fingers, make indentations all over the dough. Drizzle with the remaining 2 tablespoons oil and the remaining ½ teaspoon salt.

7. Bake for 10 minutes. Reduce the heat to 400°F., and bake until golden brown (lift up the focaccia and check the underside), 10 to 15 minutes. Slip the focaccia out of the pan onto a large cake rack and cool until warm. Serve warm or cool to room temperature.

heritage recipe

Honey Challah

Challah just may well be the ultimate Jewish food. It is much more than just something to eat; it has plenty of religious and cultural significance, too. Challah is the bread of Shabbat—the eggs and oil make it rich for the Sabbath and promote a long shelf life. (This recipe makes 2 loaves, so one can be frozen for next week's meal if it doesn't get eaten first.) For the high holy days of Rosh Hashanah and Yom Kippur, challahs are baked in round shapes to represent the continuity of life and the Jewish people. Bakers who are orthodox remove a piece of the dough and burn it, representing the ancient sacrificial rituals. So when is bread not just bread? When it is challah!

1 cup warm (105° to 115°F.)
   water
1/2 cup plus 1 tablespoon sugar
One 1/4-ounce package (or
   2 1/2 teaspoons) active dry
   yeast
1 1/4 cups cool water
1/2 cup honey
1/3 cup vegetable oil
2 large eggs, beaten
1 tablespoon kosher salt
1/2 teaspoon vanilla extract
6 1/2 cups bread flour, as needed
Yellow cornmeal, for the pans
1 large egg beaten with
   1 tablespoon water, for
   glaze
2 teaspoons sesame or poppy
   seeds (optional)

1. Mix the warm water and 1 tablespoon of the sugar in the bowl of a heavy-duty electric mixer. Sprinkle in the yeast and let stand until the mixture looks foamy, about 5 minutes.

2. Add the cool water, remaining 1/2 cup sugar, honey, oil, eggs, salt, and vanilla. Attach the bowl to the mixer, fit with the paddle blade, and mix on low speed. Gradually add enough of the flour to make a dough that pulls away from the sides of the bowl (the dough should feel somewhat tacky, so don't add too much flour). Change to the dough hook. Knead until the dough is smooth and supple, about 8 minutes.

3. Lightly oil a large bowl. Gather the dough into a ball, place in the bowl, and turn to coat on all sides with the oil. Cover tightly with plastic wrap. Let stand in a warm place until doubled in volume, about 1 1/2 hours.

4. Turn out the dough onto an unfloured work surface. Knead briefly to expel the air. Cut the dough into 6 equal portions. Working with one piece of dough at a time, roll the dough back and forth on the work surface, pressing down on the dough at the same time, slowly moving your hands apart to stretch the dough into a 15-inch-long rope. As the ropes are formed, place on an unfloured surface and cover loosely with plastic wrap. (Some challahs are created with four to six ropes. If you have excellent braiding skills, make as many ropes as you wish.)

5. Line up three ropes next to each other and pinch the ends together. Braid from the pinched ends to the other end. Repeat with the remaining three ropes of dough.

6. Sprinkle two large baking sheets with cornmeal. Place one loaf on each sheet. Cover loosely with plastic wrap and let stand until almost doubled in volume, about 1 hour.

7. Position racks in the bottom third and center of the oven and preheat the oven to 350°F. Brush the top of each loaf with some of the egg glaze, then sprinkle with the seeds, if using. Bake, switching the position of the sheets from top to bottom halfway through baking, until the loaves are golden brown and sound hollow when tapped on the bottom with your knuckles, about 35 minutes. Cool at least 30 minutes on wire racks before slicing.

heritage recipe

New York Rye Bread

Here's an authentic rye bread that will turn your typical pastrami sandwich into a masterpiece. When mixing the dough, remember that rye makes for a sticky dough, so don't try to compensate by using too much wheat flour.

SPONGE
1 cup warm (105° to 115°F.)
   water
1 tablespoon honey
Two $1/4$-ounce packages (or
   5 teaspoons) active dry yeast
1 cup rye flour

$3/4$ cup plus 2 tablespoons cool
   water
$1/2$ cup rye flour
3 tablespoons vegetable oil
3 tablespoons sugar
$2 1/4$ teaspoons kosher salt
$3 1/2$ cups bread flour, as needed
5 teaspoons caraway seeds
Yellow cornmeal, for the
   baking sheet
1 large egg beaten with
   1 tablespoon water,
   for glaze

1. Mix the warm water and honey in the bowl of a heavy-duty electric mixer. Sprinkle in the yeast and let stand until foamy, about 5 minutes. Stir in 1 cup rye flour to make a batter. Cover with plastic wrap and let stand until bubbly, about 20 minutes.

2. Add the cool water, $1/2$ cup rye flour, oil, sugar, and salt. Attach the bowl to the mixer and fit with the paddle blade. Mix on low speed until combined. Gradually add enough of the bread flour to make a dough that pulls away from the sides of the bowl. Rye dough is supposed to feel tacky; do not add too much flour. Change to the dough hook and knead on medium speed until the dough is smooth and supple, about 8 minutes. During the last minute, add 4 teaspoons of the caraway seeds.

3. Remove the bowl and hook from the mixer. Cover the bowl tightly with plastic wrap. Let the dough stand in a warm place until doubled in volume, about 1 hour.

4. Turn out the dough onto a lightly floured work surface and knead briefly to expel the air. To shape into a large round loaf, place your hands on opposite sides of the dough. Bring both hands at the same time under the dough, stretching and tucking the dough under itself. Turn the dough a quarter turn, and repeat the stretching and tucking. Repeat until the dough is shaped into a tight ball.

5. Sprinkle a baking sheet with cornmeal. Place the loaf on the baking sheet. Cover loosely with plastic wrap. Let stand in a warm place until doubled in volume.

6. Position a rack in the center of the oven and preheat the oven to 400°F. Using a serrated knife, slash 3 diagonal shallow slits across the top of the loaf. Brush lightly with the egg glaze and sprinkle with the remaining 1 teaspoon caraway seeds.

7. Bake until golden brown and the loaf sounds hollow when rapped on the bottom with your knuckles, 35 to 40 minutes. Cool for at least 30 minutes on a wire rack before slicing.

Yemenite Skillet Breads

I think of these breads as ones that even a nonbaker can make. There is no intimidating yeast, and you don't even have to turn on the oven. These are aromatic with the herb blend zahtar, and they have a satisfying chewy texture. Give them a try!

3 cups whole-wheat flour
1/2 cup all-purpose flour
1 teaspoon baking powder
1 teaspoon zahtar spice blend
   (see Note), plus more for
   sprinkling
1 teaspoon sugar
1 teaspoon kosher salt
1 1/4 cups water, or more as
   needed
1 large egg
2 tablespoons extra-virgin
   olive oil

1/4 cup extra-virgin olive oil, as
   needed, for cooking

1. Mix the whole-wheat and all-purpose flours, baking powder, zahtar, sugar, and salt in the bowl of a heavy-duty electric mixer. Attach the bowl to the mixer and fit with the paddle blade. Whisk the 1 1/4 cups water, egg, and the 2 tablespoons oil in a medium bowl until blended. With the mixer on low speed, add the liquids to the flour to create a slightly firm dough that collects on the paddle and cleans the sides of the bowl. If necessary, add tablespoons of water to the dough to correct the consistency. Change to the dough hook and knead on medium-low speed until the dough is smooth and supple, about 7 minutes.

2. Drizzle a little oil into a zip-tight plastic bag. Form the dough into a flat circle, place in the bag, and turn to coat the disk with oil. Let stand at room temperature for at least 1 and up to 2 hours. The dough will not rise, but it needs to relax before making the bread.

3. Divide the dough into 8 balls. On an unfloured surface, flatten the balls and roll into 5 1/2-inch rounds. Stack the rounds, separating them with pieces of wax paper or parchment paper.

4. Add 1 tablespoon oil to a heavy-bottomed medium skillet, and tilt the skillet so the bottom is lightly coated with oil. Heat over medium heat. Place a round of dough in the skillet and cook until golden brown on the underside, about 2 minutes. Turn and cook until the other side is splotched with dark brown spots, about 2 minutes more. Adjust the heat as needed so the bread cooks through without burning. Transfer to paper towels to drain. Repeat with the remaining dough, adding more oil as needed. Sprinkle the breads with additional zahtar and serve warm.

NOTE: Zahtar, also spelled zatar, is a popular blend of herbs and spices used in Middle Eastern cooking. It usually contains tangy ground sumac berries mixed with an aromatic dried herb or two (thyme, oregano, and/or marjoram), nutty sesame seeds, and salt. The Moroccan wild herb za'atar, a cross between oregano, marjoram, and thyme, is not the same thing. There are all kinds of misspellings and misunderstandings concerning the two, so keep in mind that you want the spice blend, and not the herb. Zahtar is available by mail order (see Sources, page 250), or use equal amounts of dried marjoram and sesame seeds.

Syrian Pita

MAKES
8
PITAS

Nothing is more representative of Middle Eastern cuisine than classic pita bread. Whether you're dipping it into a bowl of hummus, or filling the pocket with sandwich goodies, pita has found legions of new fans in America.

1/4 cup warm (105° to 115°F.) water, divided
1 1/2 teaspoons honey
1 1/4 teaspoons active dry yeast
1 cup cool water
1 1/2 teaspoons extra-virgin olive oil
1 teaspoon kosher salt
3 cups unbleached flour, as needed

1. Mix the warm water and the honey in the bowl of a heavy-duty electric mixer. Sprinkle in the yeast and let stand for 3 minutes.

2. Add the cool water, oil, and salt. Attach the bowl to the mixer and fit with the paddle blade. On low speed, mix to dissolve the yeast. Gradually add enough of the flour to make a slightly sticky dough that barely cleans the sides of the bowl. Change to the dough hook. Knead on medium speed until the dough is soft, smooth, and supple, about 8 minutes.

3. Lightly oil a large bowl. Gather the dough into a ball. Place in the bowl and turn to coat on all sides with the oil. Cover tightly with plastic wrap. Let stand in a warm place until doubled in volume, about 1 1/4 hours.

4. Turn out the dough onto a lightly floured work surface. Knead by hand until the dough is smooth and elastic, about 2 minutes. Cut the dough into 8 equal portions. Roll each piece of dough into a ball, and place the balls, 1 inch apart, on a lightly floured baking sheet or work surface. Cover the balls loosely with plastic wrap and let stand for 15 minutes to relax the gluten in the dough (this makes them easier to roll out).

5. On a lightly floured work surface, flatten 1 ball of dough with your hand into a disk. Sprinkle the top of the dough with flour, then roll out into a 5- to 6-inch-wide round. Transfer to a large baking sheet. Repeat with the remaining balls of dough, placing them at least 2 inches apart on the baking sheets. Cover the baking sheets loosely with plastic wrap. Let stand until the rounds look slightly puffy, about 30 minutes.

6. Position a rack in the center of the oven and preheat the oven thoroughly to 500°F. (allow at least 20 minutes).

7. One sheet at a time, bake until the pitas are puffed and golden brown, about 5 minutes. Do not open the oven for the first 4 minutes. Transfer the pitas to a wire rack to cool.

Matzo Frittata

MAKES
6 TO 8
SERVINGS

After a few days of matzo brei or matzo with a schmear of cream cheese during Passover, I begin to long for other ways to serve matzo at breakfast. My kids and I came up with this great recipe that we now eat nearly every day of Passover, and year-round, too.

1. Position a rack in the center of the oven and preheat the oven to 350°F. Heat the oil over medium heat in a 10-inch nonstick ovenproof skillet. Add the salami and cook, stirring occasionally, until beginning to crisp, about 3 minutes. Add the onion and red and green bell peppers. Cook, stirring occasionally, until the onion is translucent, about 5 minutes.

2. Meanwhile, soak the matzos in a large bowl of cold water just until softened and pliable, about 1 minute. Drain the matzos well and tear into large pieces. Whisk the eggs, salt, and pepper in a large bowl and stir in the matzos.

3. When the onions are translucent, pour in the egg mixture and stir to combine. Cook until the edges of the frittata look set, about 3 minutes. Transfer to the oven and cook until the frittata is cooked through, about 10 minutes.

4. Invert the frittata onto a large platter. Sprinkle with the herbs. Cut into wedges and serve, passing the honey and red pepper sauce for drizzling onto each serving.

PAREVE VARIATION
Omit the salami.

2 tablespoons extra-virgin olive oil
2 ounces ($1/4$-inch-thick) sliced beef salami, cut into $1/4$-inch strips
1 small onion, chopped
$1/2$ cup ($1/2$-inch dice) chopped red bell pepper
$1/2$ cup ($1 1/2$-inch dice) chopped green bell pepper
4 matzos
7 large eggs
$1/2$ teaspoon salt
$1/4$ teaspoon freshly ground black pepper
1 teaspoon chopped fresh rosemary, for garnish
1 teaspoon chopped fresh basil, for garnish
Honey, for serving
Hot red pepper sauce, for serving

Mediterranean Pizza with Hummus, Goat Cheese, and Cherry Peppers

It's lots of fun to make homemade pizza. You can come up with your own ideas for topping the raw dough rounds before they go into the oven (sautéed onions and beef salami come to mind), but I like to ensure that my pizza is crisp by adding toppings after baking. A thick schmear of red pepper hummus with zesty toppings makes an unusual pizza that is unusually tasty, too.

MAKES 4 INDIVIDUAL PIZZAS

PIZZA DOUGH

1/4 cup warm (105° to 115°F.) water
3 teaspoons honey
One 1/4-ounce package (or 2 1/2 teaspoons) active dry yeast
3/4 cup cool water
2 tablespoons extra-virgin olive oil, plus more for brushing
3 cups unbleached flour, as needed
1 teaspoon kosher salt
Yellow cornmeal, for sprinkling

1 1/3 cups Roasted Red Pepper Hummus (page 32)
3 pickled cherry peppers, hot or sweet, seeded and cut into thin strips
1/2 cup pitted and coarsely chopped black Mediterranean olives
3 ounces goat cheese, crumbled
3 tablespoons chopped fresh basil
Extra-virgin olive oil, for drizzling

1. To make the dough, mix the warm water and 1 teaspoon of the honey in a large glass measuring cup. Sprinkle in the yeast and let stand until foamy, about 5 minutes. Stir in the cool water, 2 tablespoons oil, and remaining 2 teaspoons honey.

2. Place the flour and salt in a food processor and pulse to combine. With the machine running, pour in the liquid through the feed tube. Process until the dough forms a ball. If the dough seems too dry to come together, add a tablespoon of water and process. If too moist and sticky, add a tablespoon of flour and process. After the dough forms a ball, process for 15 seconds to knead the dough.

3. Oil a medium bowl. Place the dough in the bowl and turn to coat on all sides with the oil. Cover tightly with plastic wrap. Let stand in a warm place until the dough doubles in volume, about 1 hour. Turn out the dough onto a lightly floured work surface and knead briefly to expel the air in the dough. Cut into 4 equal portions and form into balls. (The dough can be refrigerated for up to 1 day, each ball wrapped in plastic wrap. Or freeze for up to 1 month, overwrapping each ball of dough with aluminum foil. If frozen, defrost in the refrigerator overnight.)

4. Position a rack in the bottom third of the oven. Place a baking stone or large baking sheet on the rack and preheat the oven to 450°F. (Allow at least 20 minutes for the oven to preheat.)

5. One at a time, roll out the dough balls on an unfloured surface into a 10-inch round, sprinkling the top of the dough with a little flour so it doesn't stick to the rolling pin. (If the dough resists rolling, cover with plastic wrap, let stand and relax for a few minutes, then try again.) Cover the rounds with plastic wrap.

6. Sprinkle a baker's peel or rimless baking sheet with cornmeal, and place a round on the peel. Brush the round with olive oil and pierce the round a few times with a fork. With a sharp jerk, slide the round onto the baking stone. Close the oven door immediately and repeat with a second round. (You should be able to fit 2 pizzas on the baking stone. If not, place the dough rounds on a baking sheet, cover with plastic wrap, and refrigerate while baking the others.) Bake until the pizzas are golden brown, about 8 minutes. Use the baker's peel to remove the pizzas from the oven and repeat with the remaining rounds.

7. Spread each pizza with about $1/3$ cup of the hummus. Top each with the cherry peppers, olives, goat cheese, and basil, then drizzle with oil. Cut into wedges and serve immediately.

PAREVE VARIATION
Omit the goat cheese.

Potato and Caramelized Apple Blintzes

MAKES
4 TO 6
SERVINGS

Old-fashioned blintz recipes abound, but I wanted a blintz that spoke to contemporary diners. The familiar potato filling gets a lift from caramelized apples and a hint of rosemary to create a dish everyone at the table (even the traditionalists) will love.

CRÊPES

3/4 cup plus 2 tablespoons milk, plus more as needed

1/2 cup water

2 large eggs

5 tablespoons unsalted butter, melted

1 cup plus 2 tablespoons all-purpose flour

Pinch of kosher salt

3 tablespoons vegetable oil, for cooking

FILLING

2 pounds baking potatoes, peeled

1/4 cup sugar

1 tablespoon vegetable oil

1 Golden Delicious apple, peeled, cored, and cut into 1/2-inch dice

2 teaspoons chopped fresh rosemary

Kosher salt and freshly ground black pepper to taste

Ginger Applesauce (page 153)

Sour cream, at room temperature, for serving

1. To make the crêpes, whisk the milk, water, eggs, and 2 tablespoons of the melted butter in a medium bowl. Whisk in the flour and salt. Mix the remaining 3 tablespoons butter with the oil in a small bowl and set aside.

2. Brush a 7 1/2- to 8-inch-diameter (measured across the bottom) nonstick skillet with the butter-oil mixture, and heat over medium-high heat until the skillet is hot, about 1 1/2 minutes. Pour a scant 1/4 cup of the batter into the bottom of the skillet, and immediately tilt and swirl the skillet so the batter coats the bottom in a thin layer. Fill in any holes with dribbles of batter from the measuring cup. Cook until the edges look dry and the top is set, about 1 minute. Using a heatproof spatula, lift and turn the crêpe. Cook until the other side is splotched with golden-brown spots, about 30 seconds. Transfer to a plate. Repeat with the remaining batter, thinning as necessary with teaspoons of milk, to keep the consistency similar to heavy cream (the batter will thicken as it stands). Separate the crêpes as you stack them with pieces of wax paper or parchment paper. (The crêpes can be prepared 1 day ahead, covered with plastic wrap, and refrigerated.) Reserve the remaining butter-oil mixture.

3. To make the filling, place the potatoes in a medium saucepan and add enough lightly salted cold water to cover. Bring to a boil over high heat. Cook, partially covered, until tender, about 30 minutes. Drain well and mash in a large bowl.

4. Stirring constantly, cook the sugar and oil in a medium nonstick skillet over medium heat until the sugar is melted and caramelized, about 3 minutes. Add the apple and cook, stirring often, until it begins to soften, about $1^1/2$ minutes. Stir in the rosemary. Mix the apple and its juices into the mashed potatoes. Season with salt and pepper and cool completely.

5. To assemble the blintzes, place a crêpe, spotted side up, on the work surface. Spread about $^1/4$ cup of the filling in a strip about 1 inch from the bottom and sides of the crêpe. Fold the bottom edge up to cover the filling. Fold in the right side about 1 inch, repeat with the left side, and roll up. Place, seam side down, on a baking sheet. Repeat with the remaining crêpes and filling. Cover with plastic wrap and refrigerate until ready to serve, up to 3 hours. (The blintzes can be individually wrapped in plastic wrap and frozen for up to 2 months. Do not thaw before using.)

6. To cook the blintzes, preheat the oven to 200°F. Heat about 2 tablespoons of the remaining butter-oil mixture in a large skillet over medium heat until very hot. Add 6 blintzes and reduce the heat to medium-low. Cook, adjusting the heat as necessary so the blintzes slowly cook through without burning, until the blintzes are golden brown, about 5 minutes. (To cook frozen blintzes, reduce the heat to low. Cover and cook for 8 minutes, turning occasionally. Uncover and cook, turning once, until the blintzes are crisped and golden brown, about 4 minutes more.) Transfer the cooked blintzes to a baking sheet and place them in the oven to keep warm. Repeat with the remaining blintzes and butter-oil mixture. Serve hot, with the applesauce and sour cream passed on the side.

PAREVE VARIATION

Substitute rice milk or soy milk and pareve margarine for the milk and butter. Omit the sour cream.

Cheese Blintzes with Berry Compote

MAKES
4 TO 6
SERVINGS

Half of this recipe is a heritage recipe—the cheese blintzes are a fine example of how good they can be. But instead of the usual cherry topping, I've flavored fresh berries with a little balsamic vinegar, mint, and black pepper to bring the garnish into the twenty-first century.

BERRY COMPOTE

1 pint strawberries, hulled and quartered

1 pint blueberries

1/4 cup sugar

2 tablespoons balsamic vinegar

1 tablespoon chopped fresh mint

1/2 teaspoon coarsely cracked black pepper (crack in a mortar and pestle or under a heavy pot)

Pinch of salt

CRÊPES

3/4 cup plus 2 tablespoons milk, plus more as needed

1/2 cup water

2 large eggs

5 tablespoons unsalted butter, melted

1 cup plus 2 tablespoons all-purpose flour

Pinch of kosher salt

3 tablespoons vegetable oil, for cooking

1. To make the compote, mix the strawberries, blueberries, sugar, vinegar, mint, pepper, and salt in a medium bowl. Let stand at room temperature until the fruit gives off some juices, at least 15 minutes and up to 2 hours.

2. To make the crêpes, whisk the milk, water, eggs, and 2 tablespoons of the melted butter in a medium bowl. Whisk in the flour and salt. Mix the remaining 3 tablespoons butter with the oil in a small bowl and set aside.

3. Brush a 7 1/2- to 8-inch-diameter (measured across the bottom) nonstick skillet with the butter-oil mixture, and heat over medium-high heat until the skillet is hot, about 1 1/2 minutes. Pour a scant 1/4 cup of the batter into the bottom of the skillet and immediately tilt and swirl the skillet so the batter coats the bottom in a thin layer. Fill in any holes with dribbles of batter from the measuring cup. Cook until the edges look dry and the top is set, about 1 minute. Using a heatproof spatula, lift and turn the crêpe. Cook until the other side is splotched with golden-brown spots, about 30 seconds. Transfer to a plate. Repeat with the remaining batter, thinning as necessary with teaspoons of milk, to keep the consistency similar to heavy cream (the batter will thicken as it stands). Separate the crêpes as you stack them with pieces of wax paper. (The crêpes can be prepared 1 day ahead, covered with plastic wrap, and refrigerated.) Reserve the remaining butter-oil mixture.

4. To make the filling, drain the cottage cheese in a sieve for 5 minutes to remove any excess moisture. Mix the cottage cheese, egg, sugar, lemon juice and zest, and salt until combined.

5. To assemble the blintzes, place a crêpe, spotted side up, on the work surface. Spread about 1/4 cup of the filling in a strip about 1 inch from the bottom and sides of the crêpe. Fold the bottom edge up to cover the filling. Fold in the right side about 1 inch, repeat with the left side, and roll up. Place, seam side down, on a baking sheet. Repeat with the remaining crêpes and filling. Cover with plastic wrap and refrigerate until ready to serve, up to 3 hours. (The blintzes can be individually wrapped in plastic wrap and frozen for up to 2 months. Do not thaw before using.)

6. To cook the blintzes, preheat the oven to 200°F. Heat about 2 tablespoons of the remaining butter-oil mixture in a large skillet over medium heat until very hot. Add 6 blintzes and reduce the heat to medium-low. Cook, adjusting the heat as necessary so the blintzes slowly cook through without burning, until the blintzes are golden brown, about 5 minutes. (To cook frozen blintzes, reduce the heat to low. Cover and cook for 8 minutes, turning occasionally. Uncover and cook, turning once, until the blintzes are crisped and golden brown, about 4 minutes more.) Transfer the cooked blintzes to a baking sheet and place them in the oven to keep warm. Repeat with the remaining blintzes and butter-oil mixture.

7. Transfer the blintzes to a platter and sift confectioners' sugar on top. Serve hot, with the compote passed on the side.

FILLING

1 pound small-curd cottage cheese
1 large egg, beaten
2 tablespoons sugar
1 tablespoon fresh lemon juice
Grated zest of 1 lemon
Pinch of kosher salt

Confectioners' sugar, for serving

Cheese Blintz Casserole

This "you can make it in your sleep" recipe has been in my family for years, and we make it whenever we want the yummy (not a word I use often, but it is the right one) flavor of blintzes without the effort of making the crêpes. It features a light cheese filling sandwiched between cakelike layers. Serve with sliced berries and bananas, if you wish.

FILLING

1 pound small-curd cottage
   cheese
1 pound farmer's cheese
2 large eggs, beaten
1/4 cup sugar
2 tablespoons fresh lemon juice

BATTER

1 cup all-purpose flour
1/2 cup sugar
1 tablespoon baking powder
Pinch of kosher salt
1 cup (2 sticks) unsalted butter,
   melted and cooled slightly
1/4 cup milk
2 large eggs

1/4 cup sugar mixed with
   1 1/4 teaspoons ground
   cinnamon, for serving

1. Position a rack in the center of the oven and preheat the oven to 350°F. Lightly butter an 8 × 11 1/2-inch baking dish.

2. To make the filling, whisk the cottage cheese, farmer's cheese, eggs, sugar, and lemon juice in a medium bowl.

3. To make the batter, stir the flour, sugar, baking powder, and salt in a medium bowl to combine. Add the butter and milk, and then the eggs, and whisk until the batter is smooth. Using a large rubber spatula, spread half of the batter in the baking dish. Gently spread all of the cheese filling on the batter. Spread the remaining batter on top of the filling.

4. Bake until the top is golden brown and the casserole is pulling away from the sides of the dish, about 45 minutes.

5. Remove from the oven, sprinkle with 1 tablespoon of the cinnamon sugar, and let stand for 5 minutes. Serve hot, with the remaining cinnamon sugar passed on the side.

Mascarpone and Banana Stuffed French Toast

MAKES
6
SERVINGS

An indulgent, decadent, and downright sinful brunch dish. You will need thick slices cut by hand from a whole challah. To get 6 center slices of equal size, you may want to buy 2 challahs, and turn the ends into Challah Panzanella Salad (page 69).

1. To make the filling, heat the butter and sugar in a large skillet over medium heat, stirring occasionally to melt the sugar, until caramelized, about 3 minutes. Add the banana slices and mix to coat. Transfer to a bowl and allow to cool completely. Stir in the mascarpone.

2. Using a sharp knife, cut a deep pocket about 2 inches wide into one side of each challah slice, being sure not to cut through to the other side of the bread. Using a spoon, stuff equal portions of the filling into each pocket.

3. Whisk the rum, vanilla, and cinnamon in a large bowl until well combined, then whisk in the milk and eggs. Spread the almonds on a baking sheet. In batches, soak the challah slices in the egg mixture, turning once, for about 2 minutes. Place the slices on the baking sheet to coat one side with the almonds.

4. Position a rack in the center of the oven and preheat the oven to 350°F. Heat the oil in a large skillet over medium heat. In batches, add the challah and cook, turning once, until each side is golden, about 2 minutes. Transfer the challah, almond side up, to another clean baking sheet. Bake until golden brown, 10 to 12 minutes.

5. Sift confectioners' sugar over the almond-coated side of the French toast. Serve immediately, with the maple syrup and fresh fruit passed on the side.

2 tablespoons unsalted butter
2 tablespoons sugar
2 ripe bananas, cut into $1/2$-inch rounds
$1/2$ cup mascarpone cheese

Six 2-inch-thick slices challah bread (from 1 large or 2 medium loaves)
1 tablespoon dark rum, orange liqueur, or fruit juice
1 tablespoon vanilla extract
2 teaspoons ground cinnamon
2 cups milk
6 large eggs

1 cup sliced natural or blanched almonds
3 tablespoons vegetable oil
Confectioners' sugar, for sprinkling
Maple syrup and fresh fruit, for serving

Desserts

Desserts present a challenge to some kosher
cooks, who find the prospect of making desserts without butter and
cream or leavenings like baking powder or baking soda daunting. In
the first case, there are acceptable substitutes for dairy products, and if
you serve a dairy meal obviously no substitutes are necessary. As for
leavenings, they are only a concern at Passover. In this chapter you
will find desserts to fit every menu, whether dairy, meat, or Passover
perfect.

In many of these recipes you will note a dairy (or pareve) variation,
but it is not a good idea to automatically substitute margarine for butter in desserts. It's not just a matter of flavor; margarine has a totally
different texture than butter. Cookies that should be crisp turn out soft,
pastry doughs crumbly, and most cakes greasy. If you must substitute
margarine, don't expect the results to be the same as if you had used
butter. When I do suggest a margarine-for-butter substitution, it is in
a recipe for which I know that the change will be successful.

Another common substitute is nondairy whipped topping for
whipped cream. I much prefer the taste of freshly whipped cream to
nondairy topping, but there are many ways to make improvements. For
example, my Amaretto-Coconut Semifreddo on page 239 uses nondairy
topping for bulk, not flavor. The mixture is pumped up with additions
of Amaretto, almonds, and coconut, plus an enrichment of egg yolks,
and no one has ever commented that it was anything less than fantas-
tic. Anytime you need to make a cream-based dessert pareve, simply

substitute an equal amount of nondairy whipped topping for the *whipped* cream. Don't know how much whipped topping you'll need? Heavy cream doubles in volume when whipped, so for ¹/₂ cup heavy cream substitute 1 cup whipped topping.

The mood of the Passover meal is festive. We eat unleavened bread to commemorate the hurried exodus of the Hebrews from Egypt, an escape so rushed that the bread didn't have time to rise. I actually love Passover desserts because they give me the chance to come up with new ways to celebrate my heritage. (Check out the Matzo Napoleon with White Chocolate Mousse on page 234 to see what I mean.) Many of these desserts depend on whipped eggs for their leavening. Follow the recipe carefully to be sure you reach the proper fluffiness—this takes at least three minutes with a heavy-duty mixer, and a minute or two longer with a hand-held mixer. (Yes, it's worth it to have a Passover mixing bowl and attachments!) If the eggs aren't beaten correctly, your dessert will be heavy and sodden instead of light and tender.

Double Chocolate Chip Cookies

Are these the ultimate cookie jar cookies? I think so. They are chocolate through and through. Thanks to Abigael's pastry chef, my friend David Frank, for contributing this recipe.

1. Sift the flour and baking soda together and set aside. Mix the butter, granulated sugar, and brown sugar in the bowl of a heavy-duty electric mixer fitted with the paddle blade on medium speed until light and fluffy, about 3 minutes. Beat in the egg and vanilla. Scrape down the sides of the bowl. On low speed, beat in the cocoa, then the milk. Remove the bowl from the machine, and stir in the flour. Work in the chips.

2. On a sheet of wax paper or plastic wrap, shape half of the dough into a 12-inch log, and wrap the dough in the paper. Repeat with the remaining dough. Refrigerate until firm and chilled, at least 2 hours or overnight.

1³/₄ cups all-purpose flour
¹/₄ teaspoon baking soda
1 cup (2 sticks) unsalted butter, at room temperature
1 cup granulated sugar
¹/₂ cup packed light brown sugar
1 large egg, at room temperature (see page 227)
1 teaspoon vanilla extract
¹/₃ cup cocoa powder (not Dutch-processed)
2 tablespoons milk
1 cup (6 ounces) semisweet chocolate chips

3. Position racks in the center and top third of the oven and preheat the oven to 325°F. Line two baking sheets with parchment paper. Using a sharp knife, cut the logs into rounds about ¹/₂ inch thick. Place the rounds about 2 inches apart on the baking sheets.

4. Bake, switching the positions of the sheets from top to bottom and front to back about halfway through baking, until the cookies are barely set around the edges (the centers will look soft), about 8 minutes. Cool the cookies on the sheets for about 3 minutes, then transfer to wire racks and cool completely.

PAREVE VARIATION

Substitute 8 tablespoons (1 stick) pareve margarine and ¹/₂ cup vegetable shortening for the butter and liquid nondairy creamer for the milk.

Passover Banana Cake with Strawberry-Marsala Compote

Don't wait for Passover to enjoy this light-textured banana cake. The fruit compote is gilding the lily, because the cake is just fine by itself. The bananas must be fairly ripe—they shouldn't be black, mind you, just speckled and soft to the touch, with a distinct banana aroma. Be sure to use matzo cake flour (sometimes called cake meal), which is much more finely ground than regular matzo meal.

**MAKES
8 TO 10
SERVINGS**

BANANA CAKE

3/4 cup matzo cake flour (cake meal)

1/4 cup potato starch

1/4 teaspoon kosher salt

7 large eggs, separated, at room temperature (see page 227)

1 cup sugar

1 1/2 cups mashed ripe bananas (about 3 medium bananas)

3/4 cup toasted and coarsely chopped pecans (see page 175)

1. Position a rack in the center of the oven and preheat the oven to 350°F. Grease a 10-inch fluted tube (Bundt) pan with margarine.

2. Make the cake: Combine the matzo flour, potato starch, and salt in a small bowl. Beat the egg yolks with the sugar in a heavy-duty mixer fitted with the paddle attachment on high speed until fluffy and lightened in color, about 3 minutes. When the beater is lifted a few inches above the yolks, the mixture should fall back on itself in a thick ribbon before dissolving back into the mass. (If you use a hand mixer, the yolks may take 4 or 5 minutes to reach the correct texture.) On low speed, add the dry ingredients, then the mashed bananas, and mix just until smooth, scraping down the sides of the bowl as needed.

3. Whip the egg whites in a separate bowl until stiff peaks form. Stir one-fourth of the whites into the batter to lighten it, then fold in the remainder. Fold in the nuts. Gently transfer the batter to the pan (don't deflate the whites) and smooth the top.

4. Bake until a toothpick inserted in the center comes out clean, 45 to 55 minutes. Cool completely in the pan on a wire rack. Unmold the cake onto a serving platter.

5. Make the compote: Combine the strawberries, Marsala, pecans, and sugar in a medium bowl. Cover and let stand at room temperature until the berries give off some juices, at least 30 minutes and up to 2 hours. Just before serving, stir in the sliced bananas.

6. To serve, slice the cake, spooning some of the fruit and its juices over each serving.

1 pint strawberries, hulled and halved

$1/2$ cup Marsala or sweet red wine

$1/2$ cup toasted and coarsely chopped pecans (see page 175)

$1/4$ cup sugar

2 ripe, medium bananas, thinly sliced

Ricotta Cheesecake

MAKES
12 TO 16
SERVINGS

Who says you need cream cheese to make a great cheesecake? I've tried about fifteen cheesecake recipes on my menus over the years, and this is the keeper: The secret? Ricotta cheese and... vanilla pudding in the batter! To avoid a thick, clunky crust, I just press a small amount of graham cracker crumbs into the corners of the pan, and leave it at that.

Cheesecake of any kind is best if allowed to chill for a day before serving, so plan accordingly. Serve this with your favorite berries, if you're in the mood.

Nonstick vegetable oil spray, for the pan
1/2 cup graham cracker crumbs
4 tablespoons (1/2 stick) unsalted butter, melted
3 pounds whole-milk ricotta cheese
2 1/2 cups milk
1 cup sugar
Two 3-ounce packages instant vanilla pudding mix
2 teaspoons vanilla extract
10 large eggs, at room temperature (see page 227)

1. Position a rack in the center of the oven and preheat the oven to 350°F. Spray the inside of a 9 1/2- to 10-inch springform pan with nonstick spray.

2. Mix the crumbs and butter in a small bowl. Press the crumb mixture into the crevice where the bottom meets the sides of the pan. Wrap the outside of the pan with aluminum foil.

3. Mix the ricotta, milk, sugar, pudding mix, and vanilla in the bowl of a heavy-duty electric mixer fitted with the paddle attachment on low speed. Add the eggs one at a time, beating just until combined (overbeating contributes to a cracked cheesecake). Pour into the prepared pan and cover the top with aluminum foil, blousing the foil up to clear the surface of the cheese mixture.

4. Slide the rack halfway out of the oven. Place a deep baking pan on the rack. Place the springform pan in the baking pan. Pour enough hot water into the pan to come 1 inch up the sides of the springform pan. Carefully slide the rack back into the oven and bake the cheesecake for 1 1/2 hours. Remove the foil from the top of the pan and continue baking until the sides are slightly puffed and firm (the center will look slightly unset) and the top is golden brown, about 1 hour.

5. Carefully remove the springform pan from the water and discard the bottom sheet of foil. Cool the cheesecake completely in the pan on a wire rack. Cover with plastic wrap and refrigerate until chilled, at least 6 hours or overnight.

6. Run a sharp knife around the inside of the pan to release the cheesecake from the sides. To serve, remove the sides of the pan. Slice the cheesecake with a sharp knife dipped into hot water. Serve chilled.

SPRINGFORM PANS

Because I love both sweet and savory cheesecakes, a good springform pan is an indispensable tool in my kitchen. Purchase a well-made brand with a strong clip, because once the clip loosens, you will have batter oozing out of the pan—not good! If your pan is nonstick, remember that the dark coating will absorb the oven's heat and make the food cook more quickly. To prevent burning, reduce the oven temperature by 25°F.

In some recipes, the cheesecake is baked in a water bath, a procedure that increases moisture in the oven and promotes a moist cake. Under these circumstances, even the tightest springform pan isn't waterproof, so it is wise to enclose the underside of the pan in a protective way of aluminum foil.

Apple Cobbler
with Almond-Streusel Topping

There's only one way to make this incredible apple cobbler—in a big pan. Everyone is going to love it so much that leftovers will disappear, so don't worry about making too much. Vary the filling according to the seasons, and feel free to use pears, apricots, peaches, plums, or other appropriate fruits. A long time ago I learned that guests will consider the topping the best part, so the apples are literally smothered in a thick, almond-scented layer. The topping needs to chill for at least 4 hours, so think ahead.

MAKES 10 TO 12 SERVINGS

TOPPING

2¼ cups granulated sugar

1¼ cups (2½ sticks) pareve margarine, cut into thin slices, at room temperature

1 cup vegetable shortening

4 ounces (½ of an 8-ounce can) almond paste, crumbled

3 cups all-purpose flour

2 teaspoons pure almond extract

FILLING

¼ cup fresh lemon juice

5 pounds Golden Delicious apples (about 10 apples)

⅔ cup packed light brown sugar

⅓ cup granulated sugar

3 tablespoons cornstarch

1 teaspoon ground cinnamon

½ teaspoon freshly grated nutmeg

1½ cups golden raisins, soaked in warm water for 20 minutes and drained

2 tablespoons brandy

1 teaspoon vanilla extract

1. To make the topping: Combine the sugar, margarine, vegetable shortening, and almond paste in a heavy-duty mixer fitted with the paddle attachment. Blend until smooth. Add the flour and almond extract, and mix just until combined. Form into a thick disk and wrap in plastic wrap. Refrigerate until well chilled, about 4 hours or overnight.

2. Position a rack in the center of the oven and preheat the oven to 350°F. Lightly grease a 15 × 10-inch (3-quart) shallow baking dish with margarine.

3. To make the filling: Stir 2 tablespoons of the lemon juice in a large bowl of cold water. Peel and core the apples and cut them into ½-inch-thick wedges, dropping the cut wedges into the lemon water.

4. Mix the brown and granulated sugars, cornstarch, cinnamon, and nutmeg in a large bowl. Drain the apples well, and add to the sugar mixture. Add the raisins and sprinkle with the remaining 2 tablespoons lemon juice. Stir in the brandy and vanilla. Transfer to the baking dish. Using the large holes on a box grater, grate the streusel topping all over the filling, letting it fall randomly. Do not pack or the topping will not be delicately crunchy when baked.

5. Bake until the topping is crisp and golden brown and the apples are tender, about 1 hour. Cool slightly, then serve warm.

DAIRY VARIATION
Substitute unsalted butter for the margarine.

EGG SAFETY

Some of the recipes in this book call for raw eggs, which have been known to carry the harmful bacterium *Salmonella*. There are many ways to cut down the chances for salmonella contamination. Regardless, do not serve raw eggs to young children or the elderly, pregnant women, or anyone with an impaired immune system, because these people are especially susceptible to infections.

Check your eggs before using and discard any that have been broken. Always store eggs in the refrigerator. Keep them in their carton, and not in the egg holders found in most refrigerator doors, because the door is one of the warmest spots in the fridge. If a recipe calls for room-temperature eggs, immerse the uncracked eggs in a bowl of warm water, and let stand for 5 minutes to remove the chill before cracking.

heritage recipe

Honey Cake

What is Rosh Hashanah without honey cake? You have to start off the new year with something sweet; how else can you expect to have a year blessed with sweetness? Another reason for honey cake's popularity is that it can be made well ahead of the feast. In fact, it actually tastes better if it is aged for a day or two. My favorite part is the top, which gets nice and brown in the oven. If only I could shave off the top for myself, and then serve everyone the rest…

MAKES
8
SERVINGS

Pareve margarine, for greasing
   the pan
1³/4 cups all-purpose flour
³/4 teaspoon baking powder
¹/2 teaspoon baking soda
¹/2 teaspoon ground cinnamon
¹/2 teaspoon ground allspice
¹/8 teaspoon freshly grated
   nutmeg
¹/8 teaspoon kosher salt
2 large eggs, at room
   temperature (see page 227)
¹/2 cup granulated sugar
¹/4 cup packed light brown
   sugar
¹/2 cup honey
¹/4 cup strong brewed coffee,
   cooled
2 tablespoons apple cider
1 tablespoon vegetable oil
¹/4 teaspoon grated lemon zest

1. Position a rack in the center of the oven and preheat the oven to 300°F. Grease an 8¹/2 × 4¹/2-inch loaf pan with margarine. Line the bottom and sides of the pan with parchment paper.

2. Whisk the flour, baking powder, baking soda, cinnamon, allspice, nutmeg, and salt in a medium bowl to combine. Beat the eggs, granulated sugar, and brown sugar in a heavy-duty electric mixer fitted with the paddle attachment on high speed until thickened, about 3 minutes. Whisk the honey, coffee, apple cider, oil, and zest in another bowl to combine. On low speed, add the liquid to the eggs, and mix until blended, scraping the sides of the bowl occasionally. Beat in half of the dry ingredients until smooth, scrape down the bowl, then add the remainder, mixing just until combined. Transfer the batter to the pan.

3. Bake until a toothpick inserted in the center of the cake comes out clean, about 1 hour and 15 minutes. Cool completely in the pan on a wire rack.

4. Unmold the cake onto a serving platter and remove the paper. Slice and serve, or wrap in plastic wrap and store at room temperature for up to 5 days.

Tropical Fruit Granita

Fruity, icy granita is a cool finale for a summer dinner. It's also great to have in the freezer for a refreshing afternoon pick-me-up. This version mixes mango and pineapple for a tropical flavor. Add the syrup gradually to allow for variations in the pineapple's sweetness, but remember that the mixture should be quite sweet, as the frozen granita will dull the taste buds and seem less sweet when eaten. Start the granita the day before serving.

1. Place a 13 × 9-inch metal baking pan in the freezer and freeze until very cold.

2. Combine the sugar and water in a small, nonreactive saucepan. Heat over medium heat until it reaches a boil. Boil for 1 minute to create a sugar syrup. Cool completely, then refrigerate until chilled, at least 2 hours.

3. Purée the pineapple with half of the sugar syrup in a food processor or blender until smooth. Add the mango nectar, sparkling wine, and lime juice, and process well. Add enough of the remaining sugar syrup to make a very sweet purée. Pour into the chilled pan and freeze until semisolid, about 2 hours.

4. Remove from the freezer after 1 hour and scrape the semifrozen fruit mixture with a fork to form a slush. Refreeze overnight.

5. Scrape again with the fork and refreeze until ready to serve. (The granita should be entirely made up of ice crystals.) Serve in individual wineglasses garnished with fresh strawberries and mint.

$1/2$ cup sugar
$1/2$ cup water
3 cups peeled, cored, and
    coarsely chopped pineapple
4 cups canned mango nectar
$3/4$ cup semidry sparkling wine,
    such as Moscato d'Asti
2 tablespoons fresh lime juice
Fresh strawberries and mint
    sprigs, for garnish

Almond-Pistachio Macaroons

Macaroons are a favorite cookie, but too often they come from a box. No one will ever mistake these for ones from a factory. The pistachios give them a dramatic green coating that heralds spring. Some ethnic markets carry shelled pistachio nuts, or you can easily shell them yourself. Note that because these are made with Confectioners' sugar, which contains cornstarch, these should not be served for Passover.

Two 8-ounce cans almond
   paste (1³/4 packed cups),
   grated on the large holes of
   a box grater
³/4 cup granulated sugar
1¹/2 cups confectioners' sugar
3 large egg whites, at room
   temperature (see page 227)
1¹/2 teaspoons vanilla extract
Pinch of salt
4 ounces shelled unsalted
   pistachio nuts, finely
   chopped (1 cup)

1. Position racks in the top third and center of the oven and preheat the oven to 325°F. Line two large baking sheets with parchment paper.

2. Combine the almond paste and granulated sugar in the bowl of a heavy-duty electric mixer fitted with the paddle blade. On low speed, mix until the mixture resembles coarse crumbs, about 2 minutes. Gradually add the confectioners' sugar and mix until well combined, about 1 minute. Add the egg whites, vanilla, and salt. Increase the speed to medium and mix just until combined (the dough will be wet and sticky). Mix in a generous ¹/3 cup of the pistachios. Place the remaining pistachios in a small bowl.

3. Using a level tablespoon for each, roll the dough into balls. Dip each ball into the reserved pistachios to coat one side. Arrange the cookies, 1 inch apart on the baking sheets, pistachio sides up, pressing the cookies slightly so they adhere to the paper.

4. Bake until the tops of the macaroons are evenly colored, and the bottoms are smooth and golden brown (use a metal spatula to remove a test cookie from the sheet), 25 to 30 minutes. Cool the macaroons on the sheets. Gently pull the macaroons off the parchment paper. (The macaroons can be stored for up to 5 days in an airtight container at room temperature.)

Lemon Mousse and Blueberry Parfaits

Tart and refreshing, with a creamy richness, lemon mousse is a dessert to be reckoned with. Most recipes include gelatin, an animal product, but I don't, which makes the mousse that much more ethereal. Blueberries and lemons are a classic pairing that is difficult to improve upon. To turn this into a pareve dessert, simply use nondairy whipped topping.

1 cup sugar
2 large eggs, at room
temperature (see page 227)
¹/₃ cup fresh lemon juice
Grated zest of 1 lemon
1 cup heavy cream
1 pint fresh blueberries

1. Whisk the sugar, eggs, lemon juice, and zest well in the insert of a double boiler or a stainless-steel bowl. Place over simmering water (the bottom should not touch the water). Stir constantly with a whisk, scraping down the sides often, until the mixture is as thick as lemon pudding (an instant-read thermometer will read about 180°F.), 3 to 5 minutes.

2. Press a piece of plastic wrap directly on the surface of the lemon curd and pierce a few holes in the plastic with the tip of a knife to allow the steam to escape. Place the bowl in a larger bowl of ice water and let stand until chilled.

3. Whip the cream in a chilled medium bowl until stiff peaks form. (The cream must be quite stiff, but take care not to overwhip or you'll get butter.) Using a rubber spatula, fold the whipped cream into the chilled lemon curd.

4. Spoon the mousse into stemmed glasses. (For a fancier presentation, pipe the mousse from a large pastry bag fitted with a large open star tip.) Cover each mousse with plastic wrap and refrigerate until chilled, at least 2 hours or overnight. (The mousse can be prepared up to 1 day ahead or frozen for up to 1 week. If frozen, defrost overnight in the refrigerator.)

5. Just before serving, top each mousse with berries. Serve chilled.

PAREVE VARIATION
Substitute 2 cups nondairy whipped topping for the heavy cream.

Chocolate Mousse Flowerpots

This is the signature dessert at Abigael's, where it's served in small terra-cotta pots and topped with "dirt" made from cookie crumbs. Dig into the dessert, and you'll find chocolate mousse. Sure, they're cute, but don't let that fool you. The chocolate mousse is deeply, darkly, and intensely chocolatey.

8 ounces semisweet or bittersweet chocolate, finely chopped

3 tablespoons vegetable oil

1 tablespoon cocoa powder

1½ cups heavy cream

1 teaspoon vanilla extract

1 teaspoon dark rum

10 chocolate "sandwich" cookies with vanilla filling, such as Oreos

SPECIAL EQUIPMENT

6 (3-inch) terra-cotta flowerpots, washed in soapy water, rinsed, and air dried

6 stemmed silk flowers

1. Melt the chocolate, oil, and cocoa together in the top part of a double boiler or stainless-steel bowl over hot, not simmering, water. Remove from the heat and let stand until cool but still pourable.

2. Whip the cream, vanilla, and rum in a chilled large bowl with a hand-held electric mixer. Stir a large spoonful of the whipped cream into the chocolate to loosen it, then fold this mixture into the remaining cream until evenly colored. Spoon into the flower-pots, smoothing the tops.

3. With the machine running, drop the cookies through the feed tube of a food processor fitted with the metal blade and process to form crumbs. Apply a thick layer of the crumbs on top of each chocolate mousse to resemble dirt. Cover each pot loosely with plastic wrap and refrigerate until the mousse is chilled, at least 2 hours and up to 1 day.

4. To serve, stick a flower into each mousse. Let stand at room temperature for about 10 minutes, then serve.

PAREVE VARIATION

Substitute 2½ cups nondairy whipped topping for the heavy cream and vanilla. Substitute Paskesz or other chocolate, dairy-free cookies for the Oreos.

Matzo Napoleon with White Chocolate Mousse

For a showstopping Passover dessert, serve this sensational combo of crunchy, creamy, and sweet ingredients. It takes a bit of maneuvering to turn the matzos into crisp glazed rounds, but that's the fun of making them.

MATZO ROUNDS

1/2 cup sugar
1/2 cup water
1/2 teaspoon vanilla extract
4 unsalted matzos
1/4 cup finely chopped unsalted
    macadamia nuts
1/4 cup unsweetened coconut
    flakes, toasted (see page 180)

CHOCOLATE GANACHE

3 tablespoons heavy cream
1 teaspoon unsalted butter
2 ounces bittersweet chocolate,
    finely chopped

WHITE CHOCOLATE
MOUSSE

7 ounces white chocolate,
    finely chopped
3/4 cup heavy cream, divided

GARNISH

1/2 cup heavy cream
2 teaspoons sugar
1/4 teaspoon vanilla extract
Sliced fresh strawberries
Fresh mint sprigs

1. To make the matzo rounds, bring the sugar and water to a boil in a small saucepan over high heat, stirring constantly just until the sugar dissolves. Boil for 1 minute. Remove from the heat and cool completely. Stir in the vanilla.

2. Position racks in the top third and center of the oven and preheat the oven to 325°F. Line two large baking sheets with parchment paper.

3. Line a work surface with paper towels. Place the matzos on top and brush both sides with the cooled syrup. Let stand until slightly softened, 5 to 10 minutes. Using a 3-inch metal cookie cutter, cut out 16 rounds and arrange on the baking sheets. Gather up the scraps and spread as well as you can on the baking sheets.

4. Bake until the rounds and scraps are crisp and glazed, about 15 minutes. Cool completely on the baking sheets. Finely crush enough of the glazed scraps to make 1/4 cup (they should retain some texture, but if the bits are too big, they won't pass through the pastry tip when the mousse is piped). Mix with the macadamia nuts and coconut in a small bowl, and set the macadamia nut crunch aside.

5. To make the chocolate ganache, bring the heavy cream and butter to a simmer in a small saucepan over medium heat. Remove from the heat and add the chocolate. Let stand for 3 minutes to soften the chocolate, then whisk until smooth. Let stand until slightly thickened, about 10 minutes.

6. Using a small metal spatula, spread the underside of the rounds with the ganache. Return the rounds to the baking sheet, chocolate sides up, and refrigerate to set the ganache, about 30 minutes. (The rounds can be prepared up to 1 day ahead. Cover loosely with plastic wrap after the chocolate sets, then refrigerate.)

7. To make the white chocolate mousse, melt the white chocolate and $1/4$ cup of the heavy cream in the top part of a double boiler over very hot, but not simmering, water, stirring occasionally until melted. (If the water is too hot, the white chocolate will scorch and stiffen, so be careful.) Remove from the heat and let stand until cooled but still semiliquid.

8. Whip the remaining $1/2$ cup heavy cream in a chilled medium bowl with a hand-held electric mixer on high speed until stiff peaks form. Whisk about one-third of the whipped cream into the cooled white chocolate to loosen it, then fold in the remaining whipped cream to make a light-textured mousse. Fold in half of the macadamia nut crunch. Cover with plastic wrap and refrigerate just until stiff enough to pipe from a pastry bag, about 1 hour.

9. To assemble, transfer the white chocolate mousse to a pastry bag fitted with a $1/2$-inch star tip. Pipe large rosettes of the mousse on the chocolate-coated sides of 8 rounds. Sprinkle with the remaining macadamia nut crunch. Top with the remaining rounds, chocolate sides up. (The napoleons can be prepared up to 8 hours ahead, loosely covered with plastic wrap, and refrigerated. The chocolate mousse will firm up when chilled, so let stand at room temperature for about 30 minutes before serving.)

10. For the garnish, whip the heavy cream, sugar, and vanilla in a chilled medium bowl with a hand-held electric mixer on high speed until stiff peaks form. Transfer to a pastry bag fitted with a $1/2$-inch star tip. Place each napoleon on a chilled dessert plate. Pipe a rosette of whipped cream on top of each napoleon. Garnish with the sliced strawberries and a mint sprig. Serve immediately.

Oatmeal Lace Cookies

This lacy, caramel-flavored cookie is one of the best recipes you can have in your cookie file. Bake the cookies into rounds for afternoon snacks and casual occasions. Want to get fancy? While they're still warm and flexible, roll the cookies into cylinders to pipe whipped cream or mold them over upturned custard cups to make shells for filling with sorbet or another frozen treat. They are prone to sticking, but if you line the baking sheets with parchment paper or the new silicone baking liners you shouldn't have a problem.

> **MAKES ABOUT 48 COOKIES**

1 cup all-purpose flour
1 cup sugar
1 cup old-fashioned oatmeal (rolled oats)
$^{1}/_{2}$ teaspoon baking soda
1 cup (2 sticks) unsalted butter, melted
$^{1}/_{4}$ cup heavy cream
$^{1}/_{4}$ cup light corn syrup
2 teaspoons vanilla extract

1. Position racks in the center and top third of the oven and preheat the oven to 350°F. Line baking sheets with parchment paper or nonstick silicone baking sheet liners.

2. Whisk the flour, sugar, oatmeal, and baking soda in a medium bowl. Whisk the melted butter, heavy cream, corn syrup, and vanilla in another bowl, and stir into the dry ingredients until thoroughly mixed.

3. Using 1 teaspoon of dough for each cookie, drop the dough onto the baking sheets, spacing them at least 2 inches apart (these cookies spread, so you may want to bake a trial sheet to become familiar with the spacing). Bake, switching the pans from top to bottom and front to back halfway through the baking time, until the cookies are an even golden brown, about 8 minutes. Cool on the baking sheets for 2 to 3 minutes, then transfer the cookies to a wire rack to cool completely or shape as desired (see below). The cookies can be stored in an airtight container for up to 3 days.

LACE "CIGARS"

Remove a still-warm cookie from the baking sheet. Wrap the cookie around the handle of a wooden spoon to form a cylinder. Cool until set, about 30 seconds. Slide the cookie off the handle and place on a wire rack to cool completely. (This goes quickly if you use two or three spoons.) If the cookies cool too much to mold, reheat on the baking sheet in the oven for a minute or two until warmed and softened, then proceed. Repeat with all of the cookies.

LACE CUPS

Remove a still-warm cookie from the baking sheet. Loosely drape the cookie over a lightly oiled 5-ounce custard cup, molding it so as to have a few loose pleats. Cool until set, about 2 minutes. (This goes quickly if you use more than one custard cup.) Invert onto a wire rack to cool completely. If the cookies cool too much to mold, reheat on the baking sheet in the oven for a minute or two until warmed and softened, then proceed. Repeat with all of the cookies.

Banana Soufganiot Pudding

At Hanukkah, fried foods help us remember the miracle of the oil lamp, and soufganiot are the traditional holiday doughnuts. They are always round, usually without the central hole that you find in everyday doughnuts. For one special Hanukkah dinner menu, I wanted to serve soufganiot, but in a more elegant guise. The result was this creamy, absolutely luscious banana pudding, which eliminates the frying step by starting with store-bought doughnuts.

MAKES
8
SERVINGS

1 quart milk
2 vanilla beans, split lengthwise, or 1 teaspoon vanilla extract
12 large egg yolks
1¹/₃ cups sugar
2 store-bought cake-style doughnuts, cut into ¹/₂-inch dice
2 ripe bananas, cut into ¹/₂-inch dice

1. Position racks in the bottom third and center of the oven and preheat the oven to 300°F.

2. Place the milk in a large saucepan. If using vanilla beans, split them in half lengthwise. Scrape the vanilla bean seeds into the milk, then add the pods. Bring to a simmer over medium heat. Turn off the heat, cover, and allow to infuse for 10 minutes.

3. Whisk the yolks and sugar in a large bowl until pale and thickened. Gradually whisk in the hot milk. Pour the custard back into the saucepan. Cook over low heat, stirring constantly with a wooden spoon until the custard is thick enough to coat the spoon (if you draw your finger through the custard on the spoon, it will cut a swath), about 3 minutes. An instant-read thermometer will read 185°F. Strain the custard through a wire sieve into a bowl or 2-quart glass measuring cup. If using vanilla extract, stir it in now.

4. Distribute the doughnut pieces and bananas among eight 1¹/₄-cup dessert cups. Ladle or pour equal amounts of the custard into the cups and press on the doughnuts to be sure they are submerged. Arrange the cups in two baking pans. Pull the oven racks halfway out of the oven and place the baking pans on the racks. Pour enough hot water into each baking dish to come ¹/₂ inch up the sides of the dessert cups. Carefully slide the racks into the oven.

5. Bake until the custards are beginning to set around the edges but still look loose in the centers, about 40 minutes. Remove from the water and cool to room temperature.

6. Cover each custard with plastic wrap. Refrigerate until chilled, at least 2 hours or overnight. Serve chilled.

Amaretto-Coconut Semifreddo

Semifreddo means "partially frozen," referring to the soft, smooth texture of this ice cream relative. At the restaurant, we freeze the mixture in ramekins, then unmold them at the time of service, but this loaf-shaped presentation works beautifully in the home kitchen. This is a good make-ahead dessert, as it must chill for at least 6 hours.

1. Line a 9 × 5-inch loaf pan with plastic wrap, letting the excess hang over the sides.

2. Beat the egg yolks and sugar in the bowl of a heavy-duty electric mixer fitted with the whisk at high speed until thick and pale yellow, about 3 minutes. Beat in the liqueur and almond extract. Remove the bowl from the mixer. Stir in about one-fourth of the whipped topping to lighten the mixture, then fold in the remaining topping. Fold in ¹/₂ cup of the coconut and ¹/₃ cup of the almonds, reserving the remaining coconut and almonds for garnish.

3. Spread the mixture evenly in the pan and fold the overhanging plastic wrap over the top. Freeze until solid, at least 6 hours or overnight. (The semifreddo can be frozen for up to 2 weeks.)

4. About 2 hours before serving, gently mix the raspberries, blueberries, and sugar. Cover and refrigerate to chill.

5. To umold, pull back the plastic wrap and invert the semifreddo onto a cutting board. Slice and place each slice on a chilled dessert plate. Garnish with a spoonful of the berries, sprinkle with the reserved toasted coconut and almonds, and serve immediately.

8 large egg yolks, at room temperature (see page 227)
1 cup plus 3 tablespoons sugar
¹/₄ cup almond-flavored liqueur, such as Amaretto
1 teaspoon almond extract
1 quart nondairy whipped topping
²/₃ cup unsweetened coconut flakes, toasted (see page 180)
¹/₂ cup slivered almonds, toasted (see page 175)

¹/₂ pint fresh raspberries
1 cup fresh blueberries
2 tablespoons sugar

DAIRY VARIATION

Substitute 2 cups heavy cream, whipped, for the nondairy whipped topping.

heritage recipe

Rugelach

MAKES
45
PASTRIES

My wife's family has been using this recipe to make mountains of rugelach for years. I've never found one that is better…and I doubt that you'll have any complaints, either. Use whatever fruit preserves you like, because the choice of preserves will personalize your batch.

DOUGH
1 cup (2 sticks) unsalted butter,
  at room temperature
One 8-ounce container
  whipped cream cheese
2 tablespoons sugar
$1/2$ teaspoon vanilla extract
$1/4$ teaspoon salt
2 cups all-purpose flour

FILLING
$3/4$ cup finely chopped walnuts
$1/2$ cup dried currants
3 tablespoons sugar
$1^1/2$ teaspoons ground
  cinnamon
$3/4$ cup fruit preserves, such as
  apricot or raspberry

1. To make the dough, beat the butter and cream cheese in the bowl of a heavy-duty mixer fitted with the paddle blade on high speed until smooth and creamy, about 3 minutes. Beat in the sugar, vanilla, and salt. On low speed, gradually add the flour and mix just until combined.

2. Turn out the dough onto a lightly floured work surface and knead briefly just until smooth. Divide the dough into thirds. Shape each portion into a thick rectangle and wrap in plastic wrap. Refrigerate until chilled, at least 1 hour and up to overnight.

3. To make the filling, mix the walnuts and currants in a medium bowl. Mix the sugar and cinnamon in a small bowl.

4. Position racks in the center and top third of the oven and preheat the oven to 350°F. Line two baking sheets with parchment paper.

5. Place one portion of dough on a lightly floured work surface. Sprinkle the top lightly with flour, then roll out into a 14 × 6-inch rectangle. (If the dough cracks, let it stand at room temperature for 5 minutes to soften slightly, then try again.) Spread about $1/4$ cup of the preserves over the dough, leaving a $1/2$-inch-wide border on all sides. Sprinkle with one-third of the walnut-currant mixture, then a generous tablespoon of the cinnamon sugar. Starting at the long end, roll up into a tight cylinder. Using a sharp knife, cut crosswise into 15 pieces. Repeat with the dough and filling ingredients. Place the rugelach 1 inch apart on the baking sheets.

6. Bake until lightly browned, about 25 minutes, switching the positions of the sheets from top to bottom and front to back halfway through baking. Transfer to wire cake racks and cool completely. (The rugelach can be prepared up to 5 days ahead and stored at room temperature in airtight containers.)

Strawberry Frangipane Tart

No doubt about it—this is one heck of a dessert! Frangipane is a cakelike almond filling beloved by French bakers, and American home cooks should learn to love it, too. My version uses berry purée in the filling to complement the fruit on top. This recipe calls for strawberries, but you can substitute raspberries or blueberries if you prefer. A note of warning: Because the pastry has a lot of sugar and butter, it will probably crack when you try to fit it into the tart pan. Don't worry; just press the pieces together, as it is a very forgiving dough. You need a traditional French fluted tart pan with a removable bottom for this dessert.

> **MAKES
> 10 TO 12
> SERVINGS**

SWEET PASTRY

1¹/₂ cups all-purpose flour
3 tablespoons sugar
³/₄ cup (1¹/₂ sticks) unsalted
    butter, cut into thin slices
    and chilled
1 large egg yolk
1¹/₂ tablespoons heavy cream

FRANGIPANE FILLING

³/₄ cup sliced strawberries
One 8-ounce can almond paste,
    grated on the large holes of
    a box grater
1 cup (2 sticks) unsalted butter,
    at room temperature
1 cup sugar
1 teaspoon vanilla extract
4 large eggs
1 cup all-purpose flour

¹/₂ cup apricot preserves
2 tablespoons water
1 quart strawberries, stemmed
    and thinly sliced

1. To make the pastry: Place the flour and sugar in the bowl of a food processor. Pulse to combine. Add the butter pieces and pulse until the mixture resembles coarse meal.

2. Mix the egg yolk and cream in a small liquid measuring cup. With the motor running, pour the egg mixture into the food processor and process just until the dough is moistened. Pulse a few times until the dough forms a ball. Gather up the dough into a thick disk and wrap in plastic wrap. Refrigerate until chilled, at least 1 hour and up to overnight. (If the dough is well chilled and firm, let stand at room temperature for 10 minutes, then beat the dough all over with your rolling pin to make it malleable before rolling it out.)

3. On a lightly floured surface, roll out the dough into a 13-inch round, a little more than ¹/₈ inch thick. Transfer the dough to the pan, pressing well into the sides and at the corners. Don't worry if the dough cracks; just press it together. Trim off the excess dough flush with the edge of the pan. Refrigerate the dough-lined pan while the oven preheats.

4. Position a rack in the lower third of the oven and preheat the oven to 400°F.

5. Meanwhile, make the frangipane: Purée the strawberries in a food processor or blender and set aside. Mix the almond paste, butter, sugar, and vanilla in the bowl of a heavy-duty electric mixer fitted with the paddle blade on high speed until light and fluffy, about 2 minutes. Add the eggs, one at a time, scraping down the sides of the bowl after each addition. Reduce the mixer speed to low and add the flour and strawberry purée, mixing just until incorporated. Spread evenly in the crust.

6. Bake until the topping is golden brown and a toothpick inserted in the center of the tart comes out clean, about 35 minutes. Cool completely on a wire rack.

7. Bring the preserves and water to a boil in a small saucepan over medium heat. Cook, stirring often, until the glaze has large bubbles, about 3 minutes. Strain through a sieve into a small bowl.

8. Using a pastry brush, brush the top of the tart lightly with the glaze. Arrange the sliced strawberries, slightly overlapping as needed, in concentric circles on top of the filling. Brush the berries with the remaining glaze. Refrigerate until the glaze is set, about 30 minutes.

9. Slice and serve chilled or at room temperature.

Honey-Ginger Zabaglione Cream
with Fresh Berries

Zabaglione is often made with Marsala, but sweet sparkling wine has a delicate flavor that is more companionable. Making zabaglione is no big deal (it's harder to spell it than to make it!) if you have the right tools. A large balloon whisk is the key, as this shape really beats air into the zabaglione. If the wires are too thick or too close together, it won't work as well. (An electric hand mixer is a high-tech alternative.) If you wish to glaze the top of the dessert, use a propane kitchen torch or a butane torch, available, respectively, at kitchenware shops and hardware stores. (The zabaglione cream also makes an incredible frozen dessert. Simply freeze the mixture overnight in a tightly covered container. Scoop into bowls and serve with the berries, if you like.)

**MAKES
6
SERVINGS**

BERRIES
4 cups assorted fresh berries,
  such as blueberries,
  blackberries, raspberries, and
  sliced strawberries
2 tablespoons sparkling sweet
  wine, such as Moscato d'Asti
2 tablespoons sugar

ZABAGLIONE CREAM
6 large egg yolks
¼ cup sparkling sweet wine,
  such as Moscato d'Asti
¼ cup sugar
2 tablespoons honey
1 teaspoon finely minced fresh
  ginger, peeled, shredded on
  the large holes of a box
  grater, then minced
1 star anise (5 or 6 points)
¾ cup heavy cream

1. To prepare the berries, mix the berries, sparkling wine, and sugar in a medium bowl. Cover and refrigerate to chill and allow the berries to give off some juices, at least 2 and up to 8 hours.

2. To make the zabaglione cream, use a large balloon whisk to whisk the yolks, sparkling wine, sugar, honey, and ginger in a medium stainless-steel bowl. Add the star anise and place over a saucepan of steadily simmering, but not boiling, water (the bottom of the bowl should not touch the water). Whisk constantly (or beat with a hand-held electric mixer on high speed) until the mixture is pale yellow and fluffy, about 7 minutes. When the whisk is lifted an inch or so above the zabaglione, the mixture should be thick enough to hold its shape on the surface for a few seconds before sinking.

3. Remove from the heat and place the bowl in a larger bowl of ice water. Let stand until the zabaglione is completely cooled. Discard the star anise.

4. Whip the heavy cream in a chilled medium bowl until stiff peaks form. Fold the whipped cream into the zabaglione. (The mixture can be prepared up to 4 hours ahead, covered with plastic wrap, and refrigerated.)

5. When ready to serve, spoon the berries and their juices into 6 large martini glasses. Spoon the zabaglione over the berries. If desired, using a propane torch, pass the flame over the zabaglione until very lightly browned. Serve immediately.

PAREVE VARIATION
Substitute 1^1/$_2$ cups nondairy whipped topping for the whipped cream.

holiday menus

SHABBAT

Chicken and Veal Pâté *(page 17)*

Roast Duck with Apple–Golden Raisin Sauce *(pages 122–123)*

Sweet Noodle and Fruit Kugel *(page 186)*

Acorn Squash with Ginger-Orange Glaze *(page 180)*

Broccoli Rabe and Garlic Sauté *(page 181)*

Apple Cobbler with Almond-Streusel Topping *(page 226–227)*

Roasted Red Pepper Hummus *(page 32)*

Porcini-Crusted Striped Bass with Smoked Trout and Scallion Mashed Potatoes and Port Wine Syrup *(pages 134–135)*

Ricotta Cheesecake *(pages 224–225)*

SUKKOT

Loaded Baked Potato Soup *(pages 54–55)*

Short Ribs with Apricots and Garbanzo Beans *(pages 86–87)*

Wild Rice Salad with Toasted Walnuts and Sun-Dried Berries *(page 74)*

Apple Cobbler with Almond-Streusel Topping *(pages 226–227)*

ROSH HASHANAH

Wild Mushroom and Barley Soup *(page 56)*

Grilled Lamb Rib Chops with Ratatouille *(pages 101–101)*

Root Vegetable Tzimmes *(page 194)*

Honey Cake *(page 228)*

PURIM

Beet, Pear, and Fennel Salad with Orange Vinaigrette *(page 64)*

Savory Hamantaschen with Vegetable-Cheese Stuffing
   (pages 150–151)

Honey-Ginger Zabaglione Cream with Fresh Berries *(pages 224–245)*

Prize-Winning Rum Punch *(page 37)*

YOM KIPPUR BREAK FAST

Gefilte Fish Terrine with Carrot and Beet Salads *(pages 22–23)*

Smoked Whitefish Pinwheels *(page 28)*

Smoked Salmon Cheesecake *(pages 26–27)*

Wild Mushroom Kugel *(page 156)*

Persian Pickled Vegetables *(page 34)*

Rugelach *(pages 240–241)*

Double Chocolate Chip Cookies *(page 221)*

SHABBAT LUNCHEON

Beet, Pear, and Fennel Salad with Orange Vinaigrette *(page 64)*

Superb Sabbath Cholent *(pages 84–85)*

Israeli Couscous Salad with Summer Vegetables and
  Lime Vinaigrette *(page 67)*

Israeli Chopped Vegetable Salad *(page 75)*

Amaretto-Coconut Semifreddo *(page 239)*

PASSOVER DINNER

Sephardic Chicken Soup with Sofrito and Saffron Matzo Balls
  (pages 48–49)

Smoked Trout and Orange Salad *(page 73)*

Braised Lamb Chops with Spiced Tomato Sauce *(page 102)*

Mango-Date Haroset *(page 185)*

Passover Banana Cake with Strawberry-Marsala Compote
  (pages 222–223)

Classic Chicken Soup with Matzo Balls *(pages 46–47)*

Latin American Ceviche *(page 19)*

Rack of Veal with Wild Mushroom–Farfel Dressing *(pages 98–99)*

Mango-Date Haroset *(page 185)*

Matzo Napoleon with White Chocolate Mousse *(pages 234–235)*

Tomato–Wild Rice Soup *(page 58)*

Gefilte Fish Terrine with Carrot and Beet Salads *(pages 22–23)*

Veal Chops Milanese with Tomato Salad and Arugula
  (pages 96–97))

Mango-Date Haroset *(page 185)*

Honey-Ginger Zabaglione Cream with Fresh Berries *(pages 244–245)*

HANUKKAH

Monney's Beef Borscht *(page 44)*

Grandma's Latkes with Sour Cream and Ginger Applesauce
  (pages 152–153)

Apple Cider Brisket *(page 80)*

Apple Cobbler with Almond-
  Streusel Topping
  (pages 226–227)

mail-order sources

There are many mail-order sources for kosher food on the Web. Kosher food must be certified as such by a rabbi or kashrut inspector. There are many different organizations that provide kosher certification, but they have varying standards (although all of them will guarantee that the food does not contain any pork products). The stamp of approval you find on the labels of these foods is called a *hechscher*. Because my restaurant must provide the highest level of kosher certification to satisfy the various religious convictions of my customers, I am a stickler for using kosher foods with the strictest codes. The most reliable kosher *hechschers* are:

Ⓚ **THE ORGANIZED KASHRUS LABORATORIES**

Ⓤ **THE UNION OF ORTHODOX JEWISH CONGREGATIONS**

KOF-K KOSHER SUPERVISION

★ **STAR-K KOSHER CERTIFICATION**

There are many other certification programs, many of them localized. Choosing the kosher certification that is best for your convictions is a personal choice. I recommend these three mail-order sources because they satisfy the strict standards of the kosher restaurant industry.

Kessler Brothers Kosher
Green Street
Woodridge, NY 12789
Phone (845) 434-4500
Toll-Free (888) 228-9595
www.123kosher.com

123Kosher.com is the Website for a long-time kosher butcher in the heart of New York's "Borscht Belt" in the Catskill Mountains. They will send freezer-packed orders for kosher meats, poultry, seafood, and other perishables overnight.

Kosher Depot
Jordan Lederman
437 Railroad Avenue
Westbury, NY 11590
Phone (516) 338-4100

I depend on Kosher Depot for all kinds of hard-to-find kosher condiments, bottled goods, and other ingredients. If you aren't sure if a product exists in a kosher-certified form, don't be so sure until you call Jordan.

Spice House International Specialties Inc.
Tony Provetto
315 West John Street
Hicksville, NY 11802
Phone (516) 942-7248
Fax (516) 942-7249
www. spicehouseint.com

Spice House has an amazing selection of top-quality herbs and spices, including many that are kosher certified. Be sure to ask for the Jeff Nathan Spice Line, too!

index

American cooks use standard containers, the 8-ounce cup and a tablespoon that takes exactly 16 level fillings to fill that cup level. Measuring by cup makes it very difficult to give weight equivalents, as a cup of densely packed butter will weigh considerably more than a cup of flour. The easiest way therefore to deal with cup measurements in recipes is to take the amount by volume rather than by weight. Thus the equation reads:

1 cup = 240 ml = 8 fl. oz.   1/2 cup = 120 ml = 4 fl. oz.

In the States, butter is often measured in sticks. One stick is the equivalent of 8 tablespoons. One tablespoon of butter is therefore the equivalent to 1/2 ounce/15 grams.

LIQUID MEASURES

Fluid Ounces	U.S.	Imperial	Milliliters
	1 teaspoon	1 teaspoon	5
1/4	2 teaspoons	1 dessertspoon	10
1/2	1 tablespoon	1 tablespoon	14
1	2 tablespoons	2 tablespoons	28
2	1/4 cup	4 tablespoons	56
4	1/2 cup		120
5		1/4 pint or 1 gill	140
6	3/4 cup		170
8	1 cup		240
9			250, 1/4 liter
10	1 1/4 cups	1/2 pint	280
12	1 1/2 cups		340
15		3/4 pint	420
16	2 cups		450
18	2 1/4 cups		500, 1/2 liter
20	2 1/2 cups	1 pint	560
24	3 cups		675
25		1 1/4 pints	700
27	3 1/2 cups		750
30	3 3/4 cups	1 1/2 pints	840
32	4 cups or 1 quart		900
35		1 3/4 pints	980
36	4 1/2 cups		1000, 1 liter
40	5 cups	2 pints or 1 quart	1120

SOLID MEASURES

U.S. and Imperial Measures		Metric Measures	
Ounces	Pounds	Grams	Kilos
1		28	
2		56	
3 1/2		100	
4	1/4	112	
5		140	
6		168	
8	1/2	225	
9		250	1/4
12	3/4	340	
16	1	450	
18		500	1/2
20	1 1/4	560	
24	1 1/2	675	
27		750	3/4
28	1 3/4	780	
32	2	900	
36	2 1/4	1000	1
40	2 1/2	1100	
48	3	1350	
54		1500	1 1/2

OVEN TEMPERATURE EQUIVALENTS

Fahrenheit	Celsius	Gas Mark	Description
225	110	1/4	Cool
250	130	1/2	
275	140	1	Very Slow
300	150	2	
325	170	3	Slow
350	180	4	Moderate
375	190	5	
400	200	6	Moderately Hot
425	220	7	Fairly Hot
450	230	8	Hot
475	240	9	Very Hot
500	250	10	Extremely Hot

Any broiling recipes can be used with the grill of the oven, but beware of high-temperature grills.

EQUIVALENTS FOR INGREDIENTS

all-purpose flour—plain flour
baking sheet—oven tray
buttermilk—ordinary milk
cheesecloth—muslin
coarse salt—kitchen salt
cornstarch—cornflour
eggplant—aubergine

granulated sugar—caster sugar
half and half—12% fat milk
heavy cream—double cream
light cream—single cream
lima beans—broad beans
parchment paper—greaseproof paper
plastic wrap—cling film

scallion—spring onion
shortening—white fat
unbleached flour—strong, white flour
vanilla bean—vanilla pod
zest—rind
zucchini—courgettes or marrow